HAROLD B. SEGEL is Associate Professor of Slavic Literatures at Columbia University. His two-volume work, *The Literature of Eighteenth-Century Russia: A History and Anthology,* was published by E. P. Dutton in 1967.

THE TRILOGY OF
ALEXANDER
SUKHOVO-KOBYLIN

Alexander Sukhovo-Kobylin in later life.

THE TRILOGY OF ALEXANDER SUKHOVO-KOBYLIN

Translated and with an Introduction by

HAROLD B. SEGEL

A Dutton Paperback

E. P. Dutton & Co., Inc. New York 1969

Published simultaneously in Canada by Clarke, Irwin &
Company Limited, Toronto and Vancouver

Library of Congress Catalog Card Number: 69-14858

First Edition

For Vera Robertovna

CONTENTS

PREFACE   xi

INTRODUCTION   xiii

PRONUNCIATION GUIDE   li

Krechinsky's Wedding   1

The Case   87

The Death of Tarelkin   195

PREFACE

When Arkadina makes her first appearance in Act I of Chekhov's *The Sea Gull*, it is on the arm of retired Lieutenant Shamrayev. A conversation about the theatre is in progress. Recalling some memorable moments, Shamrayev declares:

> In 1873, at the Poltava Fair, she played astoundingly! Sheer delight! Marvelous acting! Would you happen to know where Chadin—the comedian Pavel Semyonovich Chadin—is at present? His Rasplyuev was inimitable, better than Sadovsky's, I assure you, most esteemed lady. Where is he now?*

Nowadays this allusion to Rasplyuev and the superb actor Prov Sadovsky's playing of it would require some clarification. But in Chekhov's time there would have been no need for this; the audience would have grasped the allusion at once. For Rasplyuev is a central figure in one of the most unusual works of Russian drama of the second half of the nineteenth century, the *Trilogy* of Alexander Sukhovo-Kobylin (1817–1903).

The three plays of which the *Trilogy* consists—*Krechinsky's Wedding*, *The Case*, and *The Death of Tarelkin*—represent the sole literary legacy of their aristocratic author whose involvement in a sensational murder case became one of the great scandals of contemporary Russian society. Out of the drama of his own life, Sukhovo-Kobylin fashioned a trilogy of plays remarkable for the acidity of their satire against the tsarist bureaucracy and police.

But it is not only for their pungent satire that the plays have continued to attract attention down to the present. They are, above all, splendidly theatrical and encompass not one but several different traditions of theatre from the "well-made play" of Scribe to the absurd comedy of Gogol. "As for sheer stagecraft," writes Prince D. S. Mirsky in his *A History of Russian Literature* (first Vintage edition, New York, 1958,

---

* *Chekhov: The Major Plays*, trans. Ann Dunnigan, Signet Classics, New York, 1964, 113.

251), "they have no rivals in Russian literary drama." In his *Russian Theater from the Empire to the Soviets* (Cleveland and New York, 1961, 73), Marc Slonim makes the prediction that "soon the time will come for a 'rediscovery' of Sukhovo-Kobylin in Russia and abroad . . . In the meantime, these three plays occupy a place of honor in the history of the national theater."

The same year in which this prediction was made saw the publication in the Soviet Union of a new book devoted entirely to Sukhovo-Kobylin's dramaturgy. In 1966 a new edition of the *Trilogy* was published in Moscow. And in the September 1967 issue of the prominent Soviet literary monthly *New World* (*Novy Mir*), a laudatory article appeared commemorating the hundred and fiftieth anniversary of Sukhovo-Kobylin's birth and hailing the author of the *Trilogy* as one of the masters of Russian satire and drama.

Thus, the "rediscovery" Marc Slonim anticipates has already taken place in Russia. The present book, containing the first translation of the entire *Trilogy* in English, hopefully marks the beginning of the discovery of this unique work of Russian drama in the West.

H. B. S.

INTRODUCTION

I

On the evening of November 9, 1850[1] the body of an attractive young woman in her early thirties was discovered in a pile of snow near the ramparts surrounding the Vagankovsky Cemetery on the outskirts of Moscow. Her throat was slit from ear to ear and there were multiple wounds on her body. The police lost little time in establishing that the corpse was Louise Simon-Dimanche, the French mistress for some ten years of a fashionable and handsome aristocrat, Alexander Sukhovo-Kobylin. It was Sukhovo-Kobylin, in fact, who earlier that same day had reported the French woman as missing for the past forty-eight hours.

Subsequent investigation revealed that Simon-Dimanche had been murdered elsewhere and then deposited far from the scene of the crime. As the police dug deeper, the case seemed relatively simple. Traces of blood were found in the private wing of his parents' residence occupied by Sukhovo-Kobylin, and there were rumors to the effect that the young nobleman had grown tired of his French paramour and was avidly courting a luminary of the Moscow *demi-monde* named Natalya Ivanovna Naryshkina (later the wife of Alexandre Dumas *fils*). Sukhovo-Kobylin was promptly taken into custody and the unwieldy machinery of nineteenth-century Russian justice started lumbering into action. But then there occurred a series of events in some respects unclear to this very day.

Simon-Dimanche's four servants, who received their salary from Sukhovo-Kobylin and were thus in his hire, unexpectedly reversed their earlier testimony that they knew nothing of the crime and confessed that they had jointly conspired to murder their mistress. The reason they gave was their smouldering resentment evoked by her overbearing manner and harsh treatment.

The story had the ring of plausibility. Mistreatment of

[1] The dates of events in Russia conform to the Russian Julian calendar, twelve days behind the Gregorian in the nineteenth century.

servants was hardly a novelty in Russia, but two ingredients in the case of Louise Simon-Dimanche altered the familiar circumstances. To the servants, Louise was a person of no consequence. Moreover, she was a foreigner.

The confessed murderers, two men and two women, were subjected to rigorous interrogation, tried, and sentenced finally to a public lashing, branding, and fifteen to twenty years each at hard labor. Sukhovo-Kobylin was exonerated of any guilt and freed. The matter, however, was far from over.

The conflicting testimonies of the servants and nagging doubts in some minds about certain aspects of what was fast becoming one of the most sensational cases in the annals of Russian jurisprudence led to a new investigation by a government body in 1853. The servants were run through a new gamut of interrogation and this time startled the officials charged with the reinvestigation of the case by again reversing position and insisting that they were threatened and bribed into confessing a crime they never committed. This new turn of events resulted in the reopening of the case early the next year. Now the burden of guilt came to rest again squarely on the shoulders of Sukhovo-Kobylin.

As his position worsened, he was taken into custody and incarcerated from May to November 1854. But the evidence against him was largely circumstantial and the servants' conflicting stories made it virtually impossible to determine what had actually happened. Sukhovo-Kobylin was released but remained "under suspicion" while the case now followed a tortuous path from one government office to another.

This stigma of suspicion of murder was one the Sukhovo-Kobylin family had no intention of living with, and a vigorous campaign began to be pressed to bring the case to a rapid and favorable conclusion. Neither money nor influence were stinted, and in time the sympathetic intervention of no less a personage than the Empress Alexandra Fyodorovna herself was obtained. On May 12, 1856, the Minister of Justice, Count Panin, personally informed Sukhovo-Kobylin that the empress had directed him to conclude the matter. The State Council took the case under advisement once again, and

toward the end of October 1857 issued a verdict of not guilty
on behalf of the servants. The suspicion of murder was also
removed from Sukhovo-Kobylin, but the Council sentenced
him to "ecclesiastical penitence" for his illicit love affair. On
December 3 of the same year Tsar Alexander II upheld the
decision of the Council, thereby formally bringing the sensational case to an end seven years after the battered body of
Louise Simon-Dimanche had been found in the snow. In April
1858 Sukhovo-Kobylin received a passport and left for France
shortly thereafter.

Although officially closed, the case was destined to remain
a subject of controversy down to the present.[2] The experience left an indelible impression on Sukhovo-Kobylin and
drastically altered the course of his life.

Until November 9, 1850, he had lived in a style little different from that of other young Russian aristocrats. The
family into which he was born on September 17, 1817, had
once known considerable wealth and prided itself on blood

[2] Until recent years Simon-Dimanche's murder and Sukhovo-
Kobylin's part in it tended to attract greater interest than his literary
accomplishments. This is reflected in the Russian publications on
him. Two full-length studies of the "case" itself have appeared:
Leonid Grossman, *Prestuplenie Sukhovo-Kobylina*, Leningrad, 1928,
and Viktor Grossman, *Delo Sukhovo-Kobylina*, Moscow, 1936. The
first accepts the guilt of Sukhovo-Kobylin and attempts to prove it.
The second opposes this view, assuming the position that Sukhovo-
Kobylin was innocent, that Simon-Dimanche's servants committed
the crime, and that the case against Sukhovo-Kobylin was pressed by
government officials enthusiastic about the prospects of extracting a
handsome bribe from the beleaguered aristocrat.

Older studies were similarly devoted virtually entirely to the more
sensational aspects of Sukhovo-Kobylin's life and career. These include: A. Golombievsky, "Drama v zhizni (A. V. Sukhovo-Kobylin i
frantsuzenka Simon)," *Russky Arkhiv*, II, 1910, 243–90; A. Rem-
belinsky, "Eshche o drama v zhizni pisatelya," *Russkaya Starina*, V,
1910, 269–83; "Iz dnevnika A. V. Sukhovo-Kobylina," *Russkaya
Starina*, V, 1910, 284–88. Newer materials and correspondence were
published also in 1934 and 1955: "Pisma A. V. Sukhovo-Kobylina
k rondym," *Trudy Publichnoy Biblioteki SSSR Imeni Lenina*, Vypusk
III, 1934, 185–265, and K. L. Rudnitsky, "Novye materialy o Suk-
hovo-Kobyline," *Ezhegodnik Instituta Istorii Iskusstva Teatra*, 1955,
250–303.

ties (according to the family genealogy) to the ruling Ro-
manov dynasty. His father was a former Guards officer who
saw action in the Napoleonic wars and lost an eye in the
battle of Austerlitz. As a result of the injury, he left military
service with the rank of colonel.

The philosophical and literary interests Sukhovo-Kobylin
cultivated both fashionably and sincerely stemmed less from
his father, whose fond hope was that his one son would become a priest, than from his mother, Marya Ivanovna (nee
Shepeleva), herself of aristocratic lineage and a woman of
considerable culture, possessing an enthusiasm for French
philosophical literature great enough to lead her to translate
abundantly from it. Her natural modesty, however, prevented
her from ever attempting to publish any of her translations.

Under Marya Ivanovna's aegis the Sukhovo-Kobylin home
in Moscow became a salon frequented by writers, artists, and
scholars. The atmosphere of books, paintings, and intellect
in which the family moved all but determined the careers the
Sukhovo-Kobylin children would pursue. The elder sister,
Elizaveta, became a popular writer in the second half of the
nineteenth century under the *nom de plume* of Evgenya Tur.
Sofya, the younger sister, earned a reputation as a landscape
artist and was the first woman in Russia to be awarded a
gold medal in a competition sponsored by the Imperial
Academy of Fine Arts in St. Petersburg.

Alexander's fondness for art, literature, and the theatre took
second place in his youth to a love for philosophy (Hegel,
of course, was then the rage) clearly inherited from his
mother. When he finished his course of studies in the Faculty
of Philosophy of Moscow University in 1838, he enthusiastically followed the trail of German philosophy that led to
Berlin and Heidelberg. But some time in the late 1830's or
early 1840's he seemed to forsake serious intellectual pursuits
in favor of the frenetic social life of fashionable young society
with the balls, races, and sojourns to the West such a style
of living involved.

It was on one of his trips to Paris, that cultural Mecca of
Russian aristocrats in the first half of the nineteenth century,

that he happened upon Louise Simon-Dimanche (in a café, according to some sources). In no time he found himself in love and persuaded her to come to Russia—not as his wife, but as his mistress. She arrived in Moscow in December 1842.

Their liaison, an open secret well known in Moscow society of the time, continued placidly, even uneventfully, until Natalya Naryshkina entered the picture. Sukhovo-Kobylin's ardor for his mistress declined rapidly, and Simon-Dimanche apparently accepted the inevitability of their breakup and her return to France.

The brutal murder of his paramour and the seemingly interminable investigation and bureaucratic harassment that followed in its wake left Sukhovo-Kobylin a changed man. Fashionable society ceased to attract him, and he became withdrawn, finding solace again in the world of books and prolonged stays out of Russia. He renewed his earlier love for philosophy and began to see in literature a means of giving voice to the bitterness and disillusionment the seven-year-long criminal proceedings against him had provoked.

It was out of this profound misfortune that his only literary work, the dramatic trilogy consisting of *Krechinsky's Wedding* (Svadba Krechinskogo), *The Case* (Delo), and *The Death of Tarelkin* (Smert Tarelkina), was born.[3] Despite two mar-

---

[3] The first serious attempt to study the *Trilogy* as dramatic literature was Leonid Grossman's book *Teatr Sukhovo-Kobylina*, Moscow-Leningrad, 1940. It is particularly useful for its survey of the *Trilogy* in the theatre and its bibliography. Two more recent Soviet studies are K. L. Rudnitsky, A. V. *Sukhovo-Kobylin. Ocherk zhizni i tvorchestva*, Moscow, 1957, and Isodor Kleyner, *Dramaturgiya Sukhovo-Kobylina*, Moscow, 1961. These are good for their close reading of the texts and consideration of matters of language, but suffer from an obvious socio-political bias, and an inadequate treatment of Western influences and parallels. Although a much shorter book than those of Rudnitsky and Kleyner, with a substantial part of it devoted to a review of the stage history of the *Trilogy*, Grossman's *Teatr Sukhovo-Kobylina* is more generous and objective on the matter of Western influences. See especially 54–84. The introductions to the three most recent Soviet editions of the *Trilogy* are also valuable as general surveys. These include K. L. Rudnitsky's introduction to the 1955 edition (v-xxxviii), I. D. Glikman's introduction to the 1959 edition (3–42), and K. L. Rudnitsky's intro-

riages (both to foreigners), it was this one work, this artistic realization and immortalization of his personal drama, that consumed in various ways the greater part of his life after 1857 until his death on March 11, 1903 in Beaulieu on the French Riviera.

The idea for at least the first part of the trilogy, *Krechinsky's Wedding*, was possibly conceived in the early 1840's when Sukhovo-Kobylin thought of initiating a literary career by writing a satirical social comedy along the lines of the deftly plotted *comédies-vaudevilles* he so much admired in the theatres of Paris. How much of the play was actually committed to paper in these early days nobody has ever really ascertained. Probably little. For one reason or another serious work on the comedy had to wait until 1852, nearly two years after the murder of Louise Simon-Dimanche. By now, the author's life itself resembled fiction, and the larger dimensions of *Krechinsky's Wedding* began to crystallize. Sukhovo-Kobylin's second arrest and imprisonment from May to November 1854 provided the necessary impetus to bring the play to fruition. In the six trying months during which he was behind bars Sukhovo-Kobylin spent most of his time writing. He completed the comedy three weeks before his release on November 4, and it needed only minor revisions.

The second play, *The Case*, was begun in August 1856 and definitively completed, after extensive revisions, in 1861. *The Death of Tarelkin* took the longest. It was started in 1857 and finished only in 1869, the year in which the entire *Trilogy* was published for the first time in book form.

Because of its awesome vision of evil triumphant in the form of a corrupt officialdom supported by brutal and inhuman police, opposition from the tsarist censors was anticipated, and the *Trilogy* was subtitled "Pictures of the Past"

---

duction to the 1966 edition (5–46). In general, however, it is in the area of comparative analysis that all the available Russian studies of Sukhovo-Kobylin suffer.

To date there has been only one study in English of the *Trilogy*: Nina Brodiansky's short introductory article, "Sukhovo-Kobylin (1817–1903)," *Slavonic and East European Review*, XXIV, 1946, 110–121.

(Kartiny proshedshogo) to suggest that the events depicted in the plays belonged to a bygone era. The ruse was apparently successful, for the book came off the presses in 1869.

But a "live" presentation of the *Trilogy* before theatre audiences was another matter entirely. Because the satire of *Krechinsky's Wedding* is in no way political, the play encountered virtually no opposition from the censors and was officially permitted to be staged in 1855. The last two plays, however, embroiled Sukhovo-Kobylin in a tug of war with the censors that lasted almost to the time of his death. But the dramatist had the satisfaction of seeing his most cherished dream finally come true. On September 15, 1900, almost a year and a half before his election to the Russian Academy of Sciences (on the same day as Gorky) and nearly two and a half years before his death, the third and last part of the *Trilogy* was staged for the first time. Moreover, there was the added pleasure of a taste of international recognition when in February 1902 *Krechinsky's Wedding* was performed in French at the Théâtre de Renaissance in Paris.

The hostility of the censors to the performance of *The Case* and *The Death of Tarelkin* is certainly understandable. For the young aristocrat conversant with Hegel's *Philosophy of Right and Law* (1821) and now confronted for the first time in his life by the grim reality of the omnipotence and corruption of the tsarist bureaucracy and the inhumanity and often grotesque absurdity of police methods, the confrontation came with the effect of an electric shock. His own arrests and indictment provided the once keen student of philosophy with almost an excess of material on which to reflect. And out of these reflections came the pervasive pessimism of the *Trilogy*. For the *Trilogy* is, despite its dramatic structure, a philosophical utterance, a fruition in literary form of philosophical reflection. The humorous characters and scenes, the grotesque and absurd comedy, particularly of the last play, are meant only to relieve and indeed at times heighten, but never obscure this fact.

The philosophical foundation on which the *Trilogy* rests is also the key to its essential unity. Apart from the more

obvious structural unity achieved by the repetition of characters and settings, the three plays are bound together by a
unity of philosophical vision. Sukhovo-Kobylin's world is a
perverse jungle of distorted values where virtue is torn to
shreds by the vultures of wickedness, where in the great contest between Good and Evil, a cruel Fate decides in favor of
the latter. In political terms, it is a world in which the State
in the form of a collusive bureaucracy, judiciary, and police
conspires to plunder the individual of even his most fundamental rights, using Law not as a weapon to safeguard these
rights but as the principal device against them.

Hardly renowned for their high intellectual standards, the
Russian censors of the time were riled not by the philosophical implications of the *Trilogy* (their perception of
which would have been problematical), but by the searing
exposure of a bribe-hungry officialdom and a ruthless police
functioning as little more than its coercive arm. The censors
read the *Trilogy* as a vicious satire motivated by personal
reasons. The richness of its satire, in fact, has prompted several critics to rank Sukhovo-Kobylin along with the more
familiar figures of Gogol and Saltykov-Shchedrin. But beyond
the philosophical and satirical dimensions of the *Trilogy* lies
another aspect of equal importance: the theatrical. For all the
pessimism of the author's vision of the world around him the
Trilogy is anything but a bleak exercise in didactic drama. If
Sukhovo-Kobylin sees goodness and decency mangled by the
wicked, his dramatization of this vision achieves an agile balance between the tragic and the comic. This balance reveals
itself not only in the structure of the *Trilogy* as a whole, but
by and large within the structure of each individual play,
including *The Case*, which is the most plodding and tragically
accented of the three. Juxtaposed to the somberness is the
comedy of word, image, and character. The rich colloquial
language of the plays moves rapidly from the exalted to the
ribald and is used so surely that it functions superbly as a
device for molding character and is one of the author's outstanding achievements.

In his delicate balancing of tragic and comic, Sukhovo-

Kobylin shows no reluctance in borrowing from the traditions of farce and mime theatre. The physical buffoonery of a play like Gogol's *The Inspector-General* reappears in the *Trilogy*. It may take the form of the tumbling from a ladder of the tipsy servant Tishka and the scuffling of Rasplyuev and Fyodor in *Krechinsky's Wedding*, the antics of the petty Gogolian officials in *The Case* and *The Death of Tarelkin*, the puppet-theatre routine of the clerks under Varravin's direction and the grotesque interrogation "drill" of Kachala and Shatala by Rasplyuev in *The Death of Tarelkin*, or the absurdities of situation (the fake "death" of Tarelkin) and character (Dr. Unmoeglichkeit) in the same play.

This same balance appears in the realm of Sukhovo-Kobylin's characters. With the exception of Varravin (the name is a Russianization of Barabbas), a symbol of pure evil, and of the secondary character Razuvayev who appears only in *The Case* as a man of the people (an Old Believer whose simple but eloquent faith elevates him to the level almost of a symbol of ancient Russian piety), the other characters whose meaning extends beyond the purely satirical or comic— the Muromskys, Atuyeva, Nelkin, Rasplyuev, Tarelkin—are drawn as neither wholly good nor wholly bad.

The unity of vision by which the individual plays are welded into a unique dramatic entity is reinforced structurally. Each play takes up where the preceding ends, the action of each play becoming therefore a logical progression of the action of the play before. In *Krechinsky's Wedding* Lidochka's innocent remark about the "mistake" of Krechinsky's swindle of the pawnbroker Bek is the peg on which *The Case* is hung. Out of this seemingly inconsequential remark emerges the nightmarish investigation and persecution resulting ultimately in Muromsky's death that is the substance from which the tragedy of *The Case* is evoked. The bribe money Muromsky brings as a peace offering to Varravin in this second play becomes in turn the pivot on which *The Death of Tarelkin* turns. Moreover, with the transition from one play to the next there is also a shift in mood.

In the overall scheme of the *Trilogy* the individual plays

thus become the three acts of a modern tragi-comedy. The
progression from one play to the next brings, furthermore, a
deeper descent into evil, a kind of inverted Dantesque movement. And accompanying this is the intensification of the
satire. In the final play the triumph of evil in the form of
Varravin's final victory and Tarelkin's direct appeal to the
audience for a new job assumes grotesque and absurd proportions. The satire of the entire *Trilogy* reaches a crescendo, the
irony becomes excruciatingly bitter: the police are now headed
by the totally amoral Rasplyuev, a petty criminal, and the
dominant image is that of a bloodsucking vampire—the ac-
cusation leveled against Tarelkin but operating symbolically
as the metaphor for an officialdom, its body swollen by corruption, feeding parasitically on the blood of its victims. And
who are its victims? In Sukhovo-Kobylin's vision, it is all
Russia. This is doubtless what led one recent Soviet commen-
tator to characterize *The Death of Tarelkin* in Meyerhold's
production at the Alexandrinsky Theatre in St. Petersburg in
the Spring of 1917 as the "epitaph of pre-Revolutionary Russia."[4] The implied parallel with Beaumarchais's *Le Mariage
de Figaro* in this respect is inescapable.

The elements contriving to unify the *Trilogy* as a dramatic
entity imposed no single architectural design used by Sukhovo-Kobylin in its composition. The result is that each play
is markedly different from the rest not only in structure but
also in mood. Each play represents, moreover, a different
theatrical style or styles and, in turn, a different source or
sources of technique. Sukhovo-Kobylin, it must be remembered, was an amateur dramatist who left behind only a
single dramatic work, the *Trilogy* collectively considered. Because he was not a career dramatist, he tended to use the
crutches of other dramatists' techniques longer than he
needed. But precisely because he was a talented dilettante,
Sukhovo-Kobylin could permit himself the luxury of approaching the work of other dramatists, both native and foreign, in
a casual almost irreverent manner, taking what suited his pur-

[4] M. Zlobina, "Zametki o dramaturgii Sukhovo-Kobylina," *Novy
Mir*, 19, 1967, 239.

poses, discarding the rest, bringing different and at times seemingly disparate elements together in a single work, blending always to suit his own taste. The result is an original, indeed unique, work of Russian drama.

II

Krechinsky's Wedding, the first play of the trilogy, was begun in 1852 and completed by mid-October 1854. It had its premiere on November 28, 1855, at the Moscow Maly Theatre with the brilliant actors Mikhail Shchepkin and Prov Sadovsky in the roles of Muromsky and Rasplyuev, respectively.[5] On May 7, 1856, it opened at the famous Alexandrinsky Theatre in St. Petersburg with Vasily Samoilov as Krechinsky, F. I. Burdin as Rasplyuev, and Fyodor Maksimov as Nelkin. The play was a great success and has been presented before enthusiastic audiences down to the present. The production by Meyerhold at the State Theatre in Leningrad in 1933 was one of the great moments in the relatively brief history of the Soviet theatre. In Kobylin's lifetime the play was mounted in Paris, Prague, Athens, and Constantinople— the only part of the *Trilogy* ever to achieve international renown.

The subject of *Krechinsky's Wedding* is the attempt by an impoverished nobleman, Krechinsky, to improve his financial position by marrying Lidochka (Lida, Lydia), the daughter of a wealthy provincial landowner named Muromsky. The Muromskys are simple and somewhat naïve, but good, honest country folk ill at ease in the city where they have come temporarily on business. An attractive, impressionable girl, Lidochka is ardently but vainly pursued by the young country squire, Nelkin, also a bit boorish but virtuous and sincere. Her heart, however, is won by the demon of the piece—Krechinsky, urbane, worldly, charming, cynical, ruthless, and impoverished as a result of high living and a near-fanatic passion

[5] The information on the stage history of Sukhovo-Kobylin's three plays is drawn from Leonid Grossman, *Teatr Sukhovo-Kobylina*, 31–96, and the newest edition of the *Trilogy*, edited by K. L. Rudnitsky, Moscow, 1966, 356–82.

for gambling. Krechinsky's pursuit of Lidochka's hand in marriage is promoted by her Aunt Atuyeva, a woman obsessed with social ambitions.

As his debts mount and creditors begin hounding him with the threat of public exposure, Krechinsky fears that his plans for the "marriage of convenience" he sees as the end to all his problems will be ruined by the Muromskys' discovery of his bankruptcy. In order to avoid jeopardizing so advantageous a union, he decides to acquire a certain amount of cash as quickly as possible to pay off his most demanding creditors and so avoid scandal. When the pressure on him reaches its peak he concocts the daring scheme to swindle a pawnbroker (Bek) by offering him a valuable diamond solitaire pin (obtained from Lidochka by a ruse) and then substituting in its place a worthless glass imitation the moment the pawnbroker's attention is diverted. This way he will be able to get the cash he needs to settle his outstanding debts and return the real pin to Lidochka who presumably will be none the wiser. The scheme works like a charm and Krechinsky is about to cap his victory by marrying Lidochka the day after the deception when, almost at the very end of the play, Nelkin, Bek, and the police arrive to expose the swindle and foil the criminal. When Lidochka, humiliated and in despair over the sudden realization of Krechinsky's fraudulent behavior, gives the pawnbroker the real pin, she saves Krechinsky from being arrested but unwittingly implicates herself in the swindle— the point at which the play ends and provides the link with *The Case*.

On Sukhovo-Kobylin's trips to Paris in the 1830's and 1840's he could not resist the lure of the theatre and visited it often. Through Natalya Naryshkina he made the acquaintance of Dumas *fils* and is reputed to have counted several actors and actresses among his Parisian friends. There were two aspects of contemporary French theatrical life of particular interest to Sukhovo-Kobylin and influential in the composition of his own *Trilogy*. One was the *pièce bien faite* (the "well-made play"), the masterfully plotted comedy of intrigue honed to a fine art by the highly prolific Eugène Scribe

(1791–1861),[6] then very popular in Paris, and developed further by Dumas *fils*, Emile Augier (1820–89), and Victorien Sardou (1831–1908). The other was the popular boulevard theatres of Paris, noted at that time for the remarkable on-stage multiple transformations of two outstanding comics, Marie Bouffé (1800–88) and Pierre Levassor (1808–70).

The subjects of gambling, swindling, and financial specula-tion, of *money*, generally, and the figure of the bankrupt aristocrat anxious to make a financially beneficial marriage were among the most common in French drama when Suk-hovo-Kobylin conceived the first part of the *Trilogy*.[7] These "money plays" were usually comedies of manners reflecting certain specific social conditions in France of the Second Em-pire. They were written by Scribe, but became the type of dramatic vehicle by which Scribe's successors in the genre of the *pièce bien faite* enjoyed considerable popularity in their own day, above all Augier and Sardou.

What these dramatists brought to the comedy of manners, whether satirical in the manner of Augier and Sardou or didactic in the manner of Dumas *fils*, was the sense of struc-ture, the adroit plotting inherited from Scribe. And it was precisely this marriage of social comedy and the *pièce bien faite* that Sukhovo-Kobylin sought to achieve in *Krechinsky's Wedding*. But he was no mere imitator. Through the naïveté and gullibility of both Lidochka and Atuyeva, he satirized the social ambitions of moneyed provincials in the cities; his sym-pathies are clearly with Muromsky and Nelkin who never give up their love for the soil, who preserve a simple honesty and faith, and who resist the lure of the social whirl of the city. Although Muromsky and Nelkin both fulfill, to a certain ex-tent, the role of the *raisonneur* whose opinions are those of the author, Sukhovo-Kobylin wisely avoided over-sentimental-

[6] A good English survey of Scribe's work is Neil Cole Arvin's *Eugene Scribe and the French Theater, 1815–1860*, New York, 1924.
[7] For an interesting and detailed study in English of the specu-lator, swindler, and gambler in French drama, see Hilda Laura Norman, *Swindlers and Rogues in French Drama*, Chicago, 1928.

ization and over-idealization and aimed instead for verisimili-
tude. Muromsky and Nelkin have their foibles, in spite of
their virtues, and this makes them more plausible as human
beings.

Krechinsky, too, though the villain of the piece, is made
more human by being prevented from appearing as utterly
evil. He is educated, comes apparently from a good family,
and possesses a definite charm. A rogue, he is not entirely
without honor. At one point, we learn that though women
are putty in his hands he never accepts money from them. In
Krechinsky Sukhovo-Kobylin satirizes the ne'er-do-wells of
polite society, young men of aristocratic background, leading
frivolous, aimless lives, indulging their passions (in Krechinsky's case, card playing), preying for their own gain on the
naïve, gullible, and unsuspecting. It is essentially the same
decadent *beau monde* held up to the contempt of satire a
decade and a half earlier in Lermontov's verse drama, *The
Masquerade* (Maskarada, 1835–36). The portrait is not a
flattering one, yet it can be viewed, in part, as a portrait of
the author himself as a young man-about-town in those ten
years or so from the late 1830's to 1850.

Despite the undeniable satire in *Krechinsky's Wedding*,
above all in the deft characterizations of Atuyeva, Krechinsky,
and Krechinsky's factotum and accomplice Rasplyuev, a comic
foil to his master, Sukhovo-Kobylin's goal in the first part of
his *Trilogy* cannot be defined as principally satirical. In the
overall scheme of the *Trilogy*, *Krechinsky's Wedding* sets the
stage for the persecution of the Muromskys, through which
the dramatist will expose the corruption of an officialdom in-
toxicated with the absoluteness of its power allied with the
brutality of the police. And it is this exposure with its deeper
philosophical ramifications that Sukhovo-Kobylin conceived
as his paramount objective and for which his most telling
satire is reserved.

In *Krechinsky's Wedding* the objective is more modest. The
author must first evoke interest in and sympathy for the
Muromskys and then bring them by means of Krechinsky's
swindle to the point where they are ready for their descent

into the hell of tsarist bureaucracy. Krechinsky's deception of
the Muromskys and his swindle of the pawnbroker function
as the point about which the play revolves. In common with
the tradition of the *pièce bien faite*[8] the effectiveness of
Krechinsky's Wedding depends on a meticulously designed
plot. It is structure more than character that takes precedence.
Yet to Sukhovo-Kobylin's credit is the excellent, plausible
characterization he develops within the framework of a comedy of intrigue. To succeed as a "well-made play" in the
manner of Scribe, *Krechinsky's Wedding* must be briskly
paced—it is; rich in incident—it is; suspenseful—it is; and
logically contrived—it is.

In order to capture the lively tempo of the *pièce bien faite*,
Sukhovo-Kobylin restored the unity of time, which serves him
well by enabling him to heighten for maximum effect the
mounting pressure on Krechinsky for funds to pay his creditors
and save his forthcoming marriage. Sukhovo-Kobylin uses this
pressure to make plausible the scheme to swindle Bek and, at
the same time, to prefigure the second and third plays of the
Trilogy.

As in most "well-made" plays, the suspense that is so essential an ingredient in the structure of the work is extracted in
two ways. First of all, the "secret" of Krechinsky's interest in
Lidochka is revealed to the audience in the twelfth scene of
the first act but withheld from the Muromskys until very
nearly the end of the play and the requisite "unmasking"
scene. Until the appearance of Bek and the police in the final
moments of the work, the Muromskys have only rumors about
Krechinsky's gambling and debts, but no firm evidence. Then,
the hero should also experience a series of ups and downs in
his fortunes of increasing intensity. Since Krechinsky is a
negative hero, the series of ups and downs must lead to his
eventual exposure, to the *reversal* of his fortunes. In roughly
the first half of the second act Krechinsky is driven to the

---

[8] There is an excellent discussion of the techniques of the *pièce
bien faite* and the impact of this type of drama on modern theatre
in Stephen Stanton's introduction to *Camille and Other Plays*, New
York, 1957.

point of desperation by his creditors who refuse to allow him any more time for the payment of his debts and by Rasplyuev's failure to acquire any ready cash. Out of this desperation is born the scheme to swindle Bek by means of the real and imitation diamond solitaire pins. This time it is from the audience that all the details of the swindle are withheld. The audience sees Krechinsky prepare the deception and return after its success, but it does not know how the swindle was brought off. The confusion and anxiety of Rasplyuev, left behind in Krechinsky's apartment while his master is away executing his plan, becomes the audience's as well. The mystery serves as the bridge of suspense Sukhovo-Kobylin builds between the second and third acts.

In the first half of the second act Krechinsky's fortunes suffer several blows. But the successful deception of Bek, in the second half of the act, reverses the pattern of defeats and leaves Krechinsky again triumphant at the end of the act. The same graph of ups and downs (or highs and lows) can be charted throughout the third act as well. In the first part of the act, set in Krechinsky's apartment, the Muromskys arrive to finalize plans for the wedding. Krechinsky's luck again seems in jeopardy when Rasplyuev finds himself unable to answer questions about Krechinsky's background and estate. But each time Rasplyuev falters, Krechinsky steps in at precisely the right moment to save the situation. This proceeds until the peripeteia (the greatest in a series of mishaps suffered by the hero) is reached in the fifth scene with the arrival of Nelkin and his disclosure that after acquiring Lidochka's diamond pin, Krechinsky pawned it. The *scène à faire*, or obligatory scene, marking the highest point in the hero's adventures, comes in the following scene when after a melee between Krechinsky and Nelkin, Krechinsky produces Lidochka's original pin, thereby completely vanquishing his opponent, and then gets a humbled yet perplexed Muromsky to agree never to permit Nelkin in his home again. This is Krechinsky's supreme moment.

As a positive hero, Nelkin's own peripeteia comes in the sixth scene when he has been vanquished by Krechinsky and driven from his home. His reversal of fortune and the *scène à faire* marking the highest peak of his campaign to unmask Krechinsky occurs in the eighth and last scene of the comedy when Nelkin, accompanied by Bek and the police, arrives and Krechinsky is at last exposed as a swindler.

The pattern of the play as a whole, with its suspense, mounting tension, and alternation of high and low points in the fortunes of negative and positive hero alike, is repeated within the structure of each individual act. In terms of its structure, therefore, the act becomes a microcosm of the play itself. This is the technique of the *pièce bien faite* Sukhovo-Kobylin had little difficulty in mastering. The first act of *Krechinsky's Wedding* is primarily informational; all the major characters are brought out and their personalities and inter-relationships established. The second and third acts, each constructed of a series of upsets followed by reversals of fortunes, thus reflecting the overall pattern of the play, accelerate the plot and move it steadily toward the crisis and final exposure of the villain.

Another device of the *pièce bien faite* used to good advantage by Sukhovo-Kobylin is the apparently trivial object or fact invested with a deeper significance revealed only later in the play. In Scribe, it might have been the glass of water in one of his best plays, *The Glass of Water* (Le Verre d'eau, 1840); for Sardou, the lost love-letter in *A Scrap of Paper* (Les Pattes de mouche, 1860). For Sukhovo-Kobylin, it is Lidochka's diamond pin. A barely noticeable reference is made to it early in the play (in the fifth scene of Act I) when Lidochka and Atuyeva are discussing Krechinsky's fine quali-ties (he speaks French, is a good dancer, moves freely in polite society, and so on) and mention among other things that his good taste is reflected in the way he had the diamond solitaire, which had long been lying in a strongbox, fashioned into an attractive pin. The importance of this pin and its imitation for the plot of the comedy has already been noted. Similarly, Lidochka's quite innocent remark at the end of the play, when she returns the real diamond pin to Bek, that "it was a mistake" acts as the link between *Krechinsky's Wedding* and *The Case,* and is the basis for the second part of the *Trilogy.* That is because her remark is deliberately misinterpreted by corrupt officials who use it as evidence that Lidochka and Krechinsky worked in collusion to swindle Bek. The entire burden of their case against the Muromskys rests on this single remark.

Sukhovo-Kobylin's use of apparent trivia in the manner of the *pièce bien faite* extends further to his revelation of character by means of props. One of the best examples of this in the entire *Trilogy* appears in the first few scenes of *Krechinsky's Wedding* where the small bell about which so much talk ensues clearly serves as a device to reveal character. The bell defines the social ambitions of Atuyeva, who constantly pushes Lidochka toward marriage with Krechinsky, and the simplicity and lack of pretense of both Muromsky and Nelkin. When Krechinsky arrives, it is his attitude toward the bell that enables the audience to perceive his cunning and duplicity.

For the first play of the *Trilogy* Sukhovo-Kobylin borrowed the apparatus of the *pièce bien faite.* It was a type of drama he knew well and, indeed, the most popular in France when his Parisian theatrical impressions were formed. But the above analysis should suggest that Sukhovo-Kobylin did not stop at mere imitation. While he did use most of the "tricks" of the "well-made play," he also demonstrated a capacity to utilize its conventions in a more original way. The boldest departure, of course, is the introduction of a *negative hero* and the inversion of the traditional formula of upsets and reversals. Nelkin was conceived as Krechinsky's positive counterpart and his most formidable opponent, but as the comedy unfolds the interest of the audience is centered much less on what Nelkin does than on Krechinsky's schemes and the now-increasing, now-diminishing possibilities of his exposure. Moreover, at the end of the play the conventional unmasking of the villain brings no concomitant triumph of the positive hero or of the other virtuous people of the play (the Muromskys). Krechinsky is exposed, but Lidochka's surrender of the real pin to Bek thwarts his arrest. Krechinsky's downfall does not result in a complete triumph for Nelkin, for at the end of the play there is no reunion with Lidochka, no talk of reunion, no indication that, though deeply hurt, Lidochka does not still love Krechinsky. Her desire to rescue Krechinsky at the last moment must be considered as motivated by love no less than by honor. Significantly, at the final curtain it is not Krechinsky but the Muromskys who speak of fleeing from shame. Sukhovo-Kobylin's chief departure from Scribean technique is his use of dramatic form to express a specific philosophical vision. This philosophical dimension is almost completely absent in the plays of Scribe and his followers. A moral element introduced by Dumas *fils*, Augier, and Sardou hastened the transition of the *pièce bien faite* into the *pièce à thèse* or "thesis play" dealing with contemporary social problems. The satire in Sukhovo-Kobylin's *Trilogy* is subordinated to the underlying philosophical theme—the omnipotence of evil and the helplessness of virtue in a world governed by cruel fate. That is why *Krechinsky's Wedding* has a negative hero, why attention centers on Krechinsky's machinations, and why the unmasking of the evildoer is modified in this play by Krechinsky's avoidance of any punishment for his swindle and by the absence of any successful romantic link between the positive hero, Nelkin, and the heroine, Lidochka. Moreover, the shock value of Krechinsky's fraudulence is considerably increased by the withholding of the unmasking scene until the very end of the play. Thus Sukhovo-Kobylin avoids any dissipation of the impact of Krechinsky's wrongdoing on the Muromskys and any compromise of his philosophical position.

III

The Case, originally titled *Lidochka*, was begun in August 1856 and finished in 1858. Sukhovo-Kobylin read it to the actor Shchepkin who suggested further changes. A new version was ready in 1861. Thus it was four years in the making. Sukhovo-Kobylin tried to win the censors' approval for its staging in 1861 and failed. A second attempt in 1863 also failed. The entire *Trilogy* was published six years later in

1869, but it still could not be performed. The censors re-
viewed *The Case* again in 1876 and once again rejected it.
Finally, in 1881, after the dramatist made a number of
changes aimed at blunting the sharp satire of the work, the
drama was given permission to be staged under the title *A
Bygone Time* (Otzhitoe vremya) to suggest that the satire in
the play harked back to some past era. It premiered at the
Moscow Maly Theatre on April 4, 1882 with the fine actor
I. V. Samarin in the role of Muromsky. On August 31 of the
same year it was staged at the Alexandrinsky in St. Petersburg.
Its greatest theatrical success was the production at the Alexandrinsky by Meyerhold and Lavrentev in 1917. This was the
first production for which the original text of 1861, free of
the emendations imposed by the censors, was used. The highly
talented actor Mikhail Chekhov played the meaty role of
Muromsky in a production in 1926 by the Second Studio of
the Moscow Art Theatre. Since then it has been performed
a number of times in the Soviet Union, Poland, and Czecho-
slovakia.

Although too deeply rooted in the tradition of the *pièce
bien faite* to abandon completely its techniques (which will
continue to reappear throughout the *Trilogy*), Sukhovo-Kobylin sought a different structure for his second play, one that
would set the bitterness of his satire of the tsarist bureaucracy
in the boldest relief and at the same time evoke in the audience the deepest compassion for the plight of the Muromskys.
What he finally produced was a play very different in rhythm
and mood from *Krechinsky's Wedding*.

In the first play intrigue and complications of plot were
accented; in *The Case*, it is character. The tempo of *Krechinsky's Wedding* proceeds at a good brisk pace, while that of
The Case has the slow measured pace of classical tragedy.[9] In
shifting to a somber mood, at times reaching the sublimity
of tragedy and a markedly slower, heavier rhythm, Sukhovo-
Kobylin shifted from comedy to drama, as *The Case* is desig-
nated. To accommodate the new mood, the weightier tempo,

[9] Nina Brodiansky took due notice of this in her article on Sukhovo-Kobylin for the *Slavonic Review* in 1946.

and the centrality of character, the dramatist expanded the three acts he had allowed himself for *Krechinsky's Wedding* into five.

Prior to Sukhovo-Kobylin's uncompromising assault on officialdom in *The Case*, nineteenth-century Russian bureaucracy had suffered at the hand of only one major writer, Nikolay Gogol. Whether satire was Gogol's true intent in his play *The Inspector-General* and in his Petersburg stories is irrelevant here; these works were read as satires in the nineteenth century and still continue to be by most readers. The spirit of Gogol, the Gogol of *The Inspector-General*, the Petersburg stories, and *Dead Souls*, is felt throughout *The Case*. Indeed, Sukhovo-Kobylin's diaries indicate that in planning the play he was so preoccupied with Gogol that he first named the character Tarelkin-Khlestakov (the hero of *The Inspector-General*) and Varravin-Tryapichkin (based on the name of the judge, Lyapkin-Tryapkin, in *The Inspector-General*).

Where, specifically, do we see Gogol's influence in *The Case*? First there is the matter of names. With the exception of the Old Believer Ivan Sidorov Razuvayev, Muromsky's estate steward, who was only mentioned in *Krechinsky's Wedding*, the new characters are all drawn from the bureaucratic ranks, ranging from the exalted personage identified only as the "very important person" to the petty clerks Gerts, Sherts, Shmerts, and Omega. They fall into three groups: the department heads (the "very important person" and the "important person"), the "powers" charged with the responsibility for the investigation of the Muromskys (Varravin and Tarelkin), and the "underlings" (petty clerks who are by and large comic types). There are several easily identifiable borrowings here from Gogol: a) the use of abstract names ("very important person," "important person") which Gogol had introduced in his Petersburg stories (e.g. *The Overcoat*); b) the telling name, a common Gogolian device, here used principally for the arch-villain Varravin and the petty official Zhivets (from the adjective *zhivy*, suggesting someone nimble, sprightly), a minor accomplice in the cruel deception of Muromsky; c) the absurd or comic name (e.g. that of the hero of *The Over-coat*), of which there are eight in *The Case*—Kandid Kastorovich Tarelkin (Varravin's henchman), and the petty clerks Chibisov and Ibisov, Kasyan Kasyanovich Shilo, Gerts, Sherts, Shmerts, and Omega; d) the comic pair (e.g. Gogol's Bobchinsky and Dobchinsky in *The Inspector-General*), here the clerks Chibisov and Ibisov; and e) the capsule descriptions of the characters with remarks on how they are to be played accompanying the *dramatis personae*, first introduced into Russian drama by Gogol in *The Inspector-General*.

Krechinsky's Wedding, it will be remembered, was set in Moscow; in *The Case* the setting shifts from Moscow to St. Petersburg, where the Muromskys have come because of the government investigation being conducted into Lidochka's alleged complicity in Krechinsky's swindle of Bek. The time lag between the two plays is six years.

By setting *The Case* in St. Petersburg, the capital of the Russian Empire and the seat of the bureaucracy he had come to despise, Sukhovo-Kobylin at once exposed himself to the influence of such Petersburg stories by Gogol as *Nevsky Prospekt*, *The Overcoat*, and *The Nose*. If *The Inspector-General* lent *The Case* certain dramatic devices, the contribution of Gogol's Petersburg stories was even greater. In them Sukhovo-Kobylin could grasp the whole atmosphere of bureaucratic Petersburg, here he could perceive both its tyrannical and ludicrous aspects, and could gain insight into the grotesque absurdities of its mores.

The relevance of the Petersburg stories for *The Case* can be measured not only in terms of specific devices (e.g. abstract character designation) but also in terms of specific episodes. Muromsky's shattering interview with the "important person," the prince, in the ninth scene of Act III, timed by Varravin to coincide with the prince's worst mood due to his hemorrhoids, points directly to the ill-timed visit of Akaki Akakievich to the Very Important Person in *The Overcoat* concerning the matter of his stolen outer garment, and Collegiate Assessor Kovalyov's meeting with the police inspector in *The Nose*.

But in his philosophical vision Sukhovo-Kobylin looked beyond mere satire of officialdom or a Gogol-like exploitation, however superb, of the comic potential of bureaucratic corruption or rigidity. *The Case* is conceived in terms of a direct confrontation between good and evil, between morality and immorality. The confrontation was to take place between the moral polar opposites of Muromsky, on the one hand, and Varravin, on the other. The increased number of characters compared to *Krechinsky's Wedding* and the larger dimensions of the drama should not blur the essential design. With the exception of the above antagonists, all the other characters are relatively minor, devices for the most part to define the opposing camps, as it were, and to set their respective positions into bolder relief.

In the camp of the virtuous are Atuyeva, who at last perceives the error of her ways, Nelkin, now more mature, a deeply sad Lidochka, for whom only her love for her father and her faith in God are any real sources of comfort, and the estate steward Razuvayev, the Old Believer who preaches belief in God's infinite mercy and is the closest thing to a *raisonneur* in the drama. They are important only insofar as they heighten the poignancy of Muromsky's hopeless struggle to preserve honor and decency. Of these characters it is only Muromsky himself who really grows in stature from the devoted, virtuous, conservative, simple, and somewhat boorish landowner of *Krechinsky's Wedding*. In *The Case* the more futile his struggle with the evil of bureaucratic corruption becomes, the more ennobled and tragic he grows.

Among the evil, only two figures stand out prominently: Varravin and Tarelkin. All the other officials, whether on the highest level or the lowest, serve either to exemplify the inhumanity of officialdom or, as in the case of the petty clerks, to provide the few light comic moments in an otherwise somber, bitter, and disturbing drama.

Tarelkin, who will become a more important character in the last play of the *Trilogy*, is Varravin's henchman. Like Krechinsky, he is crooked, but not wholly bad. Although he shares Varravin's corruption and relishes the thought of squeezing a sizeable bribe out of Muromsky, he is capable of feeling some compassion for the old man and is horrified at the cruel deception of Muromsky in the tense bribe scene (scene 7) of the fifth act. His remorse, when he reports Muromsky's death to Varravin, stems not only from the realization that Varravin's swindle of Muromsky's bribe money extends to him also, but also from a vague perception of the evil he has helped perpetrate. Varravin is incapable of such perception and remorse, for he is the symbol of the evils of tsarist bureaucracy: self-seeking amorality, venality, cunning, hypocrisy, and cruelty. The character is drawn with so much venom, in fact, that no trace of ordinary human decency remains. Varravin is the only figure in the entire *Trilogy* who is completely evil.

Pitted against this antichrist, Muromsky is doomed from the start. There can be no other outcome. Thus there is an inevitability about *The Case* that approaches tragedy. Struggle as he may, Muromsky can only accomplish defeat and death. The play ends with Varravin's complete triumph: the bribe money has been extracted from Muromsky so cleverly that there is no evidence of a bribe; the only outside witness to the deception, Zhivets, has been paid off; Muromsky himself is dead, and Tarelkin has been swindled out of his share and so intimidated that he is helpless to do anything. Evil is victorious.

Tarelkin's remonstrations about fate and the absence of justice in the world, a short soliloquy in the last scene of the drama, only underline the extreme pessimism of *The Case*. The device of concluding the play with Tarelkin's soliloquy satisfies two purposes: a) it immediately establishes the link with the third part of the *Trilogy*, for Tarelkin is the last speaker in *The Case* and the first in *The Death of Tarelkin*, and b) it intensifies the bitterness of the play through the irony of having the cruelty of fate and the absence of justice in the world hopelessly condemned not by Lidochka, Nelkin, Razuvayev, or even Atuyeva, but by Tarelkin, a willing partner in the scheme to swindle Muromsky.

Let us look more closely at the tragic aspects of *The Case*. In the very first scene of the play Nelkin reads a letter from Krechinsky urging Muromsky not to oppose the officials offering him a favorable resolution of their investigation of the swindle of Bek in exchange for a substantial bribe. When Krechinsky mentions at one point with some pride that he rejected the suggestion that he give testimony casting doubt on Lidochka's virtue, the audience can quickly grasp the source of conflict in the work: Muromsky's initial resistance to, but eventual acquiescence in, a bribe to save his daughter's honor. It can also sense Muromsky's imminent downfall. It observes the slow, measured progress of the old man toward the spiritual and physical destruction preordained for him. Muromsky's own virtue and the piety and religiosity of Lidochka and Razuvayev prove inconsequential in the struggle, and his fall, when it comes, is total. Throughout the *Trilogy*, Sukhovo-Kobylin uses comedy to lighten his pervading pessimism. In *The Case*, however, the introduction of humor through the antics of the petty clerks fails to provide an effective counterbalance; the sense of gloom is almost total. Moreover, the tragi-comic dimension implicit in the parallel plot of Varravin's taking Tarelkin's share of Muromsky's bribe actually intensifies the pessimism of *The Case* in the sense that even among thieves there is no honor.

Although Muromsky lacks the prerequisites of a traditional tragic hero, his growth of character in the conflict with Varravin, his ennoblement in the struggle with a destiny he cannot alter or circumvent, and his growing perception of the nature of the contest endow him with a certain tragic aspect. This dimension of tragedy is augmented in turn by the heavier rhythm of the drama, particularly in its earlier parts, the progressive imminence of the final catastrophe, and the transcendent element in the unequal contest of the protagonists. The irony of Tarelkin's bitter outcry against an unjust fate completes the circle of tragic suggestion.

If *The Case* fails as traditional tragedy, it succeeds handsomely as an example of the modern transmutation of the

classical mode.[10] As such, it is a play far removed from
Krechinsky's Wedding and the entire tradition of the *pièce
bien faite*. The blending of Gogolian and tragic elements in
The Case resulting in the very different style and pace of the
play compared to *Krechinsky's Wedding* should not obscure,
however, at least one dramatic link with the theatre of Scribe
and his followers. This is Varravin's adroit, almost sleight-of-
hand, removal of the bulk of the bribe money from Muromsky's package in the crucial seventh scene of the fifth act. It
is a deception involving a prop of the same order as Krechinsky's swindle of Bek, and drawn from the same bag of theatrical tricks.

IV

In *The Death of Tarelkin* elements of Gogolian absurdity
and grotesque merge with borrowings from the traditions of
the Parisian boulevard and domestic puppet theatres to produce a play strikingly different from the other parts of the
Trilogy and by all means the most unusual of the entire
cycle.

The initial conception of *The Death of Tarelkin* in Gogolian terms is evident in one of the first titles chosen for the
play, *Khlestakov, or Debts* (Khlestakov ili dolgi). However,
Sukhovo-Kobylin abandoned it in preference for at least three
others—*Tarelkin's Antics* (Prodelki Tarelkina), *A Great Day*
(Veliki den), and *Rasplyuev's Setup* (Rasplyuevskaya mekha-
nika)—before the final one, *The Death of Tarelkin*, was
reached, and the earlier Gogolian conception was broadened.

The play was the longest of the three in the making. It
was begun in 1857 and finished only in 1869. Sukhovo-
Kobylin considered it his best work and sought desperately to
bring it to the stage. But this was denied him for thirty-one
years. His first known attempt, in 1882, ran afoul of the
censors who took exception to the devastating satire of the

---

[10] For a fine discussion of modern tragedy and post-Renaissance
tragi-comedy, see Karl Guthke, *Modern Tragicomedy*, New York,
1966.

police and their methods of conducting investigations and securing testimony. Sukhovo-Kobylin's desire to see the play "take life" in the theatre led him to make a series of changes in the text of the play in the hope of gaining the censors' approval. The revised version of 1889, now titled *Rasplyuev's Lovely Days* (Rasplyuevskie krasnye dni), met with no more success, however, than the first draft.

The next version was submitted in 1892 under the slightly altered title *Rasplyuev's Merry Days* (Rasplyuevskie vesyolye dni). It, too, was denied approval. Another version was also denied in 1896. Finally, in 1900, when Sukhovo-Kobylin was eighty-three years old, the play was finally accepted for the stage. Its premiere was held at A. S. Suvorin's Literary-Artistic Theatre in St. Petersburg on September 15, 1900.

On three successive evenings in July 1901—the sixth, seventh, and eighth—a group of actors and actresses of the Suvorin and Alexandrinsky Theatres, on tour in Moscow, performed the entire *Trilogy*. It was the first time that all three plays were ever staged on three consecutive evenings. A repetition of the complete cycle on the next three days marked the last time that the *Trilogy* was ever so produced, although it is undoubtedly the most effective way to realize the work in the theatre.

The success of *Rasplyuev's Merry Days* in 1900 and 1901 was no guarantee, however, against further harassment from the censors. A new prohibition was levied in 1906, apparently because the line "All Russia is under arrest!" was too "touchy" in a Russia subjected to the turbulence of revolt the previous year. The ban was lifted only in 1917, and on the very eve of the Revolution, on October 23, Meyerhold staged the play at the Alexandrinsky Theatre under the title, *The Death of Tarelkin*, in the original version. It proved a great success. Five years later, Meyerhold mounted it once again, at Moscow's experimental GITIS theatre.[11] This time, however, the

---

[11] On Meyerhold's production of Sukhovo-Kobylin, see Nikolai A. Gorchakov, *The Theater in Soviet Russia*, New York, 1957, 61, 204, 205, and Marc Slonim, *Russian Theater from the Empire to the Soviets*, Cleveland and New York, 1961, 70–73, 247–48.

brilliant producer chose to make the play a vehicle for his
theories of theatrical biomechanics and constructivism. The
critics and public alike failed to appreciate the innovations of
Meyerhold's approach. The experiment was never repeated.
The play was performed again in 1922 at the New Theatre in
Leningrad, in 1924 at the Moscow MGSPS, revived again in
1936 at the Leningrad Maly, and has since appeared irregu-
larly in Soviet theatres.

The Death of Tarelkin takes up where *The Case* leaves
off. Denied his share of Muromsky's bribe money, Tarelkin
has sufficiently overcome his bitter disillusionment to hatch a
plot designed to recover his lost share—and then some. In
the interim between the end of *The Case* and the beginning
of *The Death of Tarelkin* he has stolen some papers incrimi-
nating to Varravin. With these he hopes to blackmail his
superior. When the third play opens he is busy making elabo-
rate plans to throw Varravin off his trail and free himself of
all outstanding debts by pretending that he—Tarelkin—has
died and by assuming the identity of his recently deceased
neighbor and fellow bureaucrat, Kopylov. With the collusion
of his maid Mavrusha he places a dummy resembling himself
in a coffin, and then to insure that nobody gives the bier too
close an examination, he surrounds it with a lot of dead fish.

After Varravin and a crowd of clerks have come to pay
their last respects and arrange for the funeral, Rasplyuev (in
this play cast in the role of a police official) and Varravin
return to Tarelkin's apartment to hunt for the missing papers.
In their search they discover the toupee and false teeth
Tarelkin discarded when he assumed the disguise of Kopylov.
Tarelkin-Kopylov is arrested and subjected to a merciless

OPPOSITE: *The Meyerhold production of* The Death of Tarelkin *at the Moscow GITIS (State Institute of Theatrical Art)
Theatre in 1922. Act III, Scene 8: the "grilling" of Pakhomov
by Kachala, Shatala (standing with fists raised), and Rasplyuev
(seated).*

police "grilling" bent on wringing from him the confession
that he is a *vampire* whose fellow conspirators are all Petersburg and all Moscow. Under Rasplyuev's harassment and
Varravin's threats of Siberia and death, Tarelkin cracks and
surrenders the stolen papers. He is set free as penniless as
before, but with Kopylov's papers and, as it were, a new
identity. In the last scene he turns directly to the audience
and asks if anyone would care to give him a job.

From this brief plot summary it can be seen that *The
Death of Tarelkin* is a very different type of dramatic experience than either *Krechinsky's Wedding* or *The Case*. The
Muromskys and Nelkin have completely dropped out of the
picture, and the action is played out entirely in the camp of
evil. The contest is no longer between good and evil, but
between *degrees* of evil—between Varravin and Tarelkin. As
in *Krechinsky's Wedding* and *The Case*, Sukhovo-Kobylin's
pessimism predetermines the outcome of the struggle: in the
conflict between a lesser and a greater evil the victory must
go to the utterly wicked, utterly venal, and utterly merciless.
Thus the final victor of the *Trilogy* is Varravin, the per-
sonification of all that was foul in the bureaucracy that caused
the playwright so much suffering.

Reflecting the author's personal experiences no less than
The Case, The Death of Tarelkin was conceived as a "comedy-
farce" (komediya-shutka) in which the satire of police ruth-
lessness takes on absurd and grotesque dimensions and is completely free of the bitterness and tragic doom of the second
part of the *Trilogy*. The absurd and grotesque sharpen, rather
than diminish, the effectiveness of the satire. Moreover, they
enhance the irony running throughout the play—Varravin's
swindling and harassment of Tarelkin paralleling on a comic
level the somber plot of the first two plays.

As *The Death of Tarelkin* unfolds one image gradually becomes paramount: the corrupt bureaucracy supported by a
ruthless police assumes the monstrous aspect of a gigantic
vampire feeding on the lifeblood of all Russia. This image
with its own implication of supernatural transformation gains
strength through Tarelkin's assumption of Kopylov's identity

and the investigation following his eventual arrest, instituted to prove that the metamorphosis of Tarelkin into Kopylov was no less than an act of vampirism. The transformation of Tarelkin into his neighbor and the deception of Varravin and the clerks by means of the coffin surrounded by dead fish possess an inner logic in terms of the satirical goals of the plot despite their patent absurdity. They are essential, as it were, to the full realization of the central image. The absurdity is given a grotesque dimension by the extended use of transformation throughout the play. In fact, the comedy as a whole can be viewed as an exercise in ironic inversion.

In *Krechinsky's Wedding* and *The Case* unscrupulous adventurers (Krechinsky, Rasplyuev) and corrupt government officials (Varravin, Tarelkin, and so on) prey on virtuous people (the Muromskys) for personal gain. In *The Death of Tarelkin* it is evil preying on evil: it is Tarelkin attempting to swindle Varravin by means of the stolen papers, and Varravin who has swindled Tarelkin. This basic pattern of inversion is carried through the transformation of characters. Tarelkin pretends to die and assumes the identity of his neighbor Kopylov. Varravin appears both as himself—that is, as the head of the government department investigating the Muromsky "case," and as a certain lame "hero" of the Russian wars in the Caucasus, Captain Polutatarinov ("Half Tatar"), one of Tarelkin's many creditors. The most stunning—and satirically powerful—transformation is that of Rasplyuev. From the parasitical flunkey of *Krechinsky's Wedding* he appears in the last play as a police official who takes charge of the prosecution of Tarelkin-Kopylov's vampirism and the far more menacing "plot" behind it. To carry the absurdity a step further, Sukhovo-Kobylin equips Rasplyuev with a son, Vanechka, who has a minor role as a scribe.

Sukhovo-Kobylin's preoccupation with inversion and transformation reflect his perception of their philosophical and satirical potentials, which he succeeds in exploiting to the fullest in *The Death of Tarelkin*. But they also reflect the spell cast on him by his Parisian theatrical experiences in the 1830's and 1840's. On his visits to the French capital the young

Russian aristocrat's appetite for the theatre did not stop
with visits to the traditional theatres with their classical dramatic and operatic fare. He also avidly sought out such
popular boulevard theatres as L'Ambigu, La Porte Saint-
Martin, Le Gymnase-Dramatique, Théâtre des Variétés, and
La Gaieté, where he found the *comédies-vaudevilles, opéras-
comiques, opéras-ballets, ballets-pantomimes,* and *bouffonades*
from which he learned the lessons of the "well-made play"
he was to use so effectively in the *Trilogy.*

It was also in these theatres that he was particularly fas-
cinated by the incredible facial dexterity and acting skill
demonstrated by the two outstanding comics of the age, Marie
Bouffé and Pierre Levassor in their playing of multiple parts
and transformations (often executed with lightning speed in
full view of the audience). It was primarily for these on-stage
transformations that Bouffé and Levassor gained their greatest
fame.

The transformations of Tarelkin, Varravin, and Rasplyuev,
but above all that of Tarelkin, executed before the audience
by means of the toupee, false teeth, and stoop, spring directly
from Sukhovo-Kobylin's observations at the Parisian boulevard theatres. The dramatist's own notes appended to the
text of the comedy bear this out. Among several suggestions
on how the work should be staged he calls particular attention to the technique to be used for the double on-stage transformation of Tarelkin into Kopylov. He specifically mentions
Levassor's superb muscular control enabling him to change
even the shape of his nose and his ability, with the aid of a
toupee, false beard, and moustaches, to assume the most
varied appearances almost instantaneously. So great, in fact,
was Sukhovo-Kobylin's interest in transformation, that it is
possible to see in the device the very nucleus of *The Death
of Tarelkin.* One can conceive of it as an experimental drama
built around a single stage technique and elaborated, through
a fantastic association with the transformative aspect of reve-
nantism, lycanthropism (werewolfism), and vampirism, into
a grotesque satirical comedy foreshadowing in some respects

the surrealism of the late nineteenth- and early twentieth-century European drama.

The Death of Tarelkin does not presage surrealist theatre alone, for there are also distinct hints of the verbal play and linguistic distortions of our so-called "theatre of the absurd." This is evident, for example, in Tarelkin's testimonial to himself in Act I, scene fifteen, in Dr. Unmoeglichkeit's unique prescription in Act III, scene three, in Rasplyuev's interrogation of the laundress Lyudmila Spiridonovna in the following scene, and in the attempt to wring from the thirst-crazed Tarelkin the confession that he is a vampire and a werewolf in scene eleven. None too sure of his terms (as he was previously in Act II, scene seven), Rasplyuev confuses the Russian word for vampire, *upyr*, with the Georgian for a novice monk, *mtsyri* (there is a poem by Lermontov so titled), and seems unable to settle on the proper term for werewolf, using variously *vuydalak*, *vudkoglak*, and the correct *vurdalak*.

Sukhovo-Kobylin's use of absurd language, a striking feature of *The Death of Tarelkin*, recalls the linguistic absurdities of Gogol in *The Inspector-General*, *The Nose*, and elsewhere. That Gogol's works served as a source is more than likely. Perhaps it was also from Gogol's fantasies the Sukhovo-Kobylin first derived his interest in the fantastic. Corpses rising from coffins and even the vampiric motif crop up in Gogol's tale called *Viy*, in the second *Mirgorod* collection of 1836. But Sukhovo-Kobylin also had closer sources dealing specifically with vampires, and these must also be considered. In the late 1830's and early 1840's Count Alexey Tolstoy (1817–75), famous in the history of Russian literature for his dramatic trilogy *The Death of Ivan the Terrible* (1866), *Tsar Fyodor* (1868), and *Tsar Boris* (1870), wrote three vampire tales of which Sukhovo-Kobylin doubtless was aware: *The Vampire (Upyr)* and, originally in French, *La Famille du voudalak* and *La Rendezvous dans trois cent ans*. Among Dumas *père's* less notable dramas was the play *Le Vampire*, which had its premiere in 1851, and which Sukhovo-Kobylin also could have known, particularly in the light of the elder

Dumas's travels in Russia and his friendship with the Narysh-
kin family.

The foreshadowing of surrealist and absurd theatre manifest in the grotesque absurdities of *The Death of Tarelkin* is
buttressed also by the theme of vampirism itself. The European neo-Romanticism of the late nineteenth and early twentieth centuries reawakened enthusiasm for the occult and
supernatural and opened the way for a new Gothic literature
of mysterious castles, supernatural forces, vampires, and werewolves. The tale *Carmilla* (1871) by the English writer Joseph
Sheridan Le Fanu is a relatively early manifestation; but in
1897 came that neo-Gothic classic *Dracula* by the Irishman
Abraham (Bram) Stoker, and in 1907 Strindberg's Expressionist masterpiece, *The Ghost Sonata*, with its figure of the
vampiric cook.

The Death of Tarelkin also contains some familiar Gogolian
elements previously encountered in the *Trilogy*: the absurdly
named government clerks Chibisov, Ibisov, and Omega reappear. They are joined by policemen called Kachala and
Shatala. The grotesque travesty of a muscular police interrogation in Act III, scene eight, involving an almost circus-like
clown act staged by Rasplyuev, Kachala, and Shatala, echoes
the bouncy frolicking of Dobchinsky and Bobchinsky in *The
Inspector-General*. The scene is one of the high points of the
comedy-farce. Also familiarly Gogolian is the parade of four
creditors with claims against Tarelkin (recalling the pressure
of creditors against Krechinsky in the first play of the *Trilogy*)
and the four witnesses interrogated by Rasplyuev in the
matter of Tarelkin's vampirism (the merchant Flegont
Egorych Popugaychikov, the landowner Chvankin, the yardkeeper Pakhomov, and the laundress Brandakhlystova), which
repeat the pattern of comings and goings of the local officials
and merchants in *The Inspector-General*. The number of
similarities to Gogol increases with consideration of Tarelkin's delirious raving toward the end of scene eleven in the
third act. It would not be stretching the point to draw a
parallel between Tarelkin's cry that he is going "to Algeria . . .
to Timbuktu . . ." with the remark about the Algerian bey's

nose pronounced by the insane clerk at the end of *The Diary of a Madman*. And lastly, the name of the laundress Brandakhlystova is derived from Gogol's play *The Marriage*. In Act I, scene ten, of this work, Kochkaryov mentions an Agafya Tikhonovna Brandakhlistova as the girl Podkolyossin intends marrying.

Although Gogol's influence in the *Trilogy* is more evident than that of any other Russian author, there is some evidence in *The Death of Tarelkin* that Sukhovo-Kobylin was not unaware of the early (Gogolian) Dostoevsky. *The Double*, which appeared in 1846, contains the figure of a German doctor Krestyan Ivanovich Rutenspitz. Sukhovo-Kobylin's doctor Krestyan Krestyanovich Unmoeglichkeit certainly has his origins here.

The second staging of *The Death of Tarelkin* by Meyerhold in 1922 provides additional insight into the modernity of the play in the light of the evolution of twentieth-century avant-garde drama. In his first production of the play in 1917 Meyerhold stressed its tragic elements; the mood was sinister and somber. In 1922, however, he revised his production along the lines of a circus buffonade complete with clown routines and acrobatics. By now the great producer's ideas about biomechanics and constructivism had crystallized, and the new version of *The Death of Tarelkin* represented an adaptation to these principles. Meyerhold's choice of the third part of the *Trilogy* in preference to *Krechinsky's Wedding* and *The Case* reflects his intuitive feeling for the theatrical, for of the three plays of the *Trilogy*, *The Death of Tarelkin* is the most perfectly theatrical.

Meyerhold's rejection of stage realism in favor of theatricality led him to rediscover the comic traditions of popular theatre, both Western and Eastern. Devices common to ancient mask and mime, puppetry, the *commedia dell'arte*, and circus clowns were incorporated in the practice of biomechanics and constructivism. To demonstrate the worth and significance of his vision of the theatre Meyerhold chose plays most capable of serving as proper vehicles for his theories. In *The Death of Tarelkin* he found that combina-

tion of fantasy and farce, of the grotesque and absurd, that
excited his imagination, and his exploitation of these elements in the play in no way defiled the spirit of the work.
If anything, they enhanced it, although the point was lost on
most contemporary critics.

The merging of popular theatrical forms—above all that of
the marionette—and literary drama marked one of the outstanding aspects of European theatre in the late nineteenth
and early twentieth centuries. This is anticipated in *The
Death of Tarelkin* not only in terms of structure but also in
terms of the metaphysical implications of the use of mask,
mime, and marionettes in Symbolist and Expressionist drama
and doubtless a major consideration in Meyerhold's return to
the play in 1922. Such puppet- and clown-like routines as
those between Varravin and the government clerks in Act I,
scene seven, and between Rasplyuev, Kachala, and Shatala in
the "grilling" of the yardkeeper Pakhomov in Act III, scene
eight, point directly and unequivocally to the later Strindberg,
Jarry, Andreyev, the Blok of *The Farce* (Balaganchik, 1906),
the Mayakovsky of *The Bug* (Klop, 1929) and *The Bathhouse*
(Banya, 1930), Benavente, the Grau of *El Señor de Pigmalión*
(1921), Pirandello, the Pole Stanisław Ignacy Witkiewicz,
and the contemporary exponents of the theatre of the grotesque and absurd from Ionesco to Sławomir Mrożek.

The theatrical modernity of *The Death of Tarelkin* is
paralleled also by the ideological modernity of the *Trilogy*
as a whole. Sukhovo-Kobylin anticipates not only the theatre
of the absurd in certain of its technical aspects and in its
vision of the human situation, but also the helplessness of
the individual before a monstrous governmental apparatus ex-
plicit in so vitally modern a work as Franz Kafka's symbolic
fantasy *The Trial* (written probably between 1912 and 1914
but published posthumously).[12] The nightmarish world of
The Trial is really not so far removed from that of *The Case*
and *The Death of Tarelkin*. The Court in Kafka's novel is

[12] The Sukhovo-Kobylin-Kafka parallel is also remarked by M.
Zlobina in her above-cited recent article in *Novy Mir*, 243. Zlobina,
however, sees Kafka's work as relevant only for capitalist societies.

ambiguous and never truly objectivized, while Authority in
the form of the bureaucratic apparatus and police is given
quite definite form in Sukhovo-Kobylin. Yet in both works
their power is absolute. If Josef K. never learns the crime he
is accused of in *The Trial*, he is, perhaps, only slightly worse
off than Muromsky. He suffers a whole year apparently for
no reason at all, and is eventually murdered at the behest of
Forces he but faintly understands. Muromsky's persecution
for a crime his daughter is totally innocent of is dragged out
over a period of six wretched years (nearly as long as what
Sukhovo-Kobylin personally endured) with undoubtedly
deeper psychological impact. In the end he too dies, not
much more aware of the mechanism of Power he so pitifully
contests than Josef K. In an age in which ever-growing state
authority, bureaucratic complexity and corruption, and the
uses of police power are universal concerns, the interest Sukhovo-Kobylin's *Trilogy* evokes transcends the Russia of Nicho-
las I and Alexander II. In terms of its ideological significance,
it can be as meaningful for the twentieth century as Kafka's
The Trial, Koestler's *Darkness at Noon*, or Mrożek's *The
Police*.

                                        HAROLD B. SEGEL

PRONUNCIATION GUIDE
TO THE NAMES OF THE AUTHOR
AND CHARACTERS

Súkhovo-Kobýlin

Pyótr Konstantínovich (or: Konstantínych) Múromsky

Lídochka (or: Lída, Lýdia, Lidúshechka) Petróvna

Ánna Antónovna Atúyeva

Vladímir Dmítrich Nélkin

Mikhaíl (or: Mikhaílo) Vasílevich (or: Vasílich) Krechínsky

Iván Antónovich (or: Antónych) Rasplyúev

Nikanór Sávich Bek

Shchébnev

Fyódor

Tíshka

Maksím Kuzmích Varrávin

Iván Andréyevich (or: Andréich) Zhívets

Chíbisov

Ibisov

Kasyán Kasyánovich Shílo

Iván Sídorov (or: Sídorych) Razuváyev

Paramónov

Polutatárinov

Síla Sílich Kopylov

Antiókh Elpidifórovich (or: Elpidifórych) Okh

Flégont Egórych Popugáychikov

Chvánkin

Krestyán Krestyánovich Unmoéglichkeit

Lyudmíla (or: Lyudmílushka) Spiridónovna Brandakhlýstova

Mavrúsha

Pakhómov

Kachála

Shatála

Vánechka

KRECHINSKY'S
WEDDING

A COMEDY IN THREE ACTS

Cast of Characters

PYOTR KONSTANTINOVICH MUROMSKY, a wealthy landowner in the Yaroslav district, who lives in the country, about sixty years old

LIDOCHKA, his daughter

ANNA ANTONOVNA ATUYEVA, her aunt, a middle-aged woman

VLADIMIR DMITRICH NELKIN, a young landowner and a close neighbor of the Muromskys; has served in the army; wears a moustache

MIKHAIL VASILEVICH KRECHINSKY, an attractive man, with regular and striking features; affects thick side whiskers but no moustache; close to forty

IVAN ANTONOVICH RASPLYUEV,* a short man, somewhat on the stocky side, about fifty

NIKANOR SAVICH BEK, a moneylender

SHCHEBNEV, a merchant

FYODOR, Krechinsky's valet

TISHKA, the Muromskys' porter

A POLICE OFFICER

SERVANTS

The action takes place in Moscow.

* A telling name suggesting a person who spits a lot.

ACT ONE

(Morning. The Muromskys' parlor. Directly facing the audience a large door leading to the front staircase; to the right, the door to Muromsky's quarters; to the left, the door to the rooms shared by Atuyeva and Lidochka. On a table near the sofa a tea service has been prepared.)

SCENE 1

Atuyeva, Tishka.

ATUYEVA *(entering from the door on the left, casts a glance about the room and then opens the door leading to the front staircase)*: Tishka! Hey, Tishka!

TISHKA *(offstage)*: Right away! *(Enters in livery, with a wide yellow sash across his chest, unkempt and slightly drunk.)*[1]

ATUYEVA *(Looking at him a long time)*: What a sight! . . . *(Pause.)* Why didn't you comb your hair?

TISHKA: But I did comb it, Anna Antonovna.

ATUYEVA: And didn't you wash that mug of yours?

TISHKA: But I did wash it, I most certainly did. From the time I was ordered to wash, I always wash.

ATUYEVA: Did the German bring the little bell?

TISHKA: He brought it, Madam, yes he did.

ATUYEVA: Give it here and go fetch a stepladder. *(Tishka brings the bell and a ladder.)* Now, you listen. But you're stupid—you don't understand anything.

TISHKA: If it please, Madam, why shouldn't I understand? I understand everything your ladyship says.

ATUYEVA: If a lady comes, ring twice.

---

[1] The author finds it necessary to indicate that Tishka's condition, though in all respects reprehensible, is not the coarse drunkenness frequently introduced, unfortunately, on the stage; but rather a certain pleasant state of being manifest in a zealousness to discharge his duty, the fruits of which, however, are often bitter; in a melodiousness of speech; in a barely noticeable search for equilibrium, and, most importantly, in an unperturbable serenity in the face of Anna Antonovna's rage and sober irritability.

TISHKA: Yes, Ma'am.

ATUYEVA: If a gentleman, just once.

TISHKA: Yes, Ma'am.

ATUYEVA: If it's just any lady or some female, don't ring.

TISHKA: Yes, Ma'am.

ATUYEVA: If it's a storekeeper or some merchant, don't ring either.

TISHKA: As you wish, Anna Antonovna.

ATUYEVA: You understand?

TISHKA: Everything, Madam, just as you said . . . But do I still have to announce the guests when they arrive?

ATUYEVA: Announce? Of course you have to announce.

TISHKA: So first I have to ring, then announce?

ATUYEVA: What an idiot! There's a fool for you! Listen, stupid, how can you ring first then announce?

TISHKA: As you say, Madam.

ATUYEVA: Now, climb up and start hammering. (*Tishka climbs up the ladder with the hammer and bell.*) Wait . . . There!

TISHKA (*positioning the bell*): Like this?

ATUYEVA: A little higher.

TISHKA (*going higher*): Here?

ATUYEVA: Higher I'm telling you.

TISHKA (*raising his arm higher*): Here?

ATUYEVA (*hastily*): Wait, wait . . . where? . . . Lower down!

TISHKA (*lowering his arm*): Is this all right?

ATUYEVA (*starting to get angry*): Now higher a little! Lower!! Higher!!! Lower!! Oh, my God, Tishka! What are you, a fool, don't you understand Russian at all?

TISHKA: By your leave, Ma'am, of course I do! I understand, Your Ladyship, I most certainly understand.

ATUYEVA (*impatiently*): What are you yapping about?

TISHKA (*takes the bell down completely and turns around toward Atuyeva*): I was just saying, Ma'am, that you were saying I don't understand Russian and I do understand Russian, very, very well I understand it, Ma'am.

ATUYEVA: Are you going to put up the bell or not?

TISHKA: As you wish, Madam.

ATUYEVA (*losing her patience*): Oh, you . . . Good God in Heaven! It's enough to try the patience of a saint! You're drunk, you are!!!

TISHKA: Have mercy on me, Ma'am. I was just explaining,

Your Ladyship, about your saying that I don't understand Russian when I understand it very well, Ma'am,
very well.

ATUYEVA (*crossing her hands*): Oh! Are you trying to make
a fool of me, you scoundrel you?! What is it, did you
climb up there just to carry on conversations with me?
Eh? Fasten the bell on at once, hear?!

TISHKA: Where, my lady?

ATUYEVA (*leaves completely beside herself and stamping her
feet*): Put it up wherever you want . . . Just wait, you
drunken wretch, give me time—you'll pay for this yet.

TISHKA (*hastily fitting a nail to the first place he reaches and
striking it with all his might*): I do so understand . . .
Very well . . . Your Ladyship . . . Madam . . . There,
there, that's it . . . Ouch!!! (*Tumbles from the ladder;
it falls after him.
Noise. Servants run in.*)

ATUYEVA (*shouting*): My God! . . . Help! . . . He'll break
his neck.

TISHKA (*again on his feet, smiling*): Not at all, Ma'am,
begging your pardon.
(*The servants reposition the ladder and fasten the bell.*)

SCENE 2

*The same and Muromsky, who comes in from the door on
the right, wearing a dressing gown and smoking a pipe.*

MUROMSKY: What's going on? What are you up to?

ATUYEVA: We're not up to anything. It's just Tishka drunk
again.

MUROMSKY: Drunk?

ATUYEVA: Yes! Do as you like Pyotr Konstantinych, but he's
gotten himself good and drunk this time.

TISHKA: Mercy, Sir, Pyotr Konstantinych! Drunk, says madam.
How am I drunk? If I was drunk, I ask you, how could
I fall off a contraption like that and still be standing
on my own two feet? . . . I was hammering the nail in,
Sir, when I missed, and something twisted me around . . .

MUROMSKY (*looking at him and shaking his head*): Twisted
you around, was it? . . . Go on, dunce, go back where

you belong. (*Tishka leaves, walking very cautiously; the servants remove the ladder.*)

SCENE 3

Muromsky and Atuyeva.

MUROMSKY (*following Tishka on his way out with his eyes*): Of course, drunk . . . Now what was all the fuss going on here about?

ATUYEVA: We were just putting up a little bell.

MUROMSKY (*upset*): Just a little bell! Where? What for? . . . (*Catches sight of the bell.*) What's this? Here? In the parlor?

ATUYEVA: Yes.

MUROMSKY: But what for, you plan to sound an alarm here?

ATUYEVA: Nowadays you see it everywhere.

MUROMSKY: My heavens, why it's just plain idiocy! Devil knows what it is! . . . Oh, what's the use of saying anything! . . . (*Paces the room.*) There's no sense to it . . . You'll just bite your tongue every time it goes off!

ATUYEVA: What sort of nonsense won't you think up next! Why should I bite my tongue? . . . Leave me alone, please; I know how to fix up a house better than you. (*Silence. Muromsky paces the room. Atuyeva drinks tea.*) Pyotr Konstantinych! We have to give a party.

MUROMSKY (*stopping, facing Atuyeva*): A party? What kind of a party? What party is it you're talking about?

ATUYEVA: You know what kind—the usual. As if you didn't know! Just a little ball . . . Like what we had the other day.

MUROMSKY: But you told me at the time that it was going to be the last, that there weren't going to be any more.

ATUYEVA: Impossible, Pyotr Konstantinych, completely impossible. Custom demands it, society demands it.

MUROMSKY: Isn't that lovely—society demands it! And how, tell me, does your society—to hell with it—demand it! . . . Demand of whom? Of me, demands it? . . . That's enough being so giddy! What, have you gone crazy or something?

ATUYEVA: Gone crazy? Who? Me?

MUROMSKY: Yes, you! You dragged me to Moscow, and that's when all the nonsense started: one ball after another, money flowing like water, socializing . . . a lot of fuss and bother! You turned my entire household upside down. My errand boy Petrushka—a nice fellow he used to be—you dressed up like a freak. And that idiot Tishka, a simple cobbler, you made over into a footman and decked him out in some sort of a uniform. And now (*points to the bell*) you've gone and put a bell up! The ringing carries through the whole house!

ATUYEVA: Of course, ringing. I'm telling you, everyone's got . . .

MUROMSKY: My God, woman! People go in for all kinds of stupidities—you couldn't ape them all if you tried! . . . Just look at what you've got here! (*Points to a vase with cards in it.*) What kind of a jug is it? What treasures are you collecting in it?

ATUYEVA: This? . . . It's for calling cards.

MUROMSKY (*shaking his head*): A catalogue of chatterboxes and windbags . . .

ATUYEVA: These calling cards?

MUROMSKY: Idlers, tramps from all over, people who have nothing to do but drag themselves from one house to another the whole day long, spreading dirt wherever they go, not with their boots—but with their tongues.

ATUYEVA: What, those sophisticated people?

MUROMSKY: That's right.

ATUYEVA: Ha, ha, ha! It's laughable and sad at the same time!

MUROMSKY: No, just sad.

ATUYEVA: How can you pass judgment, Pyotr Konstantinych; after all, what do you know about society?

MUROMSKY: I don't know anything and I don't want to know!

ATUYEVA: You've buried yourself your whole life in that Streshnevo of yours.

MUROMSKY: Buried myself—yes, my dear, I certainly have. But you don't have anything to complain about: if I hadn't buried myself, you wouldn't be giving those balls.

ATUYEVA: But that's your duty, Sir.

MUROMSKY: To give balls?

ATUYEVA: You have a marriageable daughter!

MUROMSKY: So I'm supposed to call people in. (*Gestures.*)

Over here! . . . This way! And then these benefactors
of mine will come up, eat us out of house and home,
drink us dry, then make a laughingstock out of us!

ATUYEVA: So it's better to waste your time yapping with
peasants?

MUROMSKY: Sure, better. When I yap with a peasant, as you
put it, either he gets something out of it, or I do, or
sometimes we both do. But who gets anything out of
your bell ringing?

ATUYEVA: A person isn't supposed to live just for gain.

MUROMSKY: He's not, is he? He certainly is!

ATUYEVA: We're not beggars.

MUROMSKY: We will be if . . . (*Throws up his hands.*) Oh,
what's the use of talking to you!

ATUYEVA: No, you'd rather hide yourself away in some God-
forsaken place and rot there with those human oddities
of yours.

MUROMSKY: Come now—they're no odder than you or I.

ATUYEVA: Well, I really don't know. The misery they caused
me at the last ball we had! The bonnet that that
Stepanida Petrovna fixed up for herself . . . and as fat
as she is she had to go sit herself down right in the
middle of the couch. Every time I looked at her, the
pain I kept getting in my heart!

MUROMSKY: For what? She was dressed nicely; she's a good
woman . . .

ATUYEVA: Who cares if she's good? Nobody's asking about
that . . . Nicely dressed! Everyone kept asking who she
was—I could have gone right through the floor.

MUROMSKY: What's wrong about people asking who she was?
I don't see anything wrong in it. But here's what is
wrong: a young girl like my daughter—and what's she
being taught? What kind of talk does she hear? Leaves
her bedroom at noon, then goes right away to have a
look at the calling cards . . . There's an occupation for
you! After that she's off chasing around the city: a
theater here, a ball there. Now I ask you, what kind of
a life is that? What are you preparing her for? What are
you teaching her? Well? To be a flirt? Make eyes at
everyone? Babble away in French, *comment vous portez-
vous?*

ATUYEVA: How, in your opinion, should she be brought up? What should she be taught?

MUROMSKY: Practical things, order.

ATUYEVA: Hire a German then.

MUROMSKY: How to manage . . .

ATUYEVA: Get a Finnish maid!

MUROMSKY: Housekeeping . . .

ATUYEVA: Get a housekeeper! . . . A slut!

MUROMSKY (*throwing his arms wide*): For God's sake, that's enough!

ATUYEVA: Why? The truth hurts, does it? . . . Well, enough of this . . . Tell me once and for all, do you want to give a party or not?

MUROMSKY: I don't want to!

ATUYEVA: Then I'll give it at my own expense; I have my own money!

MUROMSKY: Go on! I'm not your keeper!

ATUYEVA: The poor girl isn't going to be stuck in a corner, without any beaux, just because of your silly ideas. The only thing you worry about is the expenses. I'm afraid, my dear Sir, that these days you can't marry off a girl without expenses.

MUROMSKY: Aha! . . . Did you ever hear such nonsense: you can't marry off a girl without expenses! That's your idea! When they know that the girl is modest, comes from a good home, and has a dowry to boot, then some decent fellow will come along and marry her. But you marry her off spending a lot of money and putting on airs and you'll see how you'll pay for it afterward.

ATUYEVA: You think she'd be better off with some country scarecrow?

MUROMSKY: Not with some scarecrow, but with someone respectable . . .

ATUYEVA (*interrupting him*): Yes, so that this respectable person could bury her alive in the country? Go on, marry her off by force then, tie her hand and foot . . .

MUROMSKY: Catch your breath, dear lady.

ATUYEVA: What?

MUROMSKY: Catch your breath, take it easy, I say.

ATUYEVA: What's the matter with you . . .

SCENE 4

The same and Lidochka, all dressed up.

LIDOCHKA (*approaching Muromsky*): Good morning, Papa.

MUROMSKY (*regaining his spirit*): Here she is now. My little
princess! (*Takes her by the head and kisses her.*) My
spoiled child!

LIDOCHKA (*approaching Atuyeva*): Good morning, Auntie.

MUROMSKY: Well, what have you been doing? Whom did
you dance with last night?

LIDOCHKA: Oh, Papa, I danced so much!

ATUYEVA: She danced the mazurka with Mikhail Vasilevich!

MUROMSKY: With Krechinsky?

LIDOCHKA: Yes, Papa.

MUROMSKY: Great heavens—isn't it time he gave up that
sort of thing?

ATUYEVA: Why should he?

MUROMSKY: Well, he's not a young man any more; he must
be around forty.

ATUYEVA: Where did you get that idea? He's just a little over
thirty.

LIDOCHKA: He's a wonderful dancer! . . . Marvelous! . . .
Especially waltzes.

ATUYEVA: And what a handsome man!

MUROMSKY: I don't know what you see in this Krechinsky.
Grant you, he's nice-looking—and pleasant enough. But
there's talk that he's quite a gambler!

ATUYEVA: And do you have to believe everything you hear?
It's that Nelkin buzzing in your ear all the time. Well,
I ask you: where does he spend his time that he picks
up stories like that? Besides, who doesn't play cards
nowadays? Today everyone plays cards.

MUROMSKY: There are all kinds of ways of playing cards.
Anyway, Nelkin never goes near cards.

ATUYEVA: You and your Nelkin! If you saw him in society,
I think you'd be talking otherwise. He's an absolute
disgrace! Why just yesterday I finally got an invitation
to the princess's, and I got him to go along to the ball.
When he arrived, what do you think? He crawled off

to a corner and crouched there, peering around like some
kind of an animal. He didn't know a soul there. That's
what living in the country means!

MUROMSKY: So what? He's shy, he hasn't seen much of the
world. After all, it's no sin.

ATUYEVA: Who's saying it's a sin, but he'll never be accepted
in high society. Yet he'll insist on grabbing Lidochka
for a waltz! He's a poor dancer, and you'll see—he'll
stumble and pull her down with him yet. The shame
of it!

MUROMSKY (*flaring up*): I'm telling you—you're flying too
high . . . Just make sure you're not the one to stumble
and pull her down with you . . .

ATUYEVA: Don't worry about my stumbling.

MUROMSKY (*on his way out*): Watch out you don't make a
fool of yourself in front of that high society of yours.

ATUYEVA: I won't make any fool out of myself, don't worry!

MUROMSKY (*leaving*): Just the same, watch out.

ATUYEVA: Don't worry about me . . . just don't worry.

SCENE 5

The same without Muromsky.

LIDOCHKA: Auntie, why are you always making Papa angry?

ATUYEVA: I just can't take it any more. Can you imagine it?
He's fond of that Nelkin! (*Pause.*) Lida! What were
you and Krechinsky talking about during the mazurka?
You were talking quite a lot, weren't you?

LIDOCHKA (*hesitantly*): Yes, Auntie.

ATUYEVA: Were you speaking French?

LIDOCHKA: Yes, French.

ATUYEVA: I'm mad about it! I can't speak it too well myself,
but I could just die listening to it. You must be pretty
fluent in it by now, aren't you?

LIDOCHKA: Yes, I am, Auntie!

ATUYEVA: And how's his French? Does he have a good pronunciation?

LIDOCHKA: Yes, very good.

ATUYEVA: It sounds so clever when he talks French. And he
speaks it so fast, the words just seem to come pouring

out of him! And the way he says *parbleu*, it's just
wonderful! How is it, Lidochka, that you never say
parbleu?

LIDOCHKA: No, Auntie, I do say it sometimes.

ATUYEVA: That's very good! But what do you look so sad
about?

LIDOCHKA: Auntie! Honestly, I don't know how to tell you . . .

ATUYEVA: What, my dear?

LIDOCHKA: Oh, Auntie, last night he proposed to me.

ATUYEVA: Who? Krechinsky? Is that so! What did he say
to you?

LIDOCHKA: I feel somehow embarrassed telling you, Auntie . . .
He just said he loves me very much! (*Stops.*)

ATUYEVA: And what did you say to him?

LIDOCHKA: Oh, Auntie, I just couldn't say anything . . . I
only asked him, Do you really love me?

ATUYEVA: And what else did you say?

LIDOCHKA: I couldn't say anything else.

ATUYEVA: You know I noticed how you kept on twisting
some sort of ribbon in your hands. So—you mean you
really didn't say anything else to him at all? But I told
you what you were supposed to say to him, didn't I?

LIDOCHKA: Yes, Auntie, I said to him, *Parlez à ma tante et
à papa.*

ATUYEVA: That's it. You did the right thing, Lidochka.
(*Silence.*)

LIDOCHKA: Oh, Auntie, I feel like crying.

ATUYEVA: Crying? For what? You like him, don't you?

LIDOCHKA: Of course, Auntie, very much. (*Throws herself
on Atuyeva's neck and bursts out crying.*) Oh, Auntie,
Auntie, dear! I'm in love with him!

ATUYEVA: Enough, darling, enough! (*Wipes Lidochka's tears
with a handkerchief.*) There's nothing to cry about. He's
a splendid man . . . knows a lot of people . . . Is there
anyone he doesn't know?

LIDOCHKA: He knows everyone, Auntie, everyone. At every
party and ball he knows just everyone . . . Only I'm
afraid of Papa; he doesn't like him. He keeps on saying
that I should marry Nelkin.

ATUYEVA: That's just a lot of nonsense, dear. The only reason
your father wants you to marry Nelkin is because he's a
neighbor, lives in the country, and has an estate right

next to ours, furrow to furrow, as they say. That's why
he wants to see you marry Nelkin.

LIDOCHKA: Papa says he's very good.

ATUYEVA: Of course he is! That's how it always is in life,
dear: who's stupid is good; who doesn't have any teeth,
wags his tail . . . But if you marry Krechinsky—the
house he'll set up . . . the circle of friends you'll have!
Why, he has magnificent taste . . .

LIDOCHKA: Yes, Auntie, magnificent . . .

ATUYEVA: The way he took your diamond solitaire and had
it reset—just lovely! The thing was just lying around
in your father's strongbox, but now whoever sees it
simply goes crazy about it . . . Well, I'll have a little
talk about everything with your father.

LIDOCHKA: Auntie, Mikhail told me he has to leave Moscow.

ATUYEVA: Soon?

LIDOCHKA: In a few days.

ATUYEVA: Will he be gone long?

LIDOCHKA: I don't know, Auntie.

ATUYEVA: Then you have to give him an answer now.

LIDOCHKA (*sighing*): Yes, I must.

ATUYEVA: Then I'll have that talk with your father at once.

LIDOCHKA: Auntie! Wouldn't it be better if Mikhail spoke to
him himself? You know how clever he is, and smart,
and kind . . . (*Falls to musing.*)

ATUYEVA (*taking offense*): Well, do what you think is best.
I'm not your mother, after all.

LIDOCHKA: Oh, Auntie, how can you say that? Don't leave
me. You're a mother to me, a sister, you're everything
to me. You know I love him . . . (*Stops.*) Oh, Auntie,
what a word that is—love!

ATUYEVA (*smiling*): Now, now.

LIDOCHKA: I don't even know what's happening to me. My
heart beats and beats and suddenly it seems to stand still.
I don't know what it means.

ATUYEVA: It's nothing, my dear, it'll pass . . . Your father's
coming now. We'll take care of things right here and
now.

SCENE 6

The same and Muromsky.

MUROMSKY: Well, what are the two of you up to? Your Krechinsky is dragging me to the races today. Now what'll I do there? I don't especially care for racing.

ATUYEVA: So what? At least you'll have a chance to see people.

MUROMSKY: What people? We're going to look at horses, not people.

ATUYEVA: Why is it you never know anything, Pyotr Konstantinych? Why, the entire *beau monde* is going to be there.

MUROMSKY: To hell with that *beau* . . . (*A sharp ring of the bell.*) Ow! — Oh, damn you! How much can a person take? I'll break both that Tishka's arms when I get ahold of him. My patience has run out! (*Points to the bell.*) I'm telling you now, woman, please get rid of that thing or there'll be trouble!

ATUYEVA: That's impossible, Pyotr Konstantinych; do what you want, it's simply impossible. Everyone has them in their houses now.

MUROMSKY (*shouting*): What in heaven's name is the matter with you?! I don't want it, and that's all there is to it!

ATUYEVA: What on earth are you shouting for like that? Heavens! (*Points to the door and lowers her voice.*) At least have the decency to control yourself in front of strangers. (*Muromsky looks about.*)

SCENE 7

The same; Nelkin comes in, bows to the ladies and shakes hands with Muromsky.

MUROMSKY: Well, Vladimir Dmitrich, where have you been hiding yourself? I've missed you.

NELKIN: Yes, Pyotr Konstantinych (*makes a gesture with his hands*)—I've really been on a binge, what with all those balls and parties . . . (*Looks up at the door.*) Well,

Anna Antonovna, what a shrill little bell you've put up
there . . . oho!

MUROMSKY: You see, I'm not the only one who says so.

NELKIN: Yet you know, Pyotr Konstantinych, I'll tell you
something: at the ball where I was last night, at the
princess's, they had the same sort of thing (*turns his
head around in the direction of the bell*) . . . I was just
on my way up the stairs . . . everything was all lit up,
you know, just like it was daylight . . . I didn't know
my way around the house . . . swarms of servants all
over the place, all dressed up in fancy uniforms . . . So,
as I was saying, there I was on my way up the stairs,
and just as I started looking around to see where I was
the bell clanged right over my very head! It's as though
someone doused me with hot water! I can't even remember how my legs carried me into the drawing room.

ATUYEVA: But nevertheless carry you they did, and well . . .

MUROMSKY (*interrupting her*): I'm telling you, woman, you're
going to drive me out of the house yet with those bells
of yours.

NELKIN: Are you getting ready to leave for Streshnevo, Pyotr
Konstantinych?

ATUYEVA: I should say we're not! Perhaps after Shrovetide,
but before—what is there to do in the country?

MUROMSKY: There, you see?! What is there to do in the
country? Go reason with them! . . . I have to give orders
to make ready for summer. The manure has to be spread
—without the manure you won't be able to give any of
your parties.

ATUYEVA: Why have you got Ivan Sidorov there then? You
mean to tell me he can't pile the manure onto a wagon?

MUROMSKY: No, he can't.

ATUYEVA: I just don't understand . . . That's really something—so the landowner himself has to pile manure?

MUROMSKY: He has to.

ATUYEVA: A fine occupation!

MUROMSKY: That's why many an estate has fallen to ruin.

ATUYEVA: Because of manure.

MUROMSKY: That's right, from manure.

ATUYEVA: Ha, ha, ha! You better not tell that to anyone else,
Pyotr Konstantinych—you'll be the laughingstock of all.

MUROMSKY: I'm not going to worry about what . . . (*Just*

then the bell rings. Everyone starts. Muromsky bends back and bellows worse than before.) Ow! . . . God in heaven! This is driving me mad; I can't take any more of it . . . (*Goes up to Atuyeva.*) Do you understand—I can't take any more of it! What are you trying to do, finish me off?

SCENE 8

The same and Krechinsky, who makes a flamboyant entrance. He is dressed like a fop, with a cane, yellow gloves and patent-leather morning shoes.

KRECHINSKY: Good morning, Pyotr Konstantinych! (*Turns to the ladies and bows.*) Mesdames! (*Goes over to them and shakes their hands.*)

NELKIN (*somewhat at a distance; aside*): Ha! The first thing in the morning and he's here already . . . (*Krechinsky is telling a story, gesticulating with his hands, and shuffling his feet.*) A clown, a real clown. What can you do? He's entertaining, and they like him for it . . . (*The ladies laugh.*) That's women for you! What do you require, ladies? Yellow gloves, patent-leather shoes, side-whiskers as thick as felt and a lot of jabber! (*Krechinsky withdraws to a corner, puts down his hat and cane, takes off his gloves and without saying anything exchanges bows with Nelkin.*) Ah, Lydia, Lydia! (*Sighs.*)

KRECHINSKY (*pointing to the bell*): Anna Antonovna! What's that they've hung up there—a town-meeting bell?

ATUYEVA (*timidly*): Town meeting? What do you mean—town meeting?

KRECHINSKY: You know, the loud public kind.

MUROMSKY (*going over to Krechinsky and taking him by the hand*): That's the spirit, Mikhailo Vasilich! Fine fellow! Thank you, thank you from the bottom of my heart! (*To Atuyeva.*) Well, Anna Antonovna, what do you say now? Eh? I feel myself it's carrying things too far.

KRECHINSKY: What do you mean?

MUROMSKY: Good heavens! What do you think I mean? It's the work of the devil himself! I've gotten ill because of it. Town-meeting bell—precisely. It's like a meeting was being called here.

KRECHINSKY (*going up to the bell, the others following him and watching him*): Yes it's large, all right . . . Aha! What's this? It's got a spring, *à marteau* . . . Yes, I know the kind!

NELKIN (*aside*): Why shouldn't you know about bells; that's right in your line, after all.

ATUYEVA (*affirmatively*): A German made it for me.

KRECHINSKY: Yes, of course, it's a fine bell, only you ought to hang it lower down, near the staircase . . . yes, lower down.

MUROMSKY: That's it, exactly! Like a load off my shoulders . . . (*Opens the door leading to the staircase.*) Hey Tishka! You empty-headed bell-ringing sexton! Come over here! (*Tishka appears.*) Come here! Take that thing out of here! (*Tishka removes the bell and takes it away.*)

KRECHINSKY (*to Lidochka, very familiarly*): Tell me, Lydia Petrovna, did you have a chance to rest after last night's ball?

LIDOCHKA: My head still aches a little.

KRECHINSKY: Didn't we have a wonderfully gay time?

LIDOCHKA: Oh yes, wonderfully gay.

KRECHINSKY (*to Muromsky, glibly*): How lovely Lydia Petrovna was last night, how fresh and charming . . . you just couldn't help admiring her!

LIDOCHKA (*somewhat embarrassed*): Take care, Mikhailo Vasilich; you're praising yourself a little, you know.

MUROMSKY: What do you mean praising yourself? What an idea!

LIDOCHKA: Of course, Father. After all, it was Mikhailo Vasilich who picked out my entire ensemble. Auntie and I asked him to help us.

MUROMSKY: You don't say?! Really? Now isn't that something! Where'd you come by it, son—master of all trades and even trifles!

KRECHINSKY: What can I say, Pyotr Konstantinych? I've got a talent for it. And now would you be so kind as to come out to the courtyard with me and judge my talents along other lines. (*Takes Muromsky by the arm.*)

MUROMSKY: What's that you say? Why the courtyard?

KRECHINSKY (*ingratiatingly*): Have you forgotten?
MUROMSKY: Really, I don't know.
KRECHINSKY: I may freely offer my services as a consultant to
    ladies on their dress and makeup, but I still remember.
    The bullock?
MUROMSKY: Oh, yes, yes, of course! Well, what about the
    bullock? Did you bring him in from the country?
KRECHINSKY: Yes, he's already here. He's been kicking up the
    dust in your courtyard for the past half hour.
MUROMSKY (*taking his hat*): I'm curious to have a look at
    him.
KRECHINSKY: *Mesdames,* we'll be right back. (*Takes Murom-
    sky by the arm familiarly and leads him out.*)

SCENE 9

Atuyeva, Lidochka and Nelkin.

ATUYEVA (*pointing to Krechinsky on the way out*): There,
    Vladimir Dmitrich, is what I call a worldly man! . . .
    Charmant, charmant.
NELKIN: Yes, he is—what should I say?—sprightly, gay . . .
    But one hears little good about him.
ATUYEVA: Hears where? Through what crack in a wall?
NELKIN: They say he's a terrible gambler.
ATUYEVA (*obviously annoyed*): Forgive me for saying so—
    but I am tired of hearing those tales of yours. The only
    thing one ever hears from you is the gossip you pick up
    here and there. After all, you really don't know Moscow,
    so you listen to whatever anyone tells you and then
    spread it around. No, Sir, that's not the way a person
    is supposed to conduct himself in the city. You're a
    young person; you have to be more careful how you
    talk and more discriminating about the company you
    keep. Now tell me, who was it you were sitting with in
    the theater the other night? Who was he?
NELKIN: Just a local merchant I happen to know, Anna
    Antonovna!
ATUYEVA: Merchant?! You see, you've already started keeping
    company with merchants!

NELKIN: I beg your pardon, Anna Antonovna! He's a very wealthy merchant . . . you should see the house he has!

ATUYEVA: So what if he has a house? Anyone can have a house. But is a merchant fit company for you? And in public besides! Why if anyone in society sees you, they'll stop inviting you to their homes.

NELKIN: To tell you the truth, Anna Antonovna, I don't go chasing after their invitations.

LIDOCHKA (*flaring up*): What do you mean by that? Who do you think chases after them?

NELKIN (*catching himself*): Lydia Petrovna! Forgive me—I just said it like that, I assure you; I didn't mean that . . .

ATUYEVA: Well, enough of this now! God be with you, young man. But you'd do better to stop saying bad things about people. That's the way the world is, my dear—if you're good-looking, they'll say you're stupid beyond belief; if you've got money, they'll say you're ugly; if you're smart, they'll brand you a scoundrel or something even worse than that. That's the way the world is. Let God be the judge! A person is what he is.

SCENE 10

The same. Krechinsky and Muromsky come in quickly.

MUROMSKY: My dear Mikhailo Vasilich! (*Takes him by the hand.*) Thank you, thank you! But really . . . my conscience won't let me . . .

KRECHINSKY: Not a word more about it, please!

MUROMSKY: But I am embarrassed . . . I can hardly believe it. Lida! Lidochka!

LIDOCHKA: What, Papa?

MUROMSKY: Guess what, Mikhailo Vasilich here just now made a present of a bullock . . .

LIDOCHKA (*cuddling up to Muromsky*): Is it a nice one, Papa?

MUROMSKY (*closing his eyes in ecstasy*): Mag-ni-fi-cent! Just imagine: The head, the eyes, the muzzle, the horns! (*Again closes his eyes in ecstasy.*) Magnificent . . . Is he from your estate in Simbirsk?

KRECHINSKY: Yes, from my estate in Simbirsk.

MUROMSKY: So you do have an estate in Simbirsk.

KRECHINSKY: Yes, an estate.

MUROMSKY: With good cattle-raising?

KRECHINSKY: Of course, very good.

MUROMSKY: Are you fond of cattle?

KRECHINSKY: I certainly am.

MUROMSKY: Heavens! And milking cows, making cheese, that sort of thing . . .

KRECHINSKY (*smiling*): That too.

MUROMSKY: But it seems you don't really care for the country . . .

KRECHINSKY (*fervently*): Who told you that? Why I worship the country . . . In summertime the country is—paradise. The fresh air, the quiet, the peace! I go out to the garden, into the fields, through the forest—wherever I go I'm the master, it's all mine. Even the blue horizon— that's mine too! It's all so lovely!

MUROMSKY: I feel the same way too.

KRECHINSKY: As soon as I got up in the morning I headed straight for the fields. The fields are filled with warm air and fragrant scents . . . Then to the stables, the greenhouses, the vegetable garden . . .

MUROMSKY: And the threshing floor?

KRECHINSKY: And the threshing floor . . . Everything is alive; wherever you look there's activity, quiet, peaceful activity.

MUROMSKY (*sighing*): Yes indeed, quiet, peaceful activity . . . You see, Anna Antonovna, that's how intelligent people talk!

KRECHINSKY: A full day's work done, an appetite worked up, then it's homeward bound! But here's where something's needed now, Pyotr Konstantinych, right? Well, do you know what I have in mind? What's needed now?

MUROMSKY (*happily*): Tea, by all means, tea.

KRECHINSKY: No, not tea. Something more important than tea, something much higher than tea.

MUROMSKY (*puzzled*): I don't know.

KRECHINSKY: Come now, Pyotr Konstantinych! You mean to say you don't know?

MUROMSKY (*after a moment's thought*): No, I really don't know.

KRECHINSKY: A wife! That's what's needed!

MUROMSKY (*with enthusiasm*): Right, a hundred percent right! Of course!

KRECHINSKY (*continuing*): But what kind of a wife? (*Looks at Lidochka.*) Shapely, fair-haired, a quiet, gentle mistress of your home. You come home, take her head in your hands, kiss both her cheeks . . . "Greetings, wife, you say! What about some tea?"

ATUYEVA: Oh my! What kind of behavior is that? Why that way you'll ruffle your wife's hair!

KRECHINSKY: On the contrary, Anna Antonovna! Wives don't get angry when their husbands mess up their hair; it's when they don't that they're insulted. (*Muromsky laughs.*) Well, to go on with what I was saying: the samovar is already boiling. Then into the room comes the aged father—hair white as snow, leaning on a crutch. He gives his blessing to your wife, then a rascal of a little grandson hops all around him—he's afraid of his mother, but clings to his grandfather. Now that's what I call living! And that's how people live in the country . . . (*Turning to Lidochka.*) And what about you, Lydia Petrovna, do you love the country?

LIDOCHKA: I love it very much.

ATUYEVA: And since when have you loved the country, my dear girl?

LIDOCHKA: Oh, I do love it, Auntie. You know, Mikhailo Vasilich, I just adore pigeons. I feed them myself.

KRECHINSKY: And do you love flowers?

LIDOCHKA: Yes, I love flowers too.

ATUYEVA: Dear God in heaven! Now she loves everything!

KRECHINSKY: I'm afraid I've been talking some time. (*Looks at his watch. To Muromsky.*) It's already one, Pyotr Konstantinych! It's time to go, otherwise we'll be late. You'd best dress up—there's going to be a lot of people there.

MUROMSKY (*in high spirits*): Dress up? . . . Well, why not? We'll show them what country folk are like . . . It's hard to say no to so gracious a person.

LIDOCHKA (*running up to Muromsky*): Of course, Papa dear, dress up nicely. Stop pretending you're an old man already! . . . My darling (*kisses him*) . . . the two of us will go together, come . . . my dear Papa . . . (*Kisses him some more.*)

KRECHINSKY (*almost at the same time*): Bravo, Lydia Petrovna, bravo! . . . That's it, that's the way . . . splendid . . . Of course he shouldn't pretend . . .

MUROMSKY (*laughing and carressing Lidochka*): Me pretend?
More of your nonsense, eh? (*Lidochka escorts him out;
Nelkin follows them in the direction of Muromsky's
quarters.*)

SCENE 11

Atuyeva and Krechinsky.

KRECHINSKY (*looking around*): Well, Anna Antonovna, what
do you think of my picture of country life?

ATUYEVA: Now tell the truth: Do you really love the country?

KRECHINSKY: Who—me? What do you think?! I can't stand
it.

ATUYEVA: You can't stand it?

KRECHINSKY: But why shouldn't I make an old man happy?

ATUYEVA: It's such a pleasure for him when people praise
the country.

KRECHINSKY: You see! But I want you to know the real
reason for the way I talked, Anna Antonovna.

ATUYEVA: What reason is that?

KRECHINSKY: Anna Antonovna! Who doesn't esteem you,
who doesn't esteem the upbringing you gave Lydia
Petrovna?

ATUYEVA: And just imagine, Mikhailo Vasilich, Pyotr Konstantinych is always finding fault with me.

KRECHINSKY: Who? The old man? Come, Anna Antonovna
—you have to forgive him. He's a landowner, after all,
and these landowners can't see anything except their
cattle sheds and fertilizers.

ATUYEVA: Why just this very morning he was going on about
people who fall to ruin because they don't bother about
their manure.

KRECHINSKY: Exactly! You see, that's all they understand!
Your house is truly lovely. It has everything, except one
thing—a man. If you had a man, you know the kind
I mean, someone clever, worldly, someone completely

comme il faut, your house would be the first in the whole city.

ATUYEVA: I think so myself.

KRECHINSKY: I've spent a long time in society and I know what life is. True happiness is finding a well-brought-up girl and sharing everything with her. Anna Antonovna! I beg you . . . Give me that happiness . . . My fate is in your hands . . .

ATUYEVA (*putting on airs*): What do you mean? I don't understand you.

KRECHINSKY: I'm asking you for the hand of your niece, Lydia Petrovna.

ATUYEVA: Lidochka's happiness is dearer to me than anything else in the world. I'm confident that she'll be happy with you.

KRECHINSKY (*kissing her hands*): Anna Antonovna! How grateful I am to you!

ATUYEVA: You haven't spoken yet to Pyotr Konstantinych?

KRECHINSKY: Not yet.

ATUYEVA: You have to have his consent.

KRECHINSKY: I know. (*Aside.*) That's the fly in the ointment.

ATUYEVA: What did you say?

KRECHINSKY: I was saying that . . . a parent's blessing is . . . how should I put it? . . . the foundation on which everything rests.

ATUYEVA: Yes, that's true.

KRECHINSKY: How should we broach the matter to him?

ATUYEVA: To tell the truth, I'm undecided.

KRECHINSKY: I have it. Now I think is the right moment. I'll go at once to the races. The whole of society is waiting for me there. I have a big bet on with Prince Vladimir Belsky. You keep Muromsky here while I'm gone; engage him in conversation. Tell him that I was in a hurry because I was afraid of being late, and that everyone was waiting for me there. Then when you have him alone tell him about my proposal. (*Takes his hat.*)

ATUYEVA: All right, I understand.

KRECHINSKY (*pressing her hand*): Goodbye! I'm putting my fate in your hands.

ATUYEVA: Rest assured I'll do everything I can. Goodbye! (*Goes out.*)

SCENE 12

Krechinsky alone, then Nelkin.

KRECHINSKY (*musing*): Aha! There's a trick for you! A cool
million crawling right into my hands. A million! What
power! To force the issue or not to force the issue—
that's the question! (*Meditates, his hands spread apart.*)
An abyss, a bottomless abyss. Winner take all! The law
of probability—nothing more. And what are the proba-
bilities here? Against me: Papa—one; although he's an
idiot, he's a stickler for fundamentals. Nelkin—two.
Well, like they say, he's neither fish nor fowl nor good
red herring. Now in my favor, what have we? That
town-meeting bell—one; Lidochka herself—two, and . . .
yes! My bullock—three. Oh, the bullock's an important
item—he's had a splendid moral effect. (*Nelkin emerges
from a side door and stops. Krechinsky puts on his hat,
not noticing him.*) So, two against three! Hm! One
should suppose, therefore, that there's going to be a
wedding . . . (*affirmatively*) there is going to be a
wedding! (*Goes out.*)

NELKIN (*astonished*): A wedding?!! My God! Am I dreaming
it? Who's the bride-to-be? Lydia Petrovna? No, that
can't be. A lovely little berry, but it's not ripening for
you . . . But didn't he throw out a hint a little while
ago . . . "A wife," he said, "is needed, a wife." Devil
knows what else he said. Clever fellow! Real smart! A
damn daredevil! . . . But mark my words, you won't pull
the wool over the old man's eyes! He's a match for you
as it is, and he's got me behind him. No, you won't
knock him over so easily. While you're showing off your
trotters to us at the front door, we'll take a peek at the
back to see if there aren't any jades there. You city
birds are all alike—always putting up a fancy false front
with nothing behind it. But just wait—I'll smoke you
out of here yet! You've got things to hide; I've already
been told at the club that . . .

MUROMSKY (*offstage*): Write it, write it at once!

NELKIN (*going out*): I'll find out everything there is to find
out, and when I do I'll go straight to the old man and

I'll say: Can't you see what's going on? You'd better
watch out.

MUROMSKY (*appearing at the door*): Vladimir Dmitrich,
aren't you staying to have dinner with us?

NELKIN (*from the door*): If it were just with you people,
Pyotr Konstantinych. (*Leaves.*)

SCENE 13

*Muromsky, attired in evening dress, with a hat in his hand,
comes in quickly, an anxious look on his face. He is followed
by Atuyeva.*

MUROMSKY: I know them; just get them used to the habit
and they won't even pay a kopeck. (*Goes to the door
and shouts.*) Kondraty! You hear me? Write that the
lot of those peasants will have to work off their debts,
got it?! Mikhail Vasilich! Where is he? I knew it.
(*Again goes to the door. To Kondraty.*) Write to Akim
and tell him the same thing. What's he looking for?
His belly's just getting bigger! Minds his stomach and
forgets his debts—an old story . . . Mikhailo Vasilich!
(*Atuyeva comes in.*) Here's your big city Moscow life
for you, my lady!

ATUYEVA: What are you talking about?

MUROMSKY: Here's what: the peasants in Golovkovo are
seven thousand rubles in arrears.

ATUYEVA: In silver?*

MUROMSKY: Of course, silver; what did you think! (*Shouts.*)
What's the matter with you? Have you lost your mind?

ATUYEVA: But don't you have Ivan Sidorov to look after
things like that for you? What's he doing?

MUROMSKY: Why don't you ride out to him and ask him (*in
a squeaking voice*) "What are you doing, Ivan Sidorov?"
. . . Oh, God Almighty! (*Turns around.*) Mikhailo
Vasilich! Now where did he go to?

ATUYEVA: He's gone. He said he was going to be late, so
he left in a rush.

---

*In Sukhovo-Kobylin's time one ruble silver was the equivalent
of about three and a half rubles in paper currency.

MUROMSKY: Did he go to the races?

ATUYEVA: Yes, to the races. Everyone was waiting for him there—the racehorses, the club members. He has some sort of a bet on . . .

MUROMSKY: Well, I'll find him when I get there.

ATUYEVA: You and I have to have a little talk; please stay.

MUROMSKY: Ha! Now you want me to stay! What am I, a plaything? One moment go, the next moment don't go.

ATUYEVA: I have a matter I want to talk to you about.

MUROMSKY: Matter? What matter? Again some trifle or other.

ATUYEVA: You'll see. Put your hat down. I just had a long talk with Mikhail Vasilevich Krechinsky.

MUROMSKY: But you have long talks with him every day of the week—you'll never have time enough to repeat everything.

ATUYEVA: You're quite mistaken. I'm surprised that you don't understand a thing.

MUROMSKY: I don't understand a damn thing.

ATUYEVA: The man comes here every day . . . attractive, worldly, knows a lot of people . . .

MUROMSKY: He can have them!

ATUYEVA: You have a daughter, Sir.

MUROMSKY (*looking at the ceiling*): I've known for twenty years that I've got a daughter; I ought to know it better than you.

ATUYEVA: And you still don't understand anything?

MUROMSKY: I still don't understand anything.

ATUYEVA: God in heaven!

MUROMSKY (*suddenly recollecting*): What is it? A marriage proposal already?

ATUYEVA: And wouldn't he be a good match for Lida?

MUROMSKY: He's getting on in years.

ATUYEVA: Well, he's obviously not a boy anymore.

MUROMSKY: Lidochka won't marry him.

ATUYEVA: If she won't, we won't force her, but if she will— what would you say then?

MUROMSKY: Who? Me?

ATUYEVA: Yes.

MUROMSKY: I'd say . . . (*looking at her and rapidly*) hogwash!

ATUYEVA: What do you mean, hogwash!

MUROMSKY: Senselessness, nonsense, my dear woman!

ATUYEVA: It's not nonsense, my dear sir, and I'm asking you a sensible question.

MUROMSKY: If you're asking a sensible question, then give me time to think about it sensibly.

ATUYEVA: What is there to think about? You won't marry off your daughter by just thinking.

MUROMSKY: What do you want me to do? Rush off and throw her into the arms of the first man who happens to come along? You have to know who he is, what are his circumstances . . .

ATUYEVA: What do you suggest, ask him for references?

MUROMSKY: Not references, but you do have to know . . .

ATUYEVA: And you mean to say you don't know? A man comes to your house all winter and you don't know who he is. It's an open-and-shut case: he's received everywhere . . . he's known in society . . . princes and counts are his friends.

MUROMSKY: What are his circumstances?

ATUYEVA: He told you himself, didn't he, that he has an estate in Simbirsk, and he even made you a present of one of his bullocks.

MUROMSKY: What kind of an estate? There are estates and estates.

ATUYEVA: It's obvious that it's a good estate. You can see for yourself, right now all society is waiting for him at the races; if he didn't have a good estate, they wouldn't be waiting for him like that.

MUROMSKY: That's your story, not mine.

ATUYEVA: And what's *your* story?

MUROMSKY: What kind of an estate does he have?

ATUYEVA: What are you nagging me for?

MUROMSKY (*impatiently*): And what are you nagging me for?

ATUYEVA: What are you shouting about? I'm not deaf. Tell me, Pyotr Konstantinych, what is it you want? . . . Is it money? . . . Doesn't Lidochka have enough of her own? What are you so greedy about? You accumulate it and accumulate it—and it still isn't enough. The only thing that really matters is whether or not the person's good.

MUROMSKY: And is he good?

ATUYEVA: I can say that he's a splendid person.

MUROMSKY: A splendid person! And yet you hear that he

plays cards, that he hangs around clubs, that he has some debts.

ATUYEVA: Perhaps he has; who doesn't?

MUROMSKY: Whoever's in debt isn't going to be my son-in-law.

ATUYEVA: Is that so? Then you go look for one.

MUROMSKY: Fine, I'll look if I have to!

ATUYEVA: Then you'll look yourself—no help from me.

MUROMSKY: Then I'll look myself.

ATUYEVA: While your daughter remains an old maid?

MUROMSKY: Can't be helped. But I'm not going to marry her off to a goat.

ATUYEVA: So Mikhailo Vasilich is a goat, is he?

MUROMSKY: Save your energy, my dear!

ATUYEVA: Wha-a-at?

MUROMSKY: Take it easy, catch your breath.

ATUYEVA: How dare you! What are you trying to do, make a fool of me? You have nothing to say . . . that's all there is to it.

MUROMSKY: Nothing? . . . I've nothing to say? . . . I've got something to say, all right, and you just listen: you like him and Lidochka likes him, but I don't like him—so I'm not going to let her marry him.

ATUYEVA (*flaring up*): Then you should have said so in the first place: That's it and that's all there is to it! Your daughter, then, is supposed to be unhappy because of your whims? . . . And you call yourself a father?! . . . What are you, a tyrant or something?

MUROMSKY (*vehemently*): Who's a tyrant? Me? . . . Me?

ATUYEVA (*just as vehemently*): Yes, you, you!

MUROMSKY: No, you are!

ATUYEVA (*pointing a finger at him*): You, I say!

MUROMSKY (*pointing a finger at her*): No, you . . .

ATUYEVA: You! . . . What are you shaking a finger at me for like that?

SCENE 14

The same and Lidochka, who comes running in.

LIDOCHKA: Auntie, Auntie!

ATUYEVA (*still upset*): I have absolutely no more patience
left! . . . Do whatever you want, my dear.

LIDOCHKA: Papa, what's going on? What's happened?

MUROMSKY (*becoming calmer*): Nothing, darling; your aunt
and I were just having a talk . . .

ATUYEVA (*flaring up again*): Darling, is it?! Some darling!
Go on, tell your darling just what it is you were saying . . . What are you so quiet about all of a sudden?

MUROMSKY: I'm not quiet all of a sudden; I've been quiet all
along.

LIDOCHKA: Auntie! Auntie, dear! Please, for my sake!

ATUYEVA: Will you stop trying to calm me down! I'm not a
fool, after all . . . (*To Muromsky.*) What are you just
standing there for? Ask her! . . . After all, he's expecting
an answer! (*Lidochka looks at the two of them and
begins to cry.*)

MUROMSKY: Very well, I'll ask her. Tell me, Lida, would you
marry someone against my will?

LIDOCHKA: I, Papa? . . . No . . . No! . . . Never! . . . (*Em-
braces Atuyeva.*) Auntie! You see? (*Tears in her voice.*)
I'll enter a convent, Auntie . . . I'll go to grandmother
. . . I'll be better off there . . . (*Cries.*)

MUROMSKY: A convent? . . . God in heaven! . . . Where
did you get that idea! (*Bustles about her.*) Now now,
you wait a while, we'll think things over very carefully
. . . (*Dries her tears.*) Don't cry . . . we'll think things
over . . . My heavens! Who ever expected anything
like this?

SCENE 15

The same and Krechinsky, who makes a brisk entrance.

MUROMSKY: Oh, my God! Mikhailo Vasilich!

KRECHINSKY (*familiarly*): Well, Pyotr Konstantinych, looks

like we missed the races today . . . (*Stops. Muromsky and Lidochka are whispering to each other. To Atuyeva, quietly.*) How did it go?

ATUYEVA: All he says is that he wants time to think it over.

KRECHINSKY: And you got angry at him?

ATUYEVA (*straightening her bonnet*): No, not at all.

KRECHINSKY: Pyotr Konstantinych! Won't you tell me what it's about? . . . Please let me talk frankly; it's better that way. I'm a straightforward person. If we clear up the matter right away, there won't be any reason for us to have anything against each other later. After all, you're the judge, the decision is yours.

MUROMSKY: Oh, it's nothing really; we were just talking among ourselves, about another matter entirely.

KRECHINSKY (*eyeing all of them*): Another matter? I don't think so and I don't believe it . . . In my opinion, there's no point in beating about the bush. It's not my way of doing things; I like to come straight to the point. Last night I proposed to your daughter, then I had a talk with Anna Antonovna, and now I'm here in person before you.

MUROMSKY: But it's a difficult business, so difficult that I'm asking you to give us a little time to think things over.

KRECHINSKY: I should have thought, though, that you've already had time to think everything over.

MUROMSKY: No. Anna Antonovna just told me about it, in fact . . .

KRECHINSKY: That's not what I mean. For several months now I've been visiting your home—and you have had ample time to think . . .

MUROMSKY: No, I didn't give it a thought.

KRECHINSKY: Then the fault is yours, not mine. You really were obliged to think about it when you know that an honorable man doesn't frequent your home and take the chance of compromising a young lady without a special reason.

MUROMSKY: Yes, of course . . .

KRECHINSKY: Therefore I shall ask you not to postpone your decision. In a little while I have to leave here. I've already talked to Lydia Petrovna about it.

MUROMSKY (*undecided*): I don't know, I just don't know.

KRECHINSKY: May I ask what's troubling you? My circumstances?

MUROMSKY: Yes, that's part of it.

KRECHINSKY: You can see for yourself what my circumstances are; I'm not concealing anything. You notice, however, that I act differently than you do—I haven't asked you a thing about your daughter's dowry.

MUROMSKY: What's there to ask about her dowry? After all, she's all I have.

KRECHINSKY: And I'm all I have.

MUROMSKY: So far so good, Mikhailo Vasilich; but you know in matters like these a person has to have certainty, so to speak.

KRECHINSKY: I'll give you this certainty then. I have enough of my own; your daughter also has enough of her own. If you put these two enoughs together, they won't add up to poverty.

MUROMSKY: No, of course not.

KRECHINSKY: It's not wealth you're looking for, is it?

MUROMSKY: No, I'm not looking for wealth.

KRECHINSKY: Then what is it? Perhaps you heard that my affairs aren't quite in order?

MUROMSKY: I admit that there has been talk of it.

KRECHINSKY: Is there anyone living in Moscow who *isn't* somewhat unsettled! We're all unsettled! How have your own affairs been since you came to live here?

MUROMSKY: Mine? My heavens, a complete mess!

KRECHINSKY: A mess, precisely. We landowners have one curse—the city.

MUROMSKY: How true that is: one curse—the city.

KRECHINSKY: I'm leaving Moscow.

MUROMSKY: You're going back to the country?

KRECHINSKY: Yes, back to the country.

MUROMSKY: You love the country, do you?

KRECHINSKY (*with a display of emotion*): Ah, Pyotr Konstantinych! What sure means you have to make anyone around you love the country! (*Takes Lidochka by the hand.*) We love each other, love each other deeply, and shall love living in the country. We shall be with you always, and never take a step from you; we shall work together and share everything equally.

LIDOCHKA: Papa! My dear Papa!

KRECHINSKY: Remember what I said a while ago: the white-haired old man and his grandson—it's you I was talking about . . .

LIDOCHKA: Papa dear, it's you he meant . . . (*They all draw near to Muromsky.*)

MUROMSKY (*retreating*): No, no, please! Not like this . . . please . . . I haven't had a chance to think . . .

ATUYEVA: There's nothing more for you to think about, Pyotr Konstantinych—it's fate, the will of God!

MUROMSKY (*looking at all of them and heaving a sigh*): Maybe it really is the will of God! Well, God bless you! Here, Mikhailo Vasilich, here's her hand, but just see that . . .

KRECHINSKY: What?

MUROMSKY: That you keep your word about the white-haired old man.

KRECHINSKY (*leading Lidochka up to him*): Here's my guarantee! Well? Do you believe me now?

MUROMSKY: God grant it!

KRECHINSKY: Anna Antonovna! (*Leads Lidochka up to her.*) You give us your blessings, too.

ATUYEVA: You see, he didn't forget me. (*Approaches Krechinsky and Lidochka.*) My children! Be happy!

LIDOCHKA (*kissing her*): Auntie, dear Auntie! My God! How my heart is beating . . .

ATUYEVA: There's nothing to be worried about now, my dear; it's beating for joy!

MUROMSKY (*going up to Lidochka and caressing her*): Well, my darling, aren't you going to cry? Eh?

LIDOCHKA: Oh, Papa! How happy I am!

KRECHINSKY: Well, Pyotr Konstantinych, just imagine the kind of cattle farm we'll set up in Streshnevo. You'll see, I'm quite enterprising after all.

MUROMSKY (*happily*): Really?

KRECHINSKY: And how! Listen to me (*he speaks as though he were disclosing a secret*): We'll breed nothing but Tyrolean pigs.

SCENE 16

The same and Nelkin, who comes in and stops at the door in astonishment.

MUROMSKY: Yes, that kind is . . . very tender . . .
KRECHINSKY (*kissing Lidochka's hands*): No, not tender.
MUROMSKY: Yes, tender.
NELKIN (*approaching rapidly*): What? What's that? Who's tender?
KRECHINSKY (*turning around to Nelkin*): Swine!

CURTAIN

ACT TWO

(Krechinsky's apartment. Morning. A study, luxuriously furnished but in great disorder. Tables, bronze figures. On one side of the stage a bureau turned toward the audience; on the other, a table. Fyodor slowly goes about tidying the room.)

SCENE 1

Fyodor.

FYODOR: My oh my oh my! (*Sighs deeply and slowly.*) What troubles we've got . . . what troubles! You wouldn't believe it. The fourth day and we're still without heat, and the rooms are as cold as ice. But what do you expect without heat . . . (*Brief pause.*) When we lived in Petersburg, though, my God, the money we had! The gambling that went on! That's the way he's been his whole life: money—he burns it like it was straw, like it was just firewood. When he was still at the university, he had himself a merry time, but when he left it, his life became like a whirlpool, he started carrying on so! Society, counts, princes, parties, drinking bouts, cards. The young people wouldn't do a thing without him. And the fair sex—the same thing all over again . . . How many of them he's had, you couldn't even begin to imagine! Whether it's the kind of appeal he's got for them or what, he can't fight them off. The letters, notes, all kinds of things like that, and the personal calls. And the way they carry on! They plead, they love, they're jealous, they hate. Why, there was one—she was as rich and pretty as they come! She used to kneel in front of him for a whole hour, a rich woman like that, and she kept kissing his hands, like a slave. He had some power over her, no other way to describe it. The way she loved him! And money? I think she'd have pawned her body for him three times over! But no, he says, I don't want any woman's money; I don't need that kind of money, he says. Then he'd clench his fist—he's a strong fellow —and he'd say: I'm going to have money, all right; I want to have a good time. And off he'd go! Plunged into one spree after another, it was enough to make your hair stand on end! He'd blow everything he had right down to the last kopeck . . . And she—she worried herself sick and faded away to nothing, the poor woman. They say she died somewhere abroad . . . Yes, my friends, we had everything and did everything, but that's all gone and forgotten now . . . And now what's there to say? He used to have an estate in the country—nothing left of it; he doesn't even have a title. He lost the racehorses he had, and the family silver went a long time ago. Even had to give up some of his clothes . . . Everything down the drain like the earth swallowed it up! Those good friends of his, regular stalwarts they were, dropped him one after the other, and instead only this Rasplyuev tied himself around our necks. But what use is he? He couldn't even fight his way out of a paper bag . . . (A *bell rings.*) That's him! No sooner does day dawn when right away I've got to have a meal ready for him and get his playing cards sorted out, as though he were somebody worthwhile. "I can't do it myself," he says, "I play in such company." What kind of company? . . . Last night,

off he went somewhere, grabbed two decks of cards,
two of the best stacked decks . . . Well, maybe he did
win himself a little money . . . God grant it! (*Another
ring.*) Coming, coming! Ah, I'd better go let him in.

SCENE 2

Rasplyuev and Fyodor.

RASPLYUEV (*carelessly dressed, distraught, a crumpled hat on
his head*): What's the matter? You don't want to let me
in anymore, is that it?

FYODOR: Forgive me, Ivan Antonych, I didn't hear you.

RASPLYUEV (*going right to the front of the stage and stopping
there, striking a thoughtful pose*): Oh, what a life!

FYODOR (*aside*): He's out of sorts today.

RASPLYUEV: My God, my God! What does it all mean? Did
you ever hear of such misfortune?! Who'd believe it?
But there it is . . . (*Throws up his hands in a gesture
of resignation.*) Money . . . cards . . . fate . . . luck . . .
a horrible, evil delirium! Life . . . There was a time,
all right, when there was a tidy little sum. But they
consumed it, damn them all, they used it all up . . .
And now what? I'm left a beggar!

FYODOR (*approaching Rasplyuev*): How was it, Ivan Antonych? There was a game, wasn't there?

RASPLYUEV (*giving him a long look*): There was a game, all
right, there certainly was a game! (*Sits down.*) Oh-h-h,
oh my oh my! My God Almighty!

FYODOR: What's the matter with you? Did something happen?

RASPLYUEV (*giving him a long look, then spitting*): There!
—That's what happened! (*Pause.*) What can you do?
I admit it . . . I tried sneaking a change of decks . . .
and got caught . . . And then it began, ho ho! . . .
One wallop, then another, and another on top of that.
All right, have your satisfaction, I said, but enough's
enough! But he had something else in mind! He was
going to give it to me till he knocked me out! A bad
business, I see! His friends got worked up and joined
in, too. I tried giving them the slip . . . Do you know
Semipyadov?

FYODOR: I should say I do!

RASPLYUEV: The ungodliest mug you ever saw—like this. (*Makes a face.*) He wasn't even playing . . . No sooner does he get up from the table, when he rolls up his sleeves. "Give him to me," he says, "I'll teach him how to box." A fist like this he had! (*Demonstrates.*) Wham! God Almighty! "I'll splinter him into firewood," he says. (*Spreads his hands.*) He did, all right . . .

FYODOR (*moralizingly*): Ivan Antonych! Playing cards, Sir, isn't like knitting socks. Taught you a good lesson, they did!

RASPLYUEV: What lesson? There isn't a dog that could take that kind of a beating, so that's no lesson. They were just out to murder me, plain and simple.

FYODOR: Hm . . . murder? You shove your fist into someone else's pocket, so why shouldn't he give you a beating? Anyone'd do the same thing . . .

RASPLYUEV: The way he went at it though! Strong as an ox he was! . . . I've been in jams before but I can tell you I never expected a beating like that. Once in a while I managed to get my licks in too and let someone have it right in the mug—the mug's the first thing you aim for, you know—but not last night, no, that was a different story altogether . . . altogether! (*Attired in a dressing gown, Krechinsky appears at the side door. Rasplyuev does not notice him.*) The one last night's got a system: he doesn't just strike out, the dog, any old way, but gives it to you right smack in the kisser with his fist . . . No, brother, you won't get me again like that. No, Sir. I've had my lesson; I know what it is to sit with my mug in a corner for ten days at a stretch without work and food, and with a couple of black eyes the likes of which you never saw before (*demonstrates*) . . . so I know what this business is all about . . .

SCENE 3

The same and Krechinsky.

KRECHINSKY (*approaching Rasplyuev and measuring him with a stern eye*): You lost again?

RASPLYUEV: Lost? Me? Where'd you get that idea?

KRECHINSKY: I've heard. Don't try to bluff me, you blockhead!

RASPLYUEV: Why am I a blockhead? Why do you keep nee-
dling me day in and day out? God, what an existence!

KRECHINSKY: You're nothing but a windbag, a busted wheel
that churns water for nothing. (*Pause*.) Are you worth
the bread you get? Do you earn your keep? You jackass!!
After all, I'm not a member of any philanthropic societies. I need money for your keep here. So hand it
over! Understand, damn you? What have you got your
nose buried in the ground for? Talk—where were you
last night?

RASPLYUEV: Wel-l-l . . . I was . . . what's the place . . .
over there . . . (*Points*.)

KRECHINSKY: Did you bring any money?

RASPLYUEV: No, I didn't.

KRECHINSKY: Then hand over what you took to the game
the other day.

RASPLYUEV (*spreading his hands*): Gone, all gone!

KRECHINSKY: What do you mean "gone"?

RASPLYUEV: They took it away, the whole lot of it!

KRECHINSKY (*interrupting*): Blockhead! . . . I get it, they took
your money and gave you a beating on top of it.
(*Angrily*.) Ah! I ought to shake you till your teeth
started rattling! (*Starts pacing the room in obvious agitation*.)

RASPLYUEV (*mournfully*): Don't get upset, Mikhailo Vasilich;
I've already been given a good shaking! That'll hold me
a while. Strong as an ox that fellow, I'm telling you—
and how!! "I'll teach you how to box," he says! Hm!
Box! (*Krechinsky paces the room in thought. Silence*.)
Mikhailo Vasilich! Can I ask you a question? What does
he mean box, what's boxing?

KRECHINSKY: That's something you really ought to know.
Well, anyway, Ivan Antonych, this is what boxing is
(*makes a gesture with his hand*) . . . An English invention.

RASPLYUEV (*makes a gesture*): So that's what boxing is! . . .
An English invention, you say! . . . My God! (*Shakes
his head*.) Tell me . . . the English, they're a cultured
people aren't they, enlightened seafarers . . .

KRECHINSKY: I've got to lay my hands on some money! No

matter what, I've absolutely got to get money, and more
money!

RASPLYUEV (*indifferently*): I don't know what to do, Mikhailo
Vasilich, there's no money, and no way to get any.
(*Becomes pensive, then suddenly jerks his head.*) Well,
I never would have expected it! (*Raises a finger.*) The
English . . . a cultured people . . . seafarers . . . huh?

KRECHINSKY (*still pacing the room*): What's that you're
saying?

RASPLYUEV: I'm saying that they're a cultured people the
English, aren't they?

KRECHINSKY: I can see you've completely lost your mind
already. Talk to him about something important, and
devil knows what he goes on yapping about! Listen!
I've got one thing on my mind, only one thing—money,
nothing else but money. Go out and get whatever you
can—I don't care how much. My whole future, my
whole life, everything, everything depends on just three
thousand rubles silver. Go get it for me!! You hear?
Pawn your soul if you have to . . . Wait, why bother
about your soul? Steal the money, if you have to, and
bring it to me!! Go to Bek, to Sprengel, to Starov, to
all the Jews. Pay any interest they ask . . . Put down a
hundred thousand if necessary, but bring me the money!
But just see you don't come back with empty hands!
Or I'll wring your neck like a chicken's . . . Get the
money, that's all . . . Here's the story: I'm going to get
married to the Muromsky girl . . . You know her? A
good catch. I got the father's blessings yesterday, and
the wedding will take place in ten days.

RASPLYUEV (*dumbstruck*): Mikh . . . Mikh . . . Mikhailo
Vasilich! What are you saying?

KRECHINSKY: I've got fifteen hundred serfs in hand—worth
a million and a half—plus two hundred thousand
straight cash. With that kind of money I can win two
million! And I will win—I'll win for sure. I'll put one
hell of a fortune together, and after that—peace, a
house of my own, a dumb wife, and a quiet, venerable
old age. I'll give you two hundred thousand . . . enough
to last you the rest of your days, enough to give you a
free and easy life, all the fancy dinners you want, respect, friends—everything you've ever wanted.

RASPLYUEV (*bowing, rubbing his hands together, and laughing*): Two hundred thousand . . . fancy dinners . . . Ha, ha, ha . . . Mikh . . .

KRECHINSKY: But for that we have to have money; we just have to hold out for another ten days. Without three thousand I'll be bankrupt tomorrow! If I don't pay them off, the men I owe it to, Shchebnev and Halt, are going to sue me. They'll spread the story all around the club, have my name displayed on the club bulletin board— and that'll be the end of everything! You understand? (*Impetuously seizes Rasplyuev by the collar.*) You understand how this need for money is like a noose around my neck, like a terrible thirst? You've got to rescue me!

RASPLYUEV: Mikhailo Vasilich! My dear! Your words set all my bones chattering! I'm going, right away . . . ow . . . oh . . . ow . . . (*Collects himself.*) My God . . . (*Goes out.*)

SCENE 4

Krechinsky alone.

KRECHINSKY (*pacing the room*): I think he'll bring it off. That's the sort of thing he's good at—he'll comb the whole city. Those Judases know me . . . But what if he doesn't find the money! Huh? . . . God! How you need money sometimes! (*Drums with his fingers.*) How there are times in life when suddenly you see everything clearly . . . (*Thinks.*) But if there isn't any money? If Rasplyuev doesn't bring in even a single kopeck? What then? What if that fat million slips through my fingers all because of a measly three thousand rubles—when everything is already cooked, baked, roasted and all you have to do is just shove it in your mouth . . . It eats my heart out to think of it . . . (*Muses.*) It's too bad that lately I've had to tie myself up with all sorts of trash. Except for loathing and unpleasantness, I get nothing out of them. Respectable people and those stuck-up aristocrats have been shunning me. Hm . . . smelled something, I guess! It was time for me to call an end to everything or change sets . . . But then, as if by plan,

this blessed Muromsky family puts in an appearance. A
stupid waltz initiates the most banal flirtation. The business moved along swiftly: yesterday I got their consent
and in ten days I'll be married! I am making what they
call an excellent match! I'll have a house, a place in the
world, and a heap of friends and admirers . . . What's
there to talk about? (*Gaily.*) And the card playing
there'll be, the gambling! With two hundred thousand
I can win a mountain of gold! . . . Can? Must! What
a pleasure it'll be to skin the hide off all those fat
swine! But I have no intention of going to live in the
same house with that old fool. No, thank you! And as
for Lidochka, I'll have to take her more firmly in hand
and give her, as they say, a stiff training, knock all the
spirit out of her so there won't even be a peep from
her—I can't stand these whining women . . . Well, it
seems, that won't be difficult to do. This Lidochka—the
devil knows what she is! A boiled turnip, maybe, a
zero! And as for me, I'll take off to Petersburg! That's
where the real gambling is! But what do you have here?
Nothing but small fry, trash . . .

Scene 5

Krechinsky and Fyodor.

FYODOR (*coming in*): Mikhailo Vasilich! The merchant
Shchebnev is here . . . Shall I show him in?
KRECHINSKY (*after a pause*): Here's reality itself! Listen, you
fool, you should have told him that I wasn't in.
FYODOR: I couldn't, Mikhailo Vasilich! Those people aren't
like that. He'd sit calmly in the hallway for eight hours,
if he had to—it wouldn't bother him a bit.
KRECHINSKY: All right, show him in.

Scene 6

*Shchebnev and Krechinsky. Shchebnev is fashionably dressed,
with a huge gold chain, velvet checked waistcoat, and loud,
checked trousers.*

KRECHINSKY (*intimately*): Good morning, Timofey Ti-khomirych!

SHCHEBNEV: Our respects, Mikhailo Vasilich! In good health, I trust?

KRECHINSKY: I'm a little under the weather.

SHCHEBNEV: A slight cold, perhaps?

KRECHINSKY: Must be.

SHCHEBNEV: There's a little balance due me after yesterday's game. Would you care to settle it now?

KRECHINSKY: But I told you yesterday that I'd bring it to you in person.

SHCHEBNEV: Yes, that's so, Mikhailo Vasilich, but the truth is I need the money right away. So if you'd be so kind as to pay me now.

KRECHINSKY: I'll be honest with you, believe me—I just don't have the money now. I'm expecting funds any minute and I'll give you what I owe you very soon, rest assured. (*Silence.*) Well, how are things at the club?

SHCHEBNEV: Nothing much doing.

KRECHINSKY: Who joined the game after I left?

SHCHEBNEV: The same as usual. Well, what about you know what, Mikhailo Vasilich? Please do me the favor.

KRECHINSKY: You know, you're really a strange person, Timofey Tikhomirych! You be the judge: can I give you back what I owe you if I don't have any money at the moment? I simply don't have it. What am I supposed to do, bang it out of the table with a fist?

SHCHEBNEV: I see . . . as you wish . . . as you wish . . . You won't be offended then, Mikhailo Vasilich, if we go now . . . well . . . to the club . . . and enter your name in the little book.

KRECHINSKY (*obviously upset*): In the little book? You mean the club book, don't you?

SHCHEBNEV: Yes. That's the usual way.

KRECHINSKY: What do you mean "usual"? It amounts to disgracing a person, killing him on the spot . . . now the entire club will know about it, and tomorrow—the entire city!

SHCHEBNEV: Yes, of course. But it is the usual procedure.

KRECHINSKY (*jumping up from his chair*): Usual for you, but unusual for me. My whole life I've paid my debts honestly and on time, and if my memory serves me correctly, wasn't it I who waited three months precisely for *you* to pay back a debt? Do you remember?

SHCHEBNEV: That's quite true, Mikhailo Vasilich! And I'll always be grateful to you because of it. But don't you go getting yourself upset now. Do me the favor and pay up what you owe. What else can I do? It's a necessity.

KRECHINSKY: What kind of a necessity is it? Permit me . . . do you lose the right to inscribe my name in the book tomorrow, or the day after tomorrow? You don't lose it after all, do you?

SHCHEBNEV: Yes, that's quite true.

KRECHINSKY: Then why insist on doing it today?

SHCHEBNEV: That's what the rules demand. No payment, then in goes the name in the little book.

KRECHINSKY: What's the matter with you, really? Am I refusing to pay you? I'm merely asking you on my honor to wait two or three days. After all, I waited for money from you for three whole months.

SHCHEBNEV: True enough . . . that's quite true. But now it really would be better for us to settle our account, Mikhailo Vasilich! You know I don't like to do this, as God's my witness, but it is a case of necessity!

KRECHINSKY: You're as hard as a rock, damn it all! Or have you come here deliberately to play the fool? Can't I knock it into that thick skull of yours that now, this minute, I don't have any money and I can't pay you back! There is no possible way that I can! (*Advancing on Shchebnev.*) Do you understand?

SHCHEBNEV (*rising*): Why are you getting so excited, Mikhailo Vasilich? It's the usual thing . . . (*Bows.*) As you wish . . . (*After a pause, bows again and goes to the door.*) My respects! . . . However, this evening, I'll drop in on you on my way to the club; please have it ready then.

KRECHINSKY: Have what ready?

SHCHEBNEV: I'm speaking of the money again. My respects. (*Wishes to leave.*)

KRECHINSKY (*quickly taking him by the arm*): Wait! I can't do it. I sat down to play cards with you as an honorable gentleman, didn't I? An honorable gentleman, Sir, does not needlessly strangle another, does not pin another up against a wall except in extreme circumstances.

Then why are you strangling me now? What for? What did I ever do to you? Tell me, what did I ever do to you?

SHCHEBNEV: As you wish.

KRECHINSKY (*meekly*): Listen to me! If you were also without money, the way I am now, of course it'd be another matter. But you're a capitalist, you've got money lying around in that pawnshop of yours. You don't need it now. I never did you any harm, did I? I even waited for you to pay me money, while you were collecting interest on it all along.

SHCHEBNEV: For heaven's sake? How can you? God Almighty!

KRECHINSKY: Leave God out of it. What are you squeezing me for so mercilessly? You're finishing me off with a club . . . why? (*Silence.*)

SHCHEBNEV: My respects, Mikhailo Vasilich! (*Sighs, bows, and quietly slips through the door.*)

SCENE 7

Krechinsky, then Fyodor.

KRECHINSKY (*shouting after him*): Jew! (*Pause.*) He'll put my name in the club book! As sure as I'm standing here now, he'll do it. He'll scrawl my name in the book with that boorish handwriting of his, and the news is bound to reverberate throughout Moscow like a clap of thunder! And that'll be the end of it, the end of everything! The marriage'll fizzle out, and all that'll be left of that damn million'll be nothing but a puff of smoke, fumes, a hangover, and malice . . . yes, malice. (*Folds his arms.*) Well, I admit, wouldn't it be better to . . . (*Throws up his hands.*) Stuff and nonsense! . . . How would it be for me to take to my heels out of the city, a little bag over my shoulders, before they . . . (*Grabs himself by the collar. Pause.*) Me a beggar, eh? Ugh! . . . I'm in a tough spot, though!! (*Throws off his dressing gown.*) Stifling in here! (*Begins pacing in obvious agitation.*) Everything, everything depends on Rasplyuev . . . Some pass I've come to! (*Sits down at the bureau, takes a sheet of paper and begins writing with a pencil.*) Let me figure out what I need now . . . Let's see—this one, I owe fifteen hundred; that one (*pointing to the door*), twelve hundred. Now, as for this wolf—a thousand for sure. If I don't plug that insatiable gullet of his, he'll put up an awful howl . . . and how! With that trap of his . . . Let's see, small stuff—five hundred . . . six hundred. (*Adds up.*) I'll never get enough money for all that.

FYODOR (*at the door*): Mikhailo Vasilich, the coachman's here! He's asking for money.

KRECHINSKY: He'll get it all right—in the neck! (*Continues his accounting.*) This is the way the picture looks: three thousand rubles won't get me anywhere—it's a drop in the bucket . . . Then there's the wedding! The wedding? Why on earth am I making a wedding? More expenses, unavoidable expenses! Every fool'll be expecting presents and every pig'll have his hand out for a tip. On top of that those bouquets of flowers, the sweets, the meats, the silly baskets they put out . . . it's all a lot of nonsense . . . and it all takes money, money! (*Thinks.*) Money!

FYODOR (*coming in*): Mikhailo Vasilich, the laundrywoman is here. She wants money.

KRECHINSKY (*continuing his accounting*): In the neck!

FYODOR: Mikhailo Vasilich, the fellow who brings the firewood has been waiting for two hours.

KRECHINSKY (*raising his head*): Have you gone out of your mind or something? Don't you know your duty? What do you keep bothering me for with trifles?

FYODOR: As you order, Sir! I'm running out of excuses though . . . Tried just about everything . . .

KRECHINSKY (*half-rising out of his chair*): Are you going or not?! (*Fyodor disappears behind the door. The noise of voices is heard in the hallway, then fades. Silence.*)

SCENE 8

Krechinsky alone. Rasplyuev comes in, heads directly for a corner, puts his hat down and slowly removes his gloves.

KRECHINSKY (*rises, looks intently at Rasplyuev, then turns around, folds his arms slowly, and faces the audience*):

Well? . . . I knew it! (*Hangs his head.*) So that's it?!
(*Nervously runs a hand through his hair.*) That's it?!
(*Slowly approaches Rasplyuev with clenched fists. Rasplyuev retreats toward the wings. Krechinsky grabs him
by the collar with both hands.*)

RASPLYUEV (*timidly*): Mikhailo Vasilich, please . . . they ask
for security . . . secu . . . (*Krechinsky begins violently
shaking him to and fro.*)

KRECHINSKY (*stressing every syllable*): But I . . . ordered . . .
you . . . to get . . . me . . . money . . .

RASPLYUEV: Security . . . collateral . . . (*Gasps.*) Mikh . . .
Mikh . . .

KRECHINSKY: But I ordered you, you thief, to steal . . .
(*violently*) to rob!!! (*Chokes Rasplyuev.*) And to get
me money any way you can! (*Rasplyuev shouts. Krechinsky pushes him onto the sofa and takes up a position
at a corner of the stage, his face unrecognizable.*) So? . . .
He says there's no money! Liar! . . . There's money in
every house . . . there has to be . . . you just have to
know where it is . . . where it's hidden . . . (*Falls to
musing, his fingers moving.*) hm! Where it's hidden
. . . where it's hidden . . .

RASPLYUEV (*slowly getting on his feet and inspecting his
jacket*): That's the way! (*Looks for buttons on the
floor.*) Two beatings in twenty-four hours. That's certainly no way to live (*picks up a button*), that's enough
to make any dog run away from home . . . (*Picks up
another button.*) Take even a faithful dog like the
poodle—why, even he'd run away under such conditions. (*Continues looking for buttons.*) Let's suppose
what happened last night was a lesson in boxing, English style . . . but what kind is this? It seems this is
homemade stuff!

KRECHINSKY (*striking himself on the chest*): Oh!!!

RASPLYUEV (*catching sight of another button*): Ah, ah, ah!!!
(*Goes over and picks it up.*) Look where it rolled! (*Puts
it in a pocket.*) Flew at me like a wild man . . .

KRECHINSKY: What's to be done . . . what's to be done?

RASPLYUEV: First of all—stop beating me . . . (*Krechinsky
sits down at the bureau. Rasplyuev searches for a button
at the other end of the stage. Silence.*) My God! Some
people are born to happiness, to prosperity, to all the

pleasures of life, and they live, one might say, as though they were on one long continuous banquet. But others are born to be drums—to be thumped from early dawn to late at night! You see one before you now! (*Stands facing the audience.*) Well, if I'd been born skinny, delicate, puny, I'd never have survived . . . as God's my witness, I'd never have survived! I'll tell you, I'm sure I'd never have survived yesterday's beating; and that business last year— (*affirmatively*) I'd never have survived that; and the drinking-bout two years ago, in Kursk—I never, absolutely positively never, under no circumstances, would have survived that . . . and yet, after everything I've been through, here I am—alive and in one piece and I'll say this: all I need is a little food in my belly and a place I can have me a good snore . . . (*Stops and looks at Krechinsky, who is in the process of opening a bureau drawer.*) You won't find any money there, brother. (*Krechinsky opens another drawer.*) And none there either . . . (*Krechinsky opens a third drawer.*) Nor there . . . or anywhere, for that matter . . . yet he keeps on beating people! . . . What's gotten into him there? (*Krechinsky begins burrowing in the drawer.*) What's he digging around there for? What's he after in that old pile of rubbish? He's looking for money . . . the dear! But I know what's there— not a damn thing. Old dunning letters, unpaid bills. (*Krechinsky extracts a pin of rather large size.*) Look what he's got hold of—a piece of cheap costume jewelry . . . worth half a kopeck . . .

KRECHINSKY (*suddenly uttering a cry*): Aha! Eureka!

RASPLYUEV: Oho! (*Presses himself against the wall.*) He's gone off his head . . . you can see it's got the best of him . . . (*sighs*) poverty's worse than a bad relation.

KRECHINSKY (*holding the pin in his hand*): Eureka! . . . Eureka!

RASPLYUEV: Help! . . . He's gone mad . . . stark raving mad!

KRECHINSKY (*suddenly thoughtful and speaking slowly*): Eureka . . . it's Greek . . . means, I found it!

RASPLYUEV: Greek?! Whew-w-w (*Shakes his head.*) Our earthly wandering is over . . . Poor thing! My dear friend, they'll cart you off to the insane asylum and keep you, God's slave, on a chain. (*Shakes his head again.*) Yes, our earthly wandering is over. (*Deep in thought, Krechinsky moves a finger to and fro and mutters unintelligibly to himself. Rasplyuev follows him with his eyes.*) Looks bad . . . looks bad . . . Those crazy wild eyes of his . . . he's even liable to do me in . . . that's the kind of luck I have, after all. I better get away from him while I've still got my hide on . . . and that's about all I've got. (*Takes his hat and tiptoes toward the door.*) Saints preserve us and keep us! (*Goes out.*)

KRECHINSKY: Am I right? For sure? (*Rubs his forehead.*) Am I making a mistake somewhere? (*Again loses himself in thought. Rasplyuev and Fyodor appear at the door.*)

RASPLYUEV: Just see how he's carrying on, brother . . .

KRECHINSKY: This, this, then this . . . (*Jumps up.*) Bravo! Hurrah! I've got it, this time I've got it for sure!

RASPLYUEV (*hiding behind the door*): Big doings! . . . The way he's carrying on! You know what it is? I'll tell you— he's gone out of his mind, completely out of his mind!

FYODOR (*approaching timidly and embarrassed*): My dear Mikhailo Vasilich! Sir! What's the matter with you? Have a glass of water. What's bothering you, Sir? Maybe you'd like some smelling salts? Don't torture yourself so, Sir! We've been in worse jams before . . . we'll get out of this one, too . . . just say the word, and I'll carry you out on my own shoulders . . .

KRECHINSKY (*listening attentively. Then in a kindly tone*): Don't worry, Fyodor, there's nothing to worry about, I'm fine . . . (*Loudly.*) Hey, Rasplyuev! (*Rasplyuev trembles from head to foot.*) Go to that florist . . . you know . . . what's his name? . . . Fomin, that's it . . . Go to Fomin, in Petrovka, and order immediately a big bouquet of flowers, the best they've got, and all white camelias . . . understand? They've got to be white camelias. Go and bring them this minute.

RASPLYUEV (*mournfully pointing out Krechinsky to Fyodor*): What was I telling you, Fyodor? Eh? Doesn't have a kopeck to his name, and the poor dear's blowing a whole fifty rubles on a bouquet of flowers! (*Walks to and fro.*) Oh, oh, oh! My God, my God! What are we poor orphans going to do?

KRECHINSKY (*pacing about, then coming to a halt*): What's this? You're still here?! Your ears plugged, maybe? I'll unplug them for you! Did you hear me? (*Moves toward him.*) Did you hear what I ordered you?

RASPLYUEV (*retreating from him toward the wall*): Mi . . . Mi . . . Mikhailo Vasilich! Be reasonable! What am I going to use for money? I don't have a single kopeck to my name. For heaven's sake, be reasonable! What do you expect me to pay for the bouquet with?

FYODOR: On your way, Ivan Antonych, on your way! Didn't you hear what the master ordered you? On your way!

RASPLYUEV: But how can I pay for the flowers? Where's the money? I haven't got a single kopeck.

KRECHINSKY (*taking his watch and chain from the table*): Here's your money . . . Just see to it now that the flowers are right here on this table in half an hour. Hear? Now get going! (*Rasplyuev leaves.*)

SCENE 9

The same without Rasplyuev.

KRECHINSKY: Now, now, yes, right this minute I've got to send Lidochka a note to have everything ready. Time is of the essence; to business! (*Sits down at the bureau and begins to write.*)

FYODOR (*aside, casting a sidelong glance at Krechinsky*): He's all wrong, Ivan Antonych—the master hasn't gone crazy, he hasn't gone crazy at all. Just look at the way he's sitting there like a hawk.

SCENE 10

Krechinsky alone.

KRECHINSKY (*writing a letter; stopping from time to time*): That's not the way! (*Tears up the paper; writes again.*) Off to a bad start again. (*Tears up the paper once more; writes again.*) What a ticklish business! I have to write the kind of a letter that'd make the veins of a dead

woman throb, that'd excite passion. Passion, after all,
arouses passion. Ah, passion, passion! Where are you?
(*Smiles sardonically.*) My passion, my love . . . I'm
searching for firewood in a burning oven . . . He, he, he!
But I must, I absolutely must . . . (*Composes the letter,
reads it over, crosses out, writes again.*) This is what
I call real work; why I've even started sweating. (*Wipes
his face and quickly peruses the letter.*) Hm-m-m-m . . .
My gentle angel . . . family haven so dear to the heart
. . . hm . . . mm . . . hm . . . tender constellation . . .
devil knows what nonsense! But that's what they like
. . . gibberish, balderdash, tommyrot, and the like. (*Seals
the letter and writes the address.*) Let's see now: My
gentle angel! Send me one of your tiny wings—your pin
with the diamond solitaire (*parodying*), reflecting the
brilliance of your heavenly habitation. We must fit out
an enchanted vessel in which we shall sail forth under
four winds: the wind of diamonds, the wind of clubs,
the wind of spades, and the wind of hearts, over the
troubled sea of life. I shall take up my position at the
helm, Rasplyuev at the sails, and you shall be our
ballast! . . . Talking about Rasplyuev . . . he's still not
here yet . . . What a . . .

SCENE 11

Krechinsky; Rasplyuev comes in.

KRECHINSKY: Ah . . . There he is . . . at last . . .

RASPLYUEV (*carefully carrying a bouquet of flowers in his
hand. To the audience, pointing at the bouquet.*)
Twenty-five rubles silver for this broom! Pah!

KRECHINSKY: Hey, bring it over here, let's have a look at it.
(*Looks.*) Nice, it'll do. How much change left?

RASPLYUEV (*contritely*): Change? Fifty rubles. (*Hands him
the money.*)

KRECHINSKY: Now listen to me and button your lip—it's a
tricky business. Here's a letter to my fiancée, Lydia Petrovna Muromskaya. You know where she lives, right
near here on the boulevard . . . you know?

RASPLYUEV (*coming to life*): I know, Mikhailo Vasilich, I

know. A big white house with a driveway, just as you
turn the corner.

KRECHINSKY: That's the one. What time is it now, about one?

RASPLYUEV (*hopping up to the clock*): A quarter to.

KRECHINSKY: All right. The old man isn't home now; around
this time he's usually dragging around town on those
miserable nags of his. You go straight to the house and
deliver the bouquet to Lydia Petrovna personally. Wish
her a good morning for me, you know how, with a little
dash, a little swagger, ingratiate yourself . . . follow me?
And be sure and tidy yourself up nice. Put on my jacket
. . . Fyodor! (*Fyodor comes in.*) Give him my jacket! . . .
If the old man is at home, deliver the bouquet, but not
my note, get it? I ask her in it, among other things, to
send me that diamond solitaire of hers that I had made
over into a pin . . . remember it? (*Fyodor hands Rasplyuev the jacket.*)

RASPLYUEV (*putting on the jacket and straightening it out*):
I know, I remember it; twenty karats—worth thirty
thousand.

KRECHINSKY: I'm writing her that yesterday I had an argument about it with Prince Belsky and that we made a
sizable bet on it.

RASPLYUEV: Ah-h-h-h, yes-s-s . . .

KRECHINSKY: Get the thing and bring it here as carefully as
you can. (*Threatens him.*) About the bet, you can
embroider it yourself a bit.

RASPLYUEV: I'll embroider it, Mikhailo Vasilich, I'll embroider
it willingly.

KRECHINSKY: On the other hand, maybe it'd be best not to.
Everytime you start making up stories you get into
trouble. Run along, and as soon as you've got the pin—
fly back! Watch out for the old man, though; the rest
will go like clockwork . . . Everything clear?

RASPLYUEV (*in a low voice*): Clear, Mikhailo Vasilich, clear!
(*Raises his brows and the index finger of one hand
meaningfully.*) Everything understood! I'm off! (*Leaves.*)

Scene 12

Krechinsky alone.

KRECHINSKY: Clear, understood . . . The idiot didn't understand a thing. He thinks that I just want to steal it, that
I'm a thief. No, my friend, we still value honor; we
still have resources left in this pocket here (*pointing to
his head*). Well, now down to business! (*Shouts.*)
Fyodor! Hey, Fyodor! (*Fyodor comes rushing in through
the door.*) What are you doing—having yourself a nap?

FYODOR: No Sir, I've only got two legs . . .

KRECHINSKY: Well?! If two legs aren't enough, get a third! . . .
Anyway, here's some money. First of all—get the rooms
heated. But don't run away with yourself—out of sheer
joy you're liable to get the place as hot as hell. It's still
too early for that. Secondly—I'm having six people in
for tea this evening, my fiancée and her relatives, Mister
Nelkin, and perhaps a few others. See to it that everything is done right . . .

FYODOR: Yes, Sir. Will you be wanting dessert?

KRECHINSKY: I want everything just the way it should be.
Light the lamps, but not the candelabra. Tidy up the
rooms; spray them with perfume. Put up decorations,
monograms, coats-of-arms all over the place. The reception's at seven . . .

FYODOR: What about livery?

KRECHINSKY: No, there's no need for livery. The servants'll
be in evening dress, with white ties and waistcoats. And
lower the curtains—yes, definitely lower the curtains.
And as far as you're concerned, it's all the same whether
it's a gentleman giving a reception, or a merchant
marrying off his daughter.

FYODOR: As you wish, Sir. (*Leaves quickly.*)

Scene 13

Krechinsky alone.

KRECHINSKY: Now I've got to get hold of two pieces of paper
as alike as two drops of water. Hold on, whoa! (*Rum-
mages in the bureau.*) Here we are, fine, splendid!
Dunning letters! Better than anything! (*Puts one on
top of another and cuts them in half with a pair of
scissors.*) Wonderful! (*Sings an air from Karl Weber's
Der Freischütz.*)

> What would life be without wine?
> Woe and grief to make man pine. (*Repeat.*)

Is that so? Wrong, *Freischütz*, the song ought to go
like this instead:

> What would life be without brains?
> Misery to forge man chains.
> Only brains can end despair.
> If one day your pocket's bare,
> Use your head, no need to pray,
> Next day wealth will come your way. (*Repeat.*)

(*Ends the song with a most incredible roulade.*) And
when you reach "wealth" in the song, roll whatever
roulades you want. Be as wild as you please, anything
you do is all right, it's all just fine . . . Brains are everything, whatever you do, wherever you are! In society,
it's brains that count; in love—brains; in gambling—
brains; in stealing—brains! Yes, yes, that's the way it is!
Here's another philosophy sprung up. When I put all
my eggs in Rasplyuev's basket, there wasn't any philosophy, none at all. Yes, I can see that even this daughter
of Socrates prefers good soil to bad . . . But . . . I hope
Rasplyuev doesn't succeed in making a mess of things.
He's already been gone half an hour, if not longer. And
now, at this moment, at this great moment, we're crossing the Rubicon, we're mooring at the other shore, or
rushing into a bottomless whirlpool! . . . Yes, here it
is, the decisive moment, the moment when everything

hangs in the balance! (*Noise. Rasplyuev runs in in his overcoat, out of breath. Krechinsky springs up and rushes to meet him.*)

SCENE 14

Rasplyuev, followed by Fyodor, who helps him off with his coat.

KRECHINSKY: Well, Rasplyuev, victory?

RASPLYUEV: Victory, Mikhailo Vasilich, victory! Here it is, on the hook, swallowed the bait! (*Holds the pin high in the air, then hands it to Krechinsky.*)

KRECHINSKY (*happily*): Well, Rasplyuev, the Rubicon is crossed!

RASPLYUEV (*skipping*): Crossed!

KRECHINSKY: The Rubicon!

RASPLYUEV: The Rubicon!

KRECHINSKY: Idiot!

RASPLYUEV: Idi . . . oh, no, no idiot, not at all, Mikhailo Vasilich! You see how I pulled it off—remarkable. I arrive there . . . I arrive and I ask: Is the master at home? No, they say, he's not at home. I say: Is the young lady at home? Yes, they say, she is. Where, I say. In her room, they say. I say: Please announce me. They say . . .

KRECHINSKY: Well, anyone can see—brilliant work . . . (*Retreats to the bureau. Rasplyuev goes over to Fyodor and tells him what happened with frequent gestures. Krechinsky is examining the two pins.*) They're like one! (*Wraps them both separately in the pieces of paper he has prepared.*) It'll work like a charm! (*Puts them in his wallet, then turns to Rasplyuev.*) And now, Rasplyuev, it's time to get running!

RASPLYUEV (*turning around to him, quickly*): Get running?!! Oh well, I'm ready . . .

KRECHINSKY: Grab, take everything you can. Be fast about it! (*To Fyodor.*) Let's get dressed.

RASPLYUEV (*running about the room*): Come on, Fyodor, pick up everything you can! Lively now! (*Grasps some things, runs past Krechinsky, and falls down.*)

KRECHINSKY (*dressing himself*): Be fast about it, get going! The trunk, bring the trunk here! (*Rasplyuev runs into another room and brings a trunk.*) Hold on! It's no good . . . (*Rasplyuev stops as though rooted to the spot.*) What if they sent mounted guards after us? They'd catch up to us right away.

RASPLYUEV: Who? Mounted guards? They'd be sure to catch up to us in no time.

KRECHINSKY: They'll grab hold of us, and then it's the road to Siberia.

RASPLYUEV: Yes, if they grab us, then it's surely the road to Siberia.

KRECHINSKY: Then what do we do with the pin?

RASPLYUEV: Yes, Mikhailo Vasilich, what do we do with it?

KRECHINSKY: Fyodor!

RASPLYUEV: Fyodor!

KRECHINSKY: Let me have my overcoat!

RASPLYUEV: And bring mine, too.

KRECHINSKY (*quickly getting into his overcoat*): No, my dear, no overcoat for you. By all rights, you ought to have a gray prisoner's suit with the ace of diamonds on the back! (*Leaves; halts momentarily at the door. To Fyodor.*) Fyodor, don't let him leave here under any circumstances, you hear?

FYODOR: I hear, Sir! (*Stands at the door and shuts it right under Rasplyuev's nose.*)

SCENE 15

Rasplyuev and Fyodor.

RASPLYUEV (*standing as though rooted to the spot*): Wait! What are you doing? Mikhailo Vasilich! (*At the top of his lungs.*) Mikhailo Vasilich! Now where is he off to? Hold it; let me go, let me go, let me go, I'm telling you! What's the matter with you? (*Pushes Fyodor away from the door.*) What's gotten into you?

FYODOR (*holding him at arm's length*): Please stay, Sir. You heard what the master ordered.

RASPLYUEV (*becoming flustered*): What? Why this is . . . this is . . . murder!! It's treachery, that's what it is,

treachery!!! (*Goes to the door again and tries pushing
Fyodor aside.*) Out of my way, criminal, out of my way!
Let me go, I tell you! (*Fyodor turns the key in the
lock.*) Oh, saints in heaven! They're killing me, oh,
they're killing me! . . . Help! Hel . . . (*Quiets down.*)
Sh-h-h . . . What am I doing? Bringing the roof down
on myself? The hawks'll swoop down here in a matter
of seconds . . . (*Composes himself.*) Let me go, Fyodor!
Let me go, my friend! After all, what difference does
it make to you? Why should I want to destroy my
sinner's soul? In a little while now the police are going
to be here; they'll grab me right on the spot! As soon
as the old man returns home, they'll be hot on the trail
after me. Who came to see you today, they'll say. Ivan
Antonych was here, they'll say. Well, they'll say, hand
the scoundrel over to us. The old man's important, rich;
so they'll take me like this . . . (*grasps himself by the
collar*) in tow, then off to the governor-general, then
to the court, then I'll be marched off to Siberia! Oh, oh,
oh, oh, oh! (*Sits down on the trunk and weeps.*) Fyodor,
my friend! What pleasure or profit will you get out of
it if they flog me in some God-forsaken out-of-the-way
place?

FYODOR: For heaven's sake, Ivan Antonych? Flog a nobleman?
Are you serious?

RASPLYUEV: What kind of nobleman am I? That's all a lot
of nonsense, a contemptible lie. My title of nobility was
conferred on me by the King of Spades—that's all there
is to it. Fyodor, Fyodor please! Let me go, brother! For
the love of Christ the Saviour, let me go! I've got a little
nest, you know . . . with my young waiting for me to
bring home food.

FYODOR: What are you talking about? What nest?

RASPLYUEV: The usual kind, full of younglings; little children.
They'll die of cold and hunger; they'll be thrown out
onto the street like mangy pups. They're children, after
all, Fyodor—our own flesh and blood!

FYODOR: That's enough worrying yourself half to death, Ivan
Antonych. I wonder where the master went.

RASPLYUEV: What do you mean "where"? To the four winds,
of course.

FYODOR: You think he's the kind of man who'd run away?

You'll see, he'll be back all in one piece. He just went
to take care of some business; he's not running away.

RASPLYUEV: No, he's run away, he's run away without fail.
Why should he give us a thought? That trinket he's
got with him is worth all of forty thousand, I hear—
some trinket! Why should he stay here? The moment
I myself crawled into the sleigh today with the damn
thing and took a whiff of the fresh air, it began to get
to me too! But the only thing that held me back was
the thought: Where am I going to go with it, where?
He's like a hawk, he is; let him get his claws into me
and he'll rip me to pieces! But what's he got to worry
about now? Wherever he goes he's got an open road,
no Siberia ahead of him. So, off he rides . . .

FYODOR: But what's he to gain by running away, especially
with stolen goods? He'd have to be a fool to run, and
he's no fool!

RASPLYUEV: Then in your opinion it'd be better to roam
around the city with that stolen diamond on him?

FYODOR: Why is it stolen?

RASPLYUEV: Because we got it away from the Muromsky girl
by trickery. What else is there to do with it? Get out
while the getting's good, and that's all!

FYODOR: Well . . . he's gone to pawn it.

RASPLYUEV: To pawn it? But it has to be returned this evening, else the police'll come get it for them and then
haul us off to jail. And that's something none of us
wants, right? No, brother, he's flown the coop, plain
and simple! Let's you and I do the same, Fyodor, while
we still have the chance!

FYODOR: What's it got to do with me? I'm where I belong.

RASPLYUEV: Then you'll die in prison.

FYODOR: For what? I don't know anything about it. I sweep
the rooms and shine the shoes. I don't know anything
and I don't want to know anything—that's my answer.
Nonetheless, it looks like a shady business, I agree.
Maybe Mikhailo Vasilich did take off somewhere, after
all. Who knows?

RASPLYUEV: Take off somewhere? You mean, run away?!!
(*Grasps himself by the head and bustles about the
room.*) Oh, oh, oh! (*Stops and collects his senses.*)

Don't forget, Fyodor, when they ask you, be sure and
tell them how you saw me give the pin to him.

FYODOR: What?

RASPLYUEV (*shouting*): I'm telling you that with your own
eyes you saw me give the pin right here, on this very
spot, to that criminal, your master.

FYODOR: Now please, Ivan Antonych, don't go dragging me
into this business. It's got nothing to do with me. My
place is to shine shoes, sweep the rooms, and not to go
mixing into your affairs.

RASPLYUEV (*terrified*): Judas! How can you say you don't
know anything? Why, just a little while ago you saw
me give it to him before your very own eyes!

FYODOR: For heaven's sake! How am I supposed to know
what you gave him? Did you tell me what you gave him?

RASPLYUEV: Ah, you stupid peasant! You brute! (*Strikes himself on the forehead.*) You've finished me off!! Oh-h-h!
The devil's own gang! I see it all now . . . You're holding
a knife in my back! . . . No, I won't let you! (*Advances
on him in a fit of fury.*) Out of my way, I tell you, out
of my way, you soulless creature! (*Comes face to face
with him.*) You hear what I'm saying to you: let me go!
(*He leaps on him; they struggle silently, both panting
for breath. Fyodor finally pins Rasplyuev beneath him.*)

FYODOR: Give up, Ivan Antonych! It's no use, brother! Stop
wriggling, I'm telling you . . . stop . . . hold it . . .
(*Chokes him.*)

RASPLYUEV (*breathing heavily*): Oh, oh, oh! Let me go! I'm
dying . . . dying! . . . Let me go . . . oh, saints in
heaven . . . mercy . . .

FYODOR (*still clutching Rasplyuev by the throat*): I was told
to keep you here, now keep still . . .

RASPLYUEV (*breaking free, advances to the front of the stage,
straightening himself out*): Ow, oh, whew, phew! Ah-h-h!
(*To the audience.*) Would you believe it? Why that
idiot's only too happy to choke me to death. (*Muses.*)
Oh, my third beating! By God, the third! (*Folds his
arms.*) That's fate for you! (*Louder.*) Fate? Why are
you persecuting me? Why are you per . . . (*Throwing
a glance at Fyodor.*) Would you ever . . . What a wood-
goblin! Did you ever see a face like that? Again he's

standing at the door like some kind of pillar. Completely
devoid of any feelings . . . (*Fyodor gazes at him indifferently. Rasplyuev looks around on all sides.*) Oh, oh,
oh, oh, oh! And time is flying! Time is flying! Maybe
they're already on their way here! And I'm trapped!
All I'm supposed to do is be silent and wait for misfortune to overtake me! Wait for prison!! Wait for
punishment and be silent!! God in heaven! How my
heart suffers . . . how it aches! I have a pain right here,
something suffocating me!!! My babies! You're naked
and cold . . . Will I ever see you again? . . . Vanya, my
little dear! (*Cries. A bell rings.*) Oh! . . . Here they are!
. . . They're here! . . . The police, the police!! (*Races
back and forth about the room. The bell rings again.
Fyodor goes to open the door.*) They're coming!!! Oh!
My God!! (*Throws himself onto the trunk in utter
despair.*)

SCENE 16

*The same and Krechinsky, who comes in quickly. Fyodor
follows him, telling him something in a low voice.*

KRECHINSKY (*in high spirits*): Ha, ha, ha! You did very well,
Fyodor. (*To Rasplyuev.*) Well, what's the matter with
you, brother? Seems you and Fyodor have been warming
it up a bit, eh? Nothing to worry about, though: it's one
way to keep from getting bored. The only bad thing,
Ivan Antonych, is that you're always in a hurry. Everything in its own time, brother. That's the law of nature.
That police will come and you won't avoid Siberia—
but everything in its own time, don't worry. (*Goes over
to the bureau and unwraps a small package.*) Now here's
something you can keep busy with in the meantime.
(*Gives him a packet of money.*) Count all the money
here and lay it out in small piles. I've got to give it
back. It's our obligation, our sacred duty. And the pin
(*putting it on the table*) has to be returned this evening
to its rightful owner. That's how honest people do things.
And you thought . . .

RASPLYUEV (*making his way to the table, completely per-*

plexed): I just don't see a thing, nothing (*rubs his forehead*) spots, different colors . . . nothing else . . . (*Makes a gesture.*) Faugh! Let's see now . . . Money . . . this is the money . . . and this is . . . the pin . . . right, the pin! (*Takes the money and begins counting it.*) A hundred . . . two hundred . . . four hundred . . . nine hundred . . . fourteen hundred . . . phew! (*Puts it down and again begins counting money on the table. To the audience.*) I'll tell you, once upon a time in Moscow (*sighs*) we had a visit from Master Bosco, the professor of Natural Magic and Egyptian Mysteries. He could pour red and white wine out of a hat (*sobs*); he could load pistols with canaries; he could pick bouquets out of his fist, and present them to all the ladies in the audience . . . But I wager my sin-burdened soul that he could never carry off a trick like this. Compared to Mikhailo Vasilich, Bosco was little more than a babe-in-the-woods, a puppy.

KRECHINSKY (*writing at the table*): Enough of that! Count! You and that everlasting jabbering of yours! . . . He has his sentimental side, this fellow. First, it seems, he's as solid as a tree stump, and the next moment, he goes as soft as jelly.

RASPLYUEV (*in ecstasy*): God in Heaven! What balsam is it bathes my heart? What aroma engulfs me from all sides? I smell jasmine everywhere . . . and in general you can suppose that I'm talking such nonsense that afterward I'll be ashamed of it myself.

KRECHINSKY: Ha, ha, ha! You said it.

RASPLYUEV: Laugh, laugh! Why shouldn't you? The only thing you were ever meant to do in life is laugh . . . go on, don't stop! All you have to do is give a twist here, a twist there, and you're sitting on top of the world! But if you were in my shoes, it'd be a different story altogether. Yes! Go ahead and ask Fyodor. Without you, I was completely lost; everything grew cloudy before me; I was just sitting over there . . . (*points to the trunk*) howling like a wolf.

KRECHINSKY: Listen, I'm waiting, after all . . . Is this going to take very long?

RASPLYUEV: What is it Mikhailo Vasilich, is it forbidden a man to rejoice? (*Sorts out the money.*) Here they are, my darlings! My little doves, my lovely swallows! How's this for one bunch of blossoms, and a second, and a third . . . And here's the raspberries—one bunch, and a second, a thir-r-rd, and a four-r-rth . . . Ha, ha, ha! He, he, he! My God in heaven! What wouldn't I do, what wouldn't I undertake for this kind of prosperity! (*Sits down and counts. Silence.*)

KRECHINSKY (*putting on his hat and overcoat, and approaching Rasplyuev*): Well, my child, finished?

RASPLYUEV (*hastily*): In a moment . . . in a moment . . . one moment . . .

KRECHINSKY (*taking one pack of bills*): I'll deliver this money myself; you take these (*gives him the other packs*)—and get my watch out of pawn. Here's a list of whom and how much to repay. See to it you don't leave anyone out.

RASPLYUEV (*taking the money and wrapping it carefully in paper*): Mikhailo Vasilich . . . how is it possible? Isn't the money from Bek the moneylender, from Nikanor Savich?

KRECHINSKY: Yes, it's from Bek.

RASPLYUEV: But the pin . . . Wait . . . (*Examines the pin.*) Why it's my little godchild! It's the same one I got from Lydia Petrovna, isn't it? Huh?

KRECHINSKY: Of course, and this evening we've got to return it to Lydia Petrovna. (*Takes the pin from Rasplyuev's hands and locks it up in the bureau.*)

RASPLYUEV (*taking his hat*): What do you mean "of course"? The devil knows why "of course"! How can it be? Huh? Both the money and the pin! I thought you pawned it! (*Fyodor helps him into his overcoat.*)

KRECHINSKY: You're a hound-dog, Rasplyuev, but you have no scent . . . none at all . . . (*Both leave.*)

CURTAIN

ACT THREE

(Krechinsky's apartment, all tidied up and brightly illuminated. Evening.)

SCENE 1

Fyodor, in black evening-dress, white tie, waistcoat and gloves, adjusts the lamps and dusts the furniture. Rasplyuev comes in, wearing evening dress and white gloves, his hair newly waved.

RASPLYUEV: Ha, ha, ha . . . ha, ha, ha . . . ha, ha, ha . . . Oh, it's too much . . . Ha, ha, ha! I can't stop laughing! *(Hangs up his hat.)* When I think of that nasty kisser of his, the way he was sitting there, the Judas, with that little glass of his; the way he was guarding it, protecting it, the Judas—a piece of cheap crystal in worthless brass—behind seven locks—I could die laughing . . . ha, ha, ha! . . . Phew . . . *(Collects himself.)* I can just see him now rubbing his hands together. Six thousand silver he paid for it! What a pile! He's thinking to himself: Krechinsky'll go broke and the solitaire'll be mine . . . Eh, Fyodor? Our Mikhailo Vasilich is a second Napoleon, huh? Let me have a pencil. *(Fyodor hands him a pencil.)* Wait, I'll write it down! Let's see now, how did he say it, Eureka or Eudrika?

FYODOR: Eureka, I think.

RASPLYUEV: All right, Eureka then. I'll call the first bloodhound I have Eureka. Here, Eureka, come here, Eureka! Doesn't sound bad, huh? Remember how he shouted Eureka when he found it, Fyodor, and find it he did.

FYODOR: You see, Ivan Antonych! And you were all set to take him and drag him off to an insane asylum.

RASPLYUEV: What can I say, brother, I tripped up. But do you know how he pulled off that stunt?

FYODOR: How should I know? To tell the truth, you know, I've never been a fool, but this I can't figure out at all. Try as I may, it's no use; it's too deep for my mind.

RASPLYUEV: I'll spell it out for you, my friend, I'll spel-l it
    out! But remember—it's a matter of the greatest secrecy!
FYODOR: My heavens!
RASPLYUEV: Well, it's like this . . . (*Straightens his evening
    jacket and makes a gesture with his fingers.*) As soon
    as the idea came to his mind, he turned it over this
    way and that . . . Well, he says, Rasplyuev, come to
    my rescue. I'm ready, Mikhailo Vasilich, I says, ready
    for anything. Here's what, he says: Pawn your soul, if
    you must, but get me that solitaire from the Murom-
    skys. You know, the one I had made into a pin last
    fall. Remember, he says, the one like the model I've
    got in my bureau. So I began thinking.
FYODOR: You?
RASPLYUEV: Yes, me! No easy matter, I say, no easy matter.
    Nevertheless, off I went and in a quarter of an hour I
    came back with it like a hawk carrying its prey. Here, I
    say, here's the little dove! He takes it and he takes the
    model too . . . you hear, the model from which the pin
    was made . . . and slips the two of them into his wallet.
FYODOR: Into his wallet!
RASPLYUEV: Into his wallet! What a thief! He didn't give up
    the trinket . . . Get it? And that's the thing that did
    the trick! He took the solitaire and the trinket and
    headed straight to Kiselev Lane, to Nikanor Savich Bek
    the moneylender! Money, he says, give me money, Jew.
    Money? What kind of money do I have? I haven't got
    any money. But for a pawn—you've got it? For a pawn,
    he says, yes. And how much would you give me, Judas,
    he says, on this little trinket? That stirred him so, his
    mouth fell open. His eyes burned, he was shivering with
    fever. He kept turning it this way and that, testing it,
    through the glass, on the scales . . . Well, he sees it's
    something first class . . . Four thousand he offers . . .
    Four! . . . You son of a bitch, he says, it cost ten . . .
    What do you think you've got here, a fool or something.
    Give it back to me—no deal! . . . But the pawnbroker
    got all excited and couldn't let the pin out of his hands.
    But he grabbed it from him and stuck it back in his
    wallet. Will you give me seven thousand? (*In a squeaky
    voice.*) No, I can't, I can't; take five! — I want seven! —
    No! — Six then! — No! — Very well, good-bye, but

mind you don't think badly of me; Sprengel'll give me eight. The rascal trembles from head to foot, starts howling like a wolf—a regular beast of prey! Oh! Take your eight, he says. Is it a deal? A deal! . . . Then get me some sealing wax and a box. — Why a box? — That ought to be obvious. We'll tuck the solitaire away there with our hands, my dear, and I'll put a seal on the box. It'll be safe that way. Such a treasure I'm not going to give to you, Judas, he says. You understand . . . Oho!

FYODOR (nodding): Yes, yes, yes!

RASPLYUEV (continuing): He ran for the box like a quail. And don't forget the money, Krechinsky says . . . So he pulls out the money. Here, Mikhailo Vasilich, have a look! But he takes out of the wallet not the real pin, the diamond solitaire, but the model, the model, the cheap trinket . . . What is it? He twists it around in front of his eyes . . . The wealth of an entire Brazil, of an ancient Golconda . . . eh? Well?

FYODOR: God in heaven!

RASPLYUEV (excitedly): And his eyes became all bloodshot, the two of them! One, two . . . they plopped it into the box and put on the seal . . . Bek gave him the money, the master the box . . . As soon as he comes back here he tosses me on the table a bundle of money as big as this! (Demonstrates.) Take it, he says, and remember Mikhailo Vasilich!

FYODOR (folding his arms): Oh, my heavens! (Both remain standing in worshipful silence.)

RASPLYUEV (in unusually high spirits): He's a Napoleon, I tell you, a Napoleon! A great hero, a magician and sorcerer! He ran circles around him, circles I tell you! He duped a man for all time . . . A man? . . . No—he duped a moneylender, and thereby erected a great monument to himself.

FYODOR (spreading his arms out): Yes, some deal he pulled. My heavens! That's how to do things.

RASPLYEUV: And how—like a miracle! The money is here and the diamond solitaire is here, and tonight we'll return it with gratitude . . . (With inner enthusiasm.) A piece of glass is lying there under seven seals and seven locks and the Jew's crouched over it with his profane body! Not a single trace! He'll pay off all his debts at the club,

arrange a nice wedding for himself, lay his hands on a
million and then start going after some more. He'll
pile up a mountain of gold and become a big lord, great
and famous, and he won't forget us . . . eh? Fyodor? . . .
He won't forget us, will he?

FYODOR: It'll be good if he won't.

RASPLYUEV: He promised me two hundred thousand.

FYODOR: If he promised you, fine. You know the saying: The
master promised me a sheepskin coat, and his word keeps
me warm.

RASPLYUEV: Wh-a-at? Where'd you pick up that proverb?
He promised; of course, he promised. (*A bell rings.*)
That must be Mikhailo Vasilich . . . Here he is. (*Raises
his hands worshipfully.*) Great hero, magician and sorcerer! (*Goes respectfully to meet him.*)

SCENE 2

The same and Krechinsky.

KRECHINSKY (*coming in and hanging up his hat*): What a
day . . . eh? Give me a chair, Fyodor, I'm exhausted! . . .
What do you say? The first time in my life I'm exhausted. Guess I must be getting old . . . Well, is everything all set here? (*Sits down. Rasplyuev and Fyodor
stand in front of him.*)

FYODOR: Everything's all set, Mikhailo Vasilich, just as you
ordered.

KRECHINSKY (*inspects the parlor*): I see. Good. Put another
candlestick over here. An imposing looking apartment,
all right; no bridegroom would be ashamed of it. (*To
Rasplyuev, sternly.*) Well, did you take care of everything I told you?

RASPLYUEV: Everything, Mikhailo Vasilich, everything, just
as you ordered, down to the last detail. Would you like
to have the receipts?

KRECHINSKY: Of course I would; you don't expect me to
operate on faith alone. (*Takes the receipts from him
and reads them over.*) Hmmm! Good . . . Fyodor! Here,
take them and lock them up in the bureau . . .

RASPLYUEV: Here's your watch and chain, Mikhailo Vasilich. It's all here. (*Hands them over to him.*) You see how I handled everything?

KRECHINSKY (*taking the watch*): Nice! . . . Phew, am I tired! (*Puts his watch on.*) I had a fine meal at the club. I haven't had an appetite like that in a long time. That fool Nelkin was there. Kept staring at me all the time like some owl. Go on, look, my friend, I felt like saying. You've already lost your sweetheart—there's no sense in staring away at me like that now. You won't get anywhere with me, my friend; I'm so tough I can bend horseshoes . . .

RASPLYUEV: I dropped in for a good meal, too, Mikhailo Vasilich, after doing everything you told me . . .

KRECHINSKY: Aha, you didn't forget . . .

RASPLYUEV: I should say I didn't! I come in, sit myself down right in the middle of a sofa, prop myself up like this . . . Hm! I say, bring me some fish soup, I say, two fish pies, a suckling pig—in its entirety! I don't believe myself—is it me or isn't it me? They served the fish soup—nothing like it anywhere else: beads of amber loose in a bowl. I just put the first spoonful in my mouth when I remember Bek sitting there like an idiot, and I give such a roar . . . I spill the soup all over myself! I doused everything, even stained my waistcoat . . . damn it all, what a nuisance!

KRECHINSKY: All right, all right . . . Listen: when the guests arrive, keep the old man busy talking; yap about the devil knows what. I'll stay with the ladies and get this wedding wrapped up in two days. Just see, though, you don't lie any more than you have to. Out of foolishness you're liable to start running away with yourself . . .

RASPLYUEV (*complainingly*): Why should I start running away with myself? For what reason? It seems I'm the one who does everything but you never see fit to give me even a word of approval.

KRECHINSKY: The devil with you and your approval! God, what a born idiot! (*Falls to thinking.*) Wait a while . . . are you dressed decently?

RASPLYUEV: On the way home from the restaurant, Mikhailo Vasilich, I stopped in at the Frenchman's and had my

hair done *à la mouzhik* . . . And please have a look at
my gloves—I payed a ruble and a half for them. Nice,
eh? All white, white as white can be . . .

KRECHINSKY: Completely unnecessary.

RASPLYUEV: How can you say that! How?! Without white
gloves it just wouldn't do at all. And then I put on your
dress coat . . . have a look.

KRECHINSKY: Ha, ha, ha . . . Handsome, very handsome. Just
take a look, will you—he's become a real personage.
(*Turns him around.*)

RASPLYUEV: Why shouldn't I be, Mikhailo Vasilich? Money
does everything. When you don't have enough of it, you
come out at the elbows and you're always running
around doing errands for others. But when you've got
money then you can send others around doing things
for you and you can show them your displeasure when
you feel like it.

KRECHINSKY: All right, all right, that's enough now. Now
hop to it! Fyodor! (*Fyodor runs in.*) See to it that
everything is perfect, dignified. No commotion from the
servants and nothing hanging from their noses. Two
waiters in the drawing room; another candlestick over
here; the green table here. (*Looks at his watch.*) The
guests'll be here any minute! All's well that ends well!
Wait a moment, hold on! Hey, Fyodor! Over there in
the corridor I noticed the portrait of some general or
other from Catherine the Great's time . . . A mug like
this (*grimaces*). Dust it off, bring it here, and hang it
over my bureau. For the sake of genealogy. (*The candlestick, table, and portrait are arranged in the proper
order. The bell rings.*) Well, there they are now. I'll go
receive them. You, Rasplyuev, sit over here on the sofa,
like someone important. Pick up the newspaper . . . the
newspaper, you idiot, take it . . . stretch out a little! . . .
Oh, you dunce! (*Goes out.*)

RASPLYUEV: There you see, he's started picking on me again;
yet he says, handsome, handsome. You promised me
two hundred thousand, brother. You did and don't forget
it.

SCENE 3

Muromsky, Atuyeva, Lidochka, Krechinsky and Rasplyuev.
They all exchange bows and shake hands.

MUROMSKY (*looking around*): What a splendid apartment
    you have!

ATUYEVA: Oh, yes, a splendid, splendid apartment! What
    taste he has! In everything, in everything . . .

LIDOCHKA: Yes, it's very nice.

KRECHINSKY: For me, *mesdames*, it became nice only the
    moment you entered it. (*Kisses Lidochka's hand.*)

ATUYEVA: How charmingly he always responds! What a truly
    charming man he is! Do you know what, Mikhailo
    Vasilich? There's one thing I do regret.

KRECHINSKY (*courteously*): And what is that, Anna An-
    tonovna?

ATUYEVA: That I'm no longer young. If I were, I'd surely fall
    in love with you myself.

KRECHINSKY: Then I should say that I must regret not being
    older.

LIDOCHKA: That's not much of a compliment to me.

ATUYEVA: Lidochka! Don't tell me you're jealous!

KRECHINSKY (*taking Lidochka's hand and kissing it*): Because
    you're jealous, I kiss your hand; but it's not good to be
    unjust.

LIDOCHKA: In what way am I unjust?

KRECHINSKY: I said that I *must* regret but there's a great dif-
    ference between what someone *must* do and what
    actually *is*.

LIDOCHKA (*withdrawing to a side and beckoning Krechinsky*):
    Mikhailo Vasilich! Listen to me.

KRECHINSKY: What is it?

LIDOCHKA: A secret. (*Leads him farther away from the
    others.*) Do you love me?

KRECHINSKY: I love you.

LIDOCHKA: Very much?

KRECHINSKY: Very much.

LIDOCHKA: *Michel*, listen—I want you to love me terribly . . .
    beyond measure, beyond reason (*in an undertone*), the
    way I love you.

KRECHINSKY (*taking both her hands*): With all my heart and soul.

LIDOCHKA: No, only with your heart.

KRECHINSKY (*aside*): What a lovely little wench she's going to be!

ATUYEVA (*stealing up on them*): What are you consulting each other about?

LIDOCHKA: Oh, just some matter, Auntie.

ATUYEVA: The wedding dress, I'll wager.

LIDOCHKA: You lose, Auntie.

ATUYEVA: Then what?

KRECHINSKY (*pointing to his heart*): About what's under the wedding dress, Anna Antonovna!

ATUYEVA: *Under* the dress? Why what do you mean? (*Takes Lidochka aside.*) Don't tell me, my dear that you're talking about *underwear* with him?

LIDOCHKA (*laughing*): No, Auntie, not about underwear. (*Whispers into her ear.*)

KRECHINSKY (*running over to Muromsky*): Pyotr Konstantinych! Why don't you have a seat? Allow me! What kind of chair would you prefer—one with a high back or one with a low back? (*Rasplyuev draws up chairs.*)

MUROMSKY: No, no, that's all right, I'll sit down over here on the sofa. This is comfortable enough. (*Sits down.*)

KRECHINSKY: Please allow me to present my dear friend and neighbor, Ivan Antonovich Rasplyuev.

RASPLYUEV (*leaving the chairs and bowing, obviously flustered*): An honor . . . Sir . . . an honor . . . truly . . .

MUROMSKY (*rising*): A pleasure. (*Shakes hands with Rasplyuev and returns to the sofa. Rasplyuev moves up a chair and sits on the very edge of it, alongside Muromsky. Krechinsky is on the opposite side of the stage with the ladies. Tea is served. Silence.*)

MUROMSKY (*taking a cup. To Rasplyuev*): May I ask, are you in the military service or civil?

RASPLYUEV (*taking a cup*): In the civ . . . civ . . . mil . . . in the civil . . . the civil . . .

MUROMSKY (*very politely*): Do you live in Moscow, Sir, or in the country?

RASPLYUEV: In Moscow, in Moscow, that is sometimes . . . but most of the time in the country.

MUROMSKY: And tell me, if you don't mind my asking, in what province is your estate?

RASPLYUEV: In Simbirsk, Simbirsk.

MUROMSKY: Which district?

RASPLYUEV (*quickly*): Which district?

MUROMSKY (*nodding*): Yes, district.

RASPLYUEV: Oh, district! (*Leans forward and thinks.*) Let's see now . . . district . . . it's uh . . . uh . . . what is the name of it? (*Aside.*) I don't know the name of a single district in the God-forsaken place. (*Aloud and snapping his fingers.*) I've got it on the tip of my tongue . . . Oh . . . heavens . . . Mikhailo Vasilich! What's the name of the district?

KRECHINSKY: Which district?

RASPLYUEV: You know, our district. In Simbirsk.

KRECHINSKY: Ah yes! The Ardatov district.

RASPLYUEV (*gesturing to Muromsky*): That's it!

MUROMSKY: The Ardatov?

RASPLYUEV (*sipping his tea and nodding his head affirmatively*): Simbirsk province, Ardatov district.

MUROMSKY: But the Ardatov district is in the province of Nizhni-Novgorod.

RASPLYUEV (*spluttering in his cup*): Nizhni-Novgorod? How could it be in Nizhni-Novgorod? Ha, ha, ha! . . . Mikhailo Vasilich! What's all this about? They're saying that the Ardatov district is in Nizhni-Novgorod . . . how do you like that! He, he, he!

KRECHINSKY (*impatiently*): Why, of course—there are two of them: one Ardatov district in Nizhni-Novgorod, and another one in Simbirsk.

RASPLYUEV (*gesturing to Muromsky*): That's it!

MUROMSKY (*also gesturing*): Yes, you're quite right. One Ardatov district in Nizhni-Novgorod, and another one in Simbirsk.

RASPLYUEV (*again gesturing*): One Ardatov in Nizhni-Novgorod, and another one in Simbirsk. (*Straightens himself out.*)

MUROMSKY: Forgive me, my fault, you're quite right. (*Silence.*) By the way, who is your governor there?

RASPLYUEV: Come again? (*Aside.*) What's this fool latched on to me for? What's it going to lead to? (*Makes a gesture.*) Oh well, come what may! (*Aloud.*) Brevnov.

MUROMSKY: What did you say?

RASPLYUEV: Br-r-evnov!

MUROMSKY: Don't know him . . . haven't had the honor.

RASPLYUEV (*aside*): I should imagine you wouldn't.

MUROMSKY: Is he a good person?

RASPLYUEV: The worthiest! He wouldn't even hurt a fly.

MUROMSKY: In these times that's a rarity.

RASPLYUEV: Hm! A rarity! No, Pyotr Konstantinych, I'd swear to it that such people don't exist.

MUROMSKY: But, surely . . .

RASPLYUEV (*passionately*): I assure you, they don't. Go find them, if you think they do!

MUROMSKY (*sympathetically*): I can see people have caused you grief in your day.

RASPLYUEV: They have indeed! (*Straightens his dinner jacket.*) Such grief, in fact, that another person, I can tell you, would have come apart at the seams, but here I am—alive and in one piece and . . .

MUROMSKY (*with a sigh*): That's the way life is, I'm afraid . . . Tell me, just to change the subject, what kind of land do you have on your estate?

RASPLYUEV: Land, you say?! Not bad.

MUROMSKY: You must have some black soil there. After all, Simbirsk is known for its good black earth.

RASPLYUEV: Why yes, of course, of course, by all means! Black soil—amazing black soil, really black, black as can be . . . Oh, you can just imagine the kind!

MUROMSKY: And the crops must be excellent then.

RASPLYUEV: Crops? Why, the wheat grows so plentifully in that God-forsaken place I can't harvest it all . . . (*Laughs loudly.*) Word of honor, I can't.

MUROMSKY: Really?

RASPLYUEV: The truth, I can't. But the devil with it! I couldn't care less . . . (*Laughs loudly again.*)

MUROMSKY (*also laughing*): So that's the way you steppe landowners are! Tell me, what kind of a yield do you have?

RASPLYUEV (*aside*): He's doing this deliberately . . . (*Raises his eyes heavenward.*) God in heaven, what's going to happen? (*Wipes the perspiration from his brow.*) Well . . . about yields I can't tell you anything because . . .

KRECHINSKY (*turning around*): For heaven's sake, Pyotr Konstantinych! Why are you asking *him* such questions? The only time he ever goes into the fields is when he's out hunting with his dogs. When it comes to farming, he doesn't stick his nose in at all . . .

MUROMSKY: Tell me, Mikhailo Vasilich, your estate is in Simbirsk province, but all your relatives live in Mogilev province, in the West, is that right?

KRECHINSKY: The Simbirsk estate I inherited from my mother.

MUROMSKY: Ah, now I understand! And what was your mother's maiden name?

KRECHINSKY (*drawling*): Kolkhovskaya.

MUROMSKY: Oh, an old family.

KRECHINSKY: You see the portrait there of my grandfather, that is my mother's father.

MUROMSKY (*looking at the portrait*): Ah, yes, yes indeed.

KRECHINSKY: Ivan Antonych here knew him; they were neighbors. (*He winks at Rasplyuev, then leads the ladies offstage through a side door.*)

SCENE 4

Rasplyuev and Muromsky.

RASPLYUEV: Ah . . . yes, yes, of course . . . I was just a little boy at the time . . . but I can see him as clearly as if he were here now: he was a fine old man, respected—on the stout side, you know, like in the picture . . . It's a perfect likeness. (*With a sigh.*) Oh, my . . .

MUROMSKY: Is he already dead?

RASPLYUEV: What are you saying! He . . . (*pointing to the portrait*) yes, he died some time ago.

MUROMSKY (*after a short pause*): No, my dear fellow, if you tried to run an estate in our province, in Yaroslav, you'd be singing a different tune altogether. With us agronomy is really a necessity; you couldn't do a thing without agronomy.

RASPLYUEV: You really couldn't do a thing without agronomy?

MUROMSKY: Judge for yourself. Our soil is white, cold. Without fertilization, it wouldn't yield anything.

RASPLYUEV (*with obvious satisfaction*): Wouldn't yield anything like that? Who does your soil think she is?

MUROMSKY: No, it wouldn't yield anything. So whether we want to or not we've got to try out all sorts of improvements and have a look at the agricultural journals . . . The other day they had an article about the harvests the English have—as big as yours in the black soil country.

RASPLYUEV (*excitedly*): The English! He, he, he! Come on now! Who did you hear that from? What kind of agronomy could they have? They're all dying of starvation—that's their agronomy for you. Sir, that's one nation I hate!

MUROMSKY: Is that so?

RASPLYUEV: The very thought of them gives me the shivers! Imagine: every one of them is taught how to box. Do you happen to know, Sir, what boxing is?

MUROMSKY: No, I don't.

RASPLYUEV: But I know it all right . . . Oh, yes! The English have no morals! Love for their fellowman and all that . . . hm, hm, no, none at all. Why no sooner are they out of the crib when they're taught this (*makes a few boxing gestures*), so how can you expect them to ever have any love for their fellowman? (*Straightens his jacket.*) No, there's no love in them at all. Nevertheless, you do have to make allowances for them. They're the way they are because it's so crowded over there, so stuffy. There's no land, not even a square yard a person. No wonder then, whether they really wanted to or not, they started bashing each other in the teeth.

MUROMSKY: But all their inventions: factories, machines, steamships . . .

RASPLYUEV: Not on your life, Sir! It's just hunger that's driving them, hunger, I tell you. You can do anything when you're hungry enough. If you don't believe me, take any idiot, lock him up in an empty closet, starve him half to death and you'll see the stunts he'll pull! Pyotr Konstantinych! Judge for yourself, but impartially, my good man, impartially. Why, what you give your cows to eat, the English put in their soup . . . I swear it! Nowadays, it's . . .

Scene 5

The same and Nelkin, who comes in quickly, very upset, and looks all around.

MUROMSKY: Ah, Vladimir Dmitrich, my dear friend! At last! (*To Rasplyuev.*) Allow me to present Vladimir Dmitrich Nelkin, my good neighbor and friend of the family. (*Turns to Nelkin.*) Ivan Antonych Rasplyuev. (*Nelkin and Rasplyuev exchange bows.*)

RASPLYUEV: I've already had the honor . . .

NELKIN: I've had the honor, too . . .

MUROMSKY: Why are you so late, Vladimir Dmitrich?

NELKIN: Some business that detained me.

MUROMSKY: My heavens! What kind of business can it be at eight o'clock in the evening?

NELKIN: The kind, Pyotr Konstantinych, that simply burns (*looks about him*), scorches—that's the kind of business!

RASPLYUEV: Well, I see, Vladimir Dmitrich, that you're a man of affairs, and all men of affairs—no matter who— they're like quicksilver.

MUROMSKY: Vladimir Dmitrich, you ought to hear how Ivan Antonych has been blasting the English.

RASPLYUEV: A vicious nation, vicious, without a shred of honor, without . . .

NELKIN: You? You find them so?

RASPLYUEV (*gaily*): I do, I most certainly do.

NELKIN: Ha, ha, ha!

RASPLYUEV: Ha, ha, ha, ha, ha! I admit it! Ha, ha, ha!

NELKIN: What did you say your name was?

RASPLYUEV: Ivan Antonych.

NELKIN: Your last name?

RASPLYUEV: Rasplyuev.

NELKIN (*approaching him and buttonholing him*): Where is there no evil, Mister Rasplyuev? Do you know such a place?

RASPLYUEV: Oh, no! I don't share that opinion. Evil must be rooted out, torn out right by the roots.

NELKIN (*paying no attention to him*): Where? What evil? That's the question. Take, for example, meanness and

thieving in coarse heavy cloth, in the threadbare,
wretched jacket of some petty clerk—they're pitiful, vile,
but harmless. It's frightful, though, when meanness
parades in fine evening dress . . . in white gloves . . .
living off someone else . . . riding about on thoroughbred
horses, bowing and scraping in polite society, crawling
into an honest home, preying on honor . . . peace . . .
on everything! That's what's really frightful!

RASPLYUEV: Right you are! You know, Pyotr Konstantinych,
it's really so what they say about evil being everywhere.
I assure you! I'll give you an example: Once there was . . .

NELKIN: Oh, there are many examples! That's what's so
awful! When you find a black shirt under a coarse heavy
cloth jacket, there's nothing surprising about it. No,
indeed! But when you find a black shirt . . . filth . . .
under a dinner jacket like that (*points to Rasplyuev's
jacket*) . . .

RASPLYUEV (*aside*): What's he getting at? Keeps going on
about my jacket . . . (*Self-consciously straightens his
jacket.*) And I'll tell you—how often these upstarts
crawl out like badgers and start pulling tricks on us. Take
a convict, Sir: he'll fly to us like a bird of passage. And
mind you—the way he'll strut around, the airs he'll put
on . . .

NELKIN (*fixing his gaze on Rasplyuev*): Put on airs?

RASPLYUEV: Put on airs.

NELKIN (*pointing at Rasplyuev*): A scoundrel putting on
airs . . . Ha, ha, ha! (*Muromsky gaily joins in the laughter.*)

RASPLYUEV (*trying to laugh also*): Yes, imagine, a scoundrel
suddenly putting on airs—isn't that a scream? (*Aside,
gnashing his teeth.*) What I could do to you now, you
laughing hyena . . . (*Shakes himself.*)

NELKIN (*carefully enunciating his words*): Yes, it's all too
common. But it's much more frightful, Pyotr Konstantinych, when in our native country our own good-for-
nothings, Russians, mind you, rob and plunder their
fellow countrymen, as though they were infidels . . .

MUROMSKY: There's something to think about! He's got
them on the hook all right!

NELKIN (*aside*): What's the matter with him? He's completely blind! What can I do? (*To Muromsky, in a firm*

tone.) Pyotr Konstantinych! There's something I'd like
to talk to you about.

MUROMSKY (*rising*): What is it? (*Withdraws to a side.*)

NELKIN: Where are you?

MUROMSKY: Wha-a-t? I don't hear you too well!

NELKIN: I'm asking, where are you?

MUROMSKY: What do you mean "where"? Here, right here.

NELKIN: Where is here?

MUROMSKY (*getting angry*): What kind of nonsense is this!
Here I am, here! What's bothering you, Vladimir
Dmitrich? You mean to tell me you don't know that
we're now in the home of Krechinsky, of Mikhailo
Vasilich . . . Well?

NELKIN: You're in a den of thieves!

MUROMSKY: Mind your tongue! What is it with you, have
you gone crazy . . . are you mad?!

NELKIN: I haven't gone mad, but you've become blind! . . .
They're stealing your daughter from you—don't you see
it? . . . What's the matter with you?

MUROMSKY (*leading him aside*): Listen to me, Vladimir
Dmitrich, you really can't say things like that. Don't
forget—you're talking about my future son-in-law. Take
hold of yourself, man!

NELKIN: You're the one who has to take hold of himself!
You're standing on the edge of an abyss. Open your eyes;
take a look around you. Can't you see that they're just
pulling the wool over your eyes? They're stealing your
daughter, I tell you! . . . A gambler, a bankrupt swindler,
and a thief is crawling, like a snake, into your family,
into your respectable family!

RASPLYUEV (*catching Nelkin's last words*): A swindler and a
thief? Could he be speaking about us?

MUROMSKY (*to Nelkin*): Really now, Sir! What right do you
have to talk like that?

NELKIN: I have the right . . . Listen to me . . .

MUROMSKY: What is it this time?

NELKIN: Where is your diamond solitaire?

MUROMSKY: What diamond solitaire? You mean Lidochka's
pin?

NELKIN: Exactly!

MUROMSKY: She has it.

NELKIN: You know that for sure?

MUROMSKY: For sure.

NELKIN: Your daughter doesn't have it.

MUROMSKY: Now what new nonsense of yours is this?

NELKIN: Wait a moment, Pyotr Konstantinych, give me a chance! I tell you—your diamond solitaire is not in your house; it's in other hands.

MUROMSKY: What other hands?

NELKIN: A pawnbroker's! It's been pawned!

MUROMSKY: Rubbish . . . For heaven's sake! Why, I saw it myself just yesterday . . .

NELKIN: Yesterday isn't today.

MUROMSKY: Listen to me, Vladimir Dmitrich.

NELKIN (*interrupting him*): But I'm telling you that Krechinsky pawned your diamond solitaire!

RASPLYUEV (*eavesdropping*): Beginning to look bad; I better go let him know . . . (*Leaves.*)

MUROMSKY: How did the solitaire happen to fall into Krechinsky's hands?

NELKIN: You mean to tell me you don't know he took it this morning?

MUROMSKY: Took it? What do you mean "took it"?

NELKIN: That fellow (*pointing to Rasplyuev on his way out*) came for it.

MUROMSKY: Who? Rasplyuev?

NELKIN: Yes, Rasplyuev.

MUROMSKY: How do you know?

NELKIN: This morning when I came to call on you he was already there, sitting with Anna Antonovna. I saw how Lydia Petrovna brought him the pin. It jolted me . . . Aha! I thought, there's something tricky about this. Why would he ask for such a thing? I'd even be afraid to touch it, I think . . . He got into the sleigh with it . . . I followed him . . . here, there . . . all over the city, until he arrived here . . .

MUROMSKY: Go on . . . go on . . . What happened?

NELKIN: I already told you: he pawned it with the pawnbroker Bek.

MUROMSKY: That's impossible. There must be some kind of a misunderstanding.

NELKIN: But I just left him.

MUROMSKY: The pawnbroker?

NELKIN: The pawnbroker. If you want, let's go there; he'll tell you everything.

MUROMSKY (*bewildered*): What's going on here? . . . My God! What's happening? Lida! Lida! Lidochka!

LIDOCHKA (*running in from the room next door with a billiard cue in her hand*): Papa, what's the matter?

MUROMSKY: Come here! (*In a low voice.*) Tell me, Lida, your diamond solitaire . . . it's safe, isn't it?

LIDOCHKA: Of course it's safe, Papa. Oh, Papa, how could you? Why did you tear me away from the game? I'm playing with *Michel*, and he lets me win all the time . . . it's such fun.

NELKIN: You're wrong, Lydia Petrovna—it's gone.

LIDOCHKA: What's gone?

NELKIN: You gave it up . . .

LIDOCHKA: The solitaire? Yes, so what? (*Looks at him in amazement.*) This morning, Papa, I sent it over to *Michel*; he had a wager on it.

MUROMSKY: What? . . . What's that you say?

LIDOCHKA: He made a wager with Prince Belsky, about the number of karats or something like that, I don't really know.

NELKIN (*to Muromsky*): It's a lie!

LIDOCHKA: My God! But he has it; he just told me that he has it.

MUROMSKY (*anxiously*): Well?

LIDOCHKA: Well what, Papa? He'll give it back to me, that's all.

NELKIN: I don't really think so . . .

LIDOCHKA (*flaring up*): What are you saying? Why, how dare you?

NELKIN: Lydia Petrovna! For God's sake, don't get angry at me. What can I do? Is it my fault? I'm ready to die for you . . . to endure torture . . . But I must, on my honor, I must!

LIDOCHKA (*frightened*): My God! What's happening? Papa dear! I'm afraid! (*Presses close to Muromsky.*) Papa, Papa!

MUROMSKY: Don't be upset, my dear, don't worry! I myself don't know what it's all about.

SCENE 6

Atuyeva, followed by Krechinsky and Rasplyuev, who come in quickly.

ATUYEVA: What's the matter, darling? What's happened? Are you all right? (*To Nelkin.*) So it's you—I might have known it! What kind of tales are you telling now? What new dirt did you pick up? More gossip and stories. (*Silence. Everyone embarrassed. Krechinsky eyes them all attentively.*)

MUROMSKY (*indecisively*): Forgive me, Mikhailo Vasilich, I . . . that is . . . we . . . would like to have . . . a little family talk. Just a few minutes.

KRECHINSKY: A family talk? By all means. I'm hardly a stranger to the family.

MUROMSKY: Of course you're not, but could you please excuse us for just a little while?

NELKIN: What are you doing, Pyotr Konstantinych? If we're going to bring the matter out into the open, why not right here and now? My dear Sir, we're talking about the solitaire.

KRECHINSKY: About what solitaire, Pyotr Konstantinych?

MUROMSKY: You know, that diamond solitaire that you had made over into a pin for us. You took it from my daughter . . . today, didn't you?

KRECHINSKY: Yes, I took it. I'm sure she told you I took it.

MUROMSKY: Well, do you have it now or don't you?

KRECHINSKY: Aha . . . I see . . . So that's it . . . (*Runs his gaze over all of them, looking long at Nelkin then turning to Muromsky.*) So that's what it's all about! Tell me, where am I, what kind of people am I with? I'd like to know, what fool, what liar . . . or what good-for-nothing . . . (*general confusion*) dared . . . (*Nelkin rushes at Krechinsky. Atuyeva holds him back.*) Take another step and I'm warning you—I'll break your head!

NELKIN (*shouting*): No, I'll break yours . . .

KRECHINSKY (*making a rapid movement toward Nelkin, then suddenly stopping; his voice trembling*): Pyotr Konstantinych . . . I have Lydia's solitaire . . . do you understand? I tell you, I . . . have . . . it!

MUROMSKY: I never thought for a moment you didn't. But he came here and said that I was ruining my own daughter, that you're deceiving us, that you took the diamond solitaire and pawned it . . . Well, you be the judge . . .

KRECHINSKY: Ah-h-h . . . now I understand . . . But suppose he lied . . . Well? . . . Suppose he, like a bas . . . forgive me . . . told you the basest lie? What then?! (*Muromsky throws up his hands in confusion.*) Then I insist . . . Hear me—*insist* . . . that you take him by the scruff of his neck and throw him out of your house . . . Will you give me your word you will? Well? . . . And as for the solitaire—take it! (*Extracts the pin from his bureau.*) Take it! (*Gives Lidochka the pin, at the same time extending his other hand to Muromsky.*) Pyotr Konstantinych, your word now!

LIDOCHKA (*pushing the pin away*): No . . . not to me . . . (*Atuyeva takes the pin. All rush to her. General confusion, noise. Everyone talks almost at the same time.*)

NELKIN: What's this? It can't be! I tell you, it can't be!

ATUYEVA (*showing Nelkin the pin*): Well, here it is! You see, here it is!

KRECHINSKY: Pyotr Konstantinych, your word; I tell you, I demand it, I insist on it!

MUROMSKY (*beside himself, his arms spread out*): I give it! (*To Nelkin.*) That, Sir, is what I call lying! (*Looks at the pin.*) There's absolutely no doubt it's the one!

NELKIN (*as though regaining consciousness*): My God! Where am I? Who's playing games at my expense? (*Goes over to Lidochka and takes her by a sleeve.*) Lydia Petrovna! Please listen to me!

KRECHINSKY: Away from her! (*Brushes Lidochka's sleeve.*) You'll only dirty her!

NELKIN (*clutching his head*): God in heaven! What's happening? My God!

MUROMSKY (*to Nelkin*): Who ever could have told you such rubbish? Where did you hear it?

KRECHINSKY (*interrupting him*): Please, let me handle this! This isn't the time now for questions. Polite conversations are over. We're dealing here with facts, Sir, not tales . . . Is this your pin?

MUROMSKY (*dumbstruck*): It is.

KRECHINSKY (*showing Nelkin the door*): Out!

MUROMSKY (*to Nelkin*): There's nothing more for you to do here now. Go on.

NELKIN (*taking his hat and approaching Krechinsky*): If you wish satisfaction as a gentleman, I'm prepared to oblige . . . (*Krechinsky points to the door. Nelkin comes closer to him and shouts.*) This very minute . . . and to the death! (*General confusion. Muromsky, Lidochka, Atuyeva, and Rasplyuev surround Krechinsky. Nelkin stands alone. They speak almost at the same time.*)

LIDOCHKA: No, no, never! I don't want you to. (*To Nelkin.*) Go away, go away!

ATUYEVA: Go away, my dear. God be with you, go away.

MUROMSKY: Stop gentlemen, I beg you!

KRECHINSKY (*stepping out of the group*): Wh-a-a-at? (*Folding his arms.*) Ah, so that's it! . . . Satisfaction . . . What kind of satisfaction? About what, may I ask you? You want to fight a duel, is that it? Ha, ha, ha, ha . . . I should stick a pistol in your hands and you'll take aim at me? That's what you're after? . . . Then again, I accept with one condition: that I spit in your eyes for every shot you fire. Those are my conditions. Tomorrow, even, if you wish; but now . . . Hey, any servants there?

RASPLYUEV: Hey, any servants there? That's the best way to handle him. (*Fyodor comes in, followed by two servants.*)

KRECHINSKY: Take him by the scruff of his neck and chuck him out.

NELKIN: My God? Am I dreaming this? Am I really alive? (*Pinches himself. Bitterly.*) Truth, truth! Where is your power? (*Leaves, bewildered.*)

RASPLYUEV (*locking the door after Nelkin*): Adieu!! He, he, he! So that's what he's after! (*Withdraws to a side.*) My blessings, son! There's no faster way to become a beggar! Go ahead, search for truth, my friend; you're still young yet, go look for it . . . (*Silence. Muromsky has a troubled look on his face. Lidochka remains motionless. Atuyeva looks angrily at Muromsky.*)

SCENE 7

The same, except for Nelkin.

KRECHINSKY (*after a pause*): Well, are you satisfied, Pyotr Konstantinych?

MUROMSKY: Completely satisfied. Poor fellow, he's simply gone mad.

KRECHINSKY: And I'm also satisfied. Well now, I imagine we can end things.

MUROMSKY (*perplexed*): End things? How?

KRECHINSKY: The way people usually do! We've just been involved in a scandalous affair; my reputation's even been compromised by you, hasn't it? With such a stigma, what sort of a husband would I be for your daughter? Pyotr Konstantinych! To you I must return your consent, and to you, Lydia, your heart. Take it, be happy, and . . . forget me . . .

LIDOCHKA: What do you mean?! *Michel!* What are you saying? I don't understand you. A heart isn't given back. My heart belongs to you . . . Papa! Why don't you say something? For God's sake, why don't you say something! We're the guilty ones. (*In despair.*) It's all our doing!

MUROMSKY (*hastily*): Yes, I . . . please, Mikhailo Vasilich, how can you? I never . . . he's a complete half-wit. How can you pay any attention to what he says?

KRECHINSKY: How can you act the way you have? Tell me? If that gossip monger could insult me, then think how much more you've insulted me. And what if tomorrow someone else comes to tell you I'm a gambler and a swindler? What will you do then? Take it all in, I suppose, and then start making inquiries.

MUROMSKY: Mikhailo Vasilich! How can you?

KRECHINSKY: I know these principles of middle-class morality. But what you have to realize is that my pride forbids me to accept them. Either I trust a person or I don't; there's no happy medium. I don't need your diamond solitaires or your money. If anyone says anything about your money to me again, I'll smash him in the face with it!

LIDOCHKA (*taking him by the hand*): Michel! For God's sake! If you still love me even a little . . .

MUROMSKY: Mikhailo Vasilich! I beg you, forgive me; forgive me, I beg you . . .

KRECHINSKY (*something coming to mind; aside*): He headed straight for Bek's I'll bet.

LIDOCHKA: You're not saying anything. Are you offended? I know you don't have either forgiveness or pity in your heart . . . What more do you want? We'll do anything . . .

KRECHINSKY (*grasping her hands, with emotion*): Oh, what a heart you have, Lydia! What a good heart! Am I worth it?

LIDOCHKA: Michel! Aren't you ashamed to talk like that?

KRECHINSKY: Well, Pyotr Konstantinych, give me your hand!

MUROMSKY: That's the way now! (*They shake hands.*) That's the way!

KRECHINSKY: Listen, I have an idea: let's have the wedding tomorrow in order to put an end once and for all to all the gossip.

MUROMSKY: Tomorrow, if you like.

KRECHINSKY: And right after it, we'll leave for the country, for Streshnevo.

MUROMSKY: Good, right for Streshnevo.

KRECHINSKY: Don't have any more to do with Nelkin.

MUROMSKY: God be with him! What more do I have to do with him now?

KRECHINSKY: You give me your word, on your honor?

MUROMSKY: Whatever you want; I agree to everything. My head is spinning. (*Makes a rotating gesture with a hand.*) There's only one thing . . . she's all . . . (*His voice breaks.*) I only have . . .

KRECHINSKY (*looking at his watch*): Ten o'clock already; time for you to go home. (*To Lidochka.*) Lydia, you're still upset, I can see!

LIDOCHKA: No, it's nothing. (*Takes him by the hand.*) You've forgotten everything . . . haven't you? Please say yes!

KRECHINSKY (*holding her hand*): Yes, a hundred times yes! I've forgotten everything . . . except one thing: that you belong to me. Tomorrow you'll become mine . . . all mine . . .

LIDOCHKA: Yes, yours, *Michel*, yours! Tell me again that you love me!

KRECHINSKY (*looking at her*): Don't you believe it?

LIDOCHKA: It's not that. I just want to hear that word once again; there's something special in it! I don't know what it is . . . fear and a kind of pain.

KRECHINSKY (*uneasily*): Pain? . . . What makes you say that?

LIDOCHKA: Don't be afraid . . . I wouldn't exchange that pain for any pleasures. Well, why are you waiting? Aren't you going to say you love me?

KRECHINSKY (*in a whisper*): I love you . . .

LIDOCHKA (*taking him by one hand and with the other covering her eyes*): You know, *Michel*, the moment you said that my heart completely froze . . . it's not beating any more. Tell me, is that what love is?

KRECHINSKY: No, my angel, that's only half of it.

LIDOCHKA (*smiling*): Half? What a cheat you are . . . when I'm ready now to give up everything for it . . . (*Krechinsky kisses her hand.*) Yes, everything, everything . . . (*in a low voice*) the whole world.

KRECHINSKY (*kissing Lidochka's hand again; to Muromsky*): Well, Pyotr Konstantinych! It's time for you to go.

MUROMSKY: Yes, we'll be on our way now.

KRECHINSKY: Go on then, and please put Lidochka to bed; she needs the rest. Lydia! Tomorrow you'll be fresh, rosy-cheeked, lovely, the way a bride should be . . . (*Thinks.*) Or better yet, I'll take you all home myself and see to everything. (*Muromsky, Atuyeva, and Lidochka get ready to leave.*)

RASPLYUEV (*to Krechinsky*): Just what I was thinking, Mikhailo Vasilich—it'd be better for you to see to everything yourself.

KRECHINSKY (*leading Rasplyuev aside*): Stay here and keep your eyes open. If that Nelkin tries to push his way in again, let him in and keep him here even if you have to hit him over the head with a log from the fireplace . . . understand? Make sure you don't let him go until I get back . . . remember . . .

RASPLYUEV: Don't worry, don't worry. That's one bird I won't let out of the cage.

KRECHINSKY: Everything else I've got firmly under control.

The Muromskys won't let him into the house, I'll see to that. He won't crawl there any more.

MUROMSKY: Well, Mikhailo Vasilich, let's be off; we're all ready.

KRECHINSKY: Let's be off, come now. (*Quickly takes his hat. The doorbell rings abruptly. They all stop as though rooted to the spot.*) Huh? What? What's that? Eh? (*Shouts.*) Hey! Servants! Fyodor! Who's there? Don't let anyone in . . . you hear me? (*Noise, followed by another ring of the bell. Voices.*) Ah-h-h! That's it! (*Fyodor comes in.*) What is it? Who's here?

FYODOR: Mister Nelkin, Sir . . . and someone else with him. He's shouting to open the door. (*Voices are heard off-stage: "Open the doors! Open the doors!" More ringing of the bell.*)

KRECHINSKY (*in a violent outburst*): So he wants me to kill him on the spot! (*Breaks the arm off a chair. Muromsky and Lidochka seize him by the hand.*)

LIDOCHKA: *Michel! Michel!*

MUROMSKY: Mikhailo Vasilich, for heaven's sake, calm yourself! What's come over you? (*They all surround him.*)

KRECHINSKY (*to Rasplyuev*): Go and toss him out on his ear.

RASPLYUEV (*running to the door*): Right away. (*Returns hurriedly. To Krechinsky.*) Mikhailo Vasilich, there's at least five of them there! Five, I tell you!

KRECHINSKY (*advancing on him threateningly*): Go back and get rid of them, even if you have to die in the attempt!

RASPLYUEV: Die? Die?! Mikhailo Vasilich, have mercy! Is it so light a matter, dying? (*The noise keeps up. Voices: "Open the door! Break it down!"*)

KRECHINSKY (*tearing free of Muromsky and Lidochka and running to the door*): Let me go; I'm the only one who can put an end to it. (*Clenches his teeth.*) I'll kill him like a dog.

FYODOR: Mikhailo Vasilich! The police are here and they're ordering us to open the door.

KRECHINSKY (*beside himself*): Hold it, don't let them in! I'll crack the skull of the first person who moves! (*Holds the chair arm in his hand. Suddenly stops.*) The police! (*In a lifeless voice.*) Aa . . . (*Throws the chair arm into a corner.*) It's all over! (*Withdraws to a side.*) Open the door . . . (*Noise. The door is opened.*)

SCENE 8

The same and Nelkin, who rushes in and throws himself at Lidochka. Bek comes running in after him, in an overcoat, his eyes searching for Krechinsky. When he spots him he rushes to him and stops directly in front of him, his arms spread wide to block his path. A police officer appears in the doorway.

BEK: There he is, the thief! Robber! Oh, you thief—thought you could pawn a plain piece of glass! Took money from me for a piece of glass, the thief! (*Runs about. Krechinsky stands calmly, his arms folded.*) Seize him—there he is! Seize him, seize him!

LIDOCHKA (*screaming shrilly*): Ay-y-y!!! (*Nelkin, Muromsky, and Atuyeva rush to her. Krechinsky also makes a move to approach her.*)

BEK: Stop, stop! Where are you going, thief? Oh, you robber! (*Rasplyuev hides behind Krechinsky.*)

POLICE OFFICER: Calm down, Nikanor Savich, please, calm down! (*To Krechinsky.*) May I have your full name, please.

KRECHINSKY: Mikhailo Vasilich Krechinsky.

POLICE OFFICER (*to Rasplyuev*): And yours, Sir?

RASPLYUEV (*completely beside himself.*): M . . . i . . . khailo Va . . . ch . . . What . . . should I . . . do? Mikhailo Vasilich . . . What . . . what . . . tell me? (*Krechinsky looks him straight in the eyes.*) I . . . don't . . . have . . . a name . . . That's . . . how . . . I am . . . no name.

POLICE OFFICER: I am asking you for your full name.

RASPLYUEV: But, please, since I don't have a name . . .

KRECHINSKY (*calmly*): His name is Ivan Antonov Rasplyuev. (*The police officer proceeds to the other group and quietly converses with Muromsky until almost the end of the play. Krechinsky makes a sudden movement.*)

BEK (*shouting*): Stop, stop! Hold him, don't let him go! (*Screams.*) Hold him! (*Stands directly in front of Krechinsky, his arms spread wide.*)

POLICE OFFICER: Nikanor Savich! I beg you—calm yourself!

BEK (*shouting*): He's a beast, a beast! He'll get away! Hold him! I gave out six thousand for a piece of glass, for a

fake diamond pin! It's forgery! He should go to jail!
Arrest him!

LIDOCHKA (*separating from the group, crossing the entire
stage, and coming over to Bek*): Please, Sir: let him go!
Here's the pin . . . that should have been pawned. Take
it . . . it was . . . (*dissolves in tears*) a mistake!

MUROMSKY and ATUYEVA: Lidochka, do you know what you're
saying? Lidochka!

BEK: Huh? What's that, young lady? (*Looks at the pin.*) This
is the real one? Eh? The real pin? It is? It is!! Praise
God! What a girl! Heavenly kindness! Angelic meek-
ness . . . (*Lidochka covers her face with her hands and
sobs.*)

KRECHINSKY (*facing the audience, aside*): What luck! (*Puts
a hand to his brow.*) Saved by a woman again!

ATUYEVA: Oh, Pyotr Konstantinych, what are we to do now?

MUROMSKY: Run, my dear, as fast as we can! Run away from
the shame! (*Lidochka rushes headlong off the stage,
followed by Nelkin, Muromsky, and Atuyeva.*)

CURTAIN

THE CASE

A DRAMA IN FIVE ACTS

Written in the year 1862:

The play herein offered to the public under the title *The Case* is not, as it used to be called, a *labor of love,* nor, as it is nowadays known, a *specimen of literary art,* but rather a real case torn flesh and blood from truest life.

If someone—I am not speaking about the class of *literati,* which is as alien to me as the remaining fourteen ranks of the bureaucracy—but if someone of those whom I esteem should doubt the veracity or even the possibility of the event described by me, then I herewith declare that I have at hand facts of sufficiently bright colors to convince any and all disbelief that I invented nothing impossible and fabricated nothing unimaginable. As for the rest, I am indifferent.

To those who seek here raw allusions to certain individuals and piquant pasquinades, I say that I hold in low esteem those who merit pasquinades and myself in too high esteem to permit myself such literary misconduct.

About the so-called literary value of this Drama I myself have nothing to say, of course. But if some Mr. Conscientious or other of the Critics' Guild should approach it with his official measure and scales of judgment, such a Dignitary of the Department of Literature and Periodical Affairs could scarcely to form an opinion of the indifference with which I view his tribunal . . . It is high time that such a tribunal became public. It is high time even for it to free itself from literary bureaucracy. It is high time indeed that in the privacy of its own emotions and in the stirrings of its own nature the public itself seek the judgment of what is good or bad on the stage—without any literary Recommendation or other such Patronage, without any Staging or Decoration, but only by means of these inner stirrings and turbulences. For seven years now Krechinsky has been serving on the Russian stage, a service which at the same time functions as the tribunal by which he is judged. I thank the public for such a flattering sentence for me; I greet it and its beginning independence—and now my sincere and burning desire is only that my *Case* be heard in this same tribunal and judged by this same court.

March 26, 1862
Hairos

P.S. Six years have passed! My desire, alas, could not be fulfilled and now I regretfully deliver to the press what I did for the stage.

February 21, 1868
Kobylinka

Six years have passed since the breakup of Krechinsky's wedding plans.

The scene is set in St. Petersburg, partly in the Muromskys' apartment, partly in the offices and quarters of a certain official department.

Cast of Characters

I. Authorities.

A VERY IMPORTANT PERSON, before whom everyone, including the author, is silent.

AN IMPORTANT PERSON, by birth, a prince; by rank, a privy council-lor; by club, a pleasant sort; in the service, a beast. He enjoys good health, but has a hankering for strawberries, which he often indulges to satiety, and as a result of which he suffers from hemorrhoids.

II. Powers.

MAKSIM KUZMICH VARRAVIN, director of affairs and driving wheel of a certain official department, actual state councillor, once decorated. At his birth nature endowed him with a juglike snout.

KANDID KASTOROVICH TARELKIN, collegiate councillor and a close associate of Varravin; an exhausted and utterly emaciated type, about forty years old; dresses well—his linen impeccable; wears a toupee, but keeps the fact a great secret. The movements of his jaws also suggest that several of his teeth, and perhaps all of them, are false. He talks like Demosthenes, particularly when the latter attempted to address the roaring ocean with stones in his mouth in order to overcome stuttering.

IVAN ANDREYEVICH ZHIVETS. He has achieved a career on the field of honor. Having received there several shares of the cudgel and because of that naturally thrust himself forward, he has attained the rank of a nonstaff officer. At present he zealously serves Throne and Fatherland as a sergeant-at-arms.

III. Underlings.

CHIBISOV, a decent, presentable appearance, dressed fashionably; speaks softly, with feeling and, in general, the way people speak who in St. Petersburg are called *warm*, in diametric opposition to Moscow where *warm* means *thieving*.

IBISOV, a bon vivant and superficial type who is the friend of everyone and no one.

KASYAN KASYANOVICH SHILO, the physiognomy of a Corsican bandit; dresses carelessly; looks at everyone and everything with a jaundiced eye. From the anxieties and storms of the sea of life he suffers from moral seasickness, and from an excessive bitterness of taste in the mouth he often halts in the middle of a sentence and sometimes completely stutters.

Officials:

GERTS
SHERTS } Wheels, pulleys, and pinions of bureaucracy.
SHMERTS

The official OMEGA. He has a good heart and disposition, but he is weak and unstable.

IV. *Nonentities, or private personages.*

PYOTR KONSTANTINOVICH MUROMSKY, the same simplicity and directness of nature, sculptured with a fine chisel by the late S. Schchepkin. In the last five years he has grown thin, weak, and as white as paper.

ANNA ANTONOVNA ATUYEVA. She has fallen low morally, but has prospered physically.

LIDOCHKA. What is there to say? To some she has grown rather plain; to others, she has become pretty. She is thinner and pale. Her movements are steady and precise; her gaze is stern and penetrating. She goes about dressed in black, wears Berget plaid and a hat with a thick black veil.

NELKIN. He has traveled—and become more complex. He has lost his feelers and acquired a pair of well-cared-for whiskers, which are of no offense, however, to any moral sensitivity. He parts his hair from the back, but without any affectation.

IVAN SIDOROV RAZUVAYEV. [Throughout the play he is generally referred to just by his given name and patronymic, Ivan Sidorov, or on occasion by the familiar form of his patronymic, Sidorych.] He manages Muromsky's possessions and affairs. Previously he himself had an interest in commerce, conducted trade, raised himself up by the bootstraps and acquired something. Now he is over sixty. He is married, but has no children. He preserves the old faith and wears a beard in the Byzantine style. He is dressed in the style of all officials: a blue double-breasted frock coat, high boots, and a sash around his waist.

V. *No Personage.*

TISHKA. Even he has known the limits of grandeur! After such tumult he has ripped off his gallooned livery, pulled the boots from his feet, and with composed inner satisfaction gone back to a gray frock coat and to plain canvas pantaloons.

ACT ONE

(The Muromsky apartment. The parlor. Three doors. The one on the right leads to Lidochka's and Atuyeva's room; the one on the left to Muromsky's study; the third, directly in front of the audience, leads into the hallway. A bureau; sofa; a large chair by a window.)

SCENE 1

Atuyeva is drinking tea as Nelkin enters.

NELKIN *(bowing)*: Good morning, Anna Antonovna!

ATUYEVA: How are you?

NELKIN *(looking about)*: Perhaps I've come too early?

ATUYEVA: Not at all. Even the old man is getting up.

NELKIN: Lydia Petrovna hasn't gotten up yet?

ATUYEVA: You think things are just the way they used to be. No, now Lydia gets up earlier than everyone else. She's at morning mass now, but should be back in a little while.

NELKIN *(seating himself)*: We haven't seen each other for some time. It will soon be five years.

ATUYEVA: Yes, a long time. Well, where did you travel out of the country?

NELKIN: Many places. In fact, I just returned. You know how much I love you all here.

ATUYEVA: Thank you. Nowadays there are precious few who love us . . . you can count them on the fingers of one hand. You did a good thing in coming here right away.

NELKIN: Why, I was just waiting to come to you. You should have written long ago. You see—I lost no time . . . *(They embrace firmly. Atuyeva wipes away tears.)* Now, now—why the tears?

ATUYEVA: Why not?!

NELKIN: What's going on here?

ATUYEVA *(sighing)*: Oh—it's no good at all!

NELKIN: What is?

ATUYEVA: This case on our hands.

NELKIN: Won't you tell me what it's about? What sort of case can there be?

ATUYEVA: My dear, I see it all clearly now. Ivan Sidorov is

A 1962 production of The Case at The Teatr Nowy in Łódź, Poland. Directed by Bohdan Korzeniewski. Left to right: Varravin, The Very Important Person, and The Important Person.

right when he says that there can be a case for anything. Here they've started the whole business, now go
do something about it. They drag you from one torture
to another. They drag it out and determine that there
are opinions and disagreements. It's been going on five
years now and there's no peace for us. And you know
it's all fallen on her.

NELKIN: On her? Why in Heaven's name on her?

ATUYEVA: Because of the suspicion.

NELKIN: Suspicion? About what?

ATUYEVA: First of all, that she knew, they say, that Krechinsky wanted to rob Pyotr Konstantinovich.

NELKIN (*shaking his head*): She *what*?

ATUYEVA: And second, they're even saying that she must have
been helping him.

NELKIN (*raising his eyes*): My God!

ATUYEVA: And third, and one can say, the cruelest and evilest
of all, they're saying that the reason she was helping
him was because the two of them were having a love
affair. She's an innocent victim, but he enticed her . . .

NELKIN: Yes, that's how it was, that no good Krechinsky . . .

ATUYEVA (*interrupting him*): No, no, don't you sin.

NELKIN: I'm afraid I can't help it.

ATUYEVA (*interrupting him*): Wait a moment . . . when the
whole affair first started . . .

NELKIN (*interrupting her*): You mean to say you still haven't
cured yourself of that illness?

ATUYEVA: Cure myself of what?

NELKIN (*waving his hands*): No—don't say anything.

ATUYEVA (*jumping up*): Oh, God! (*Takes a piece of paper
out of a desk drawer.*) Here, read this.

NELKIN (*twisting the paper in his hand*): What is it?

ATUYEVA: This letter here Krechinsky wrote to Pyotr Konstantinovich when the case first started.

NELKIN: Krechinsky?! A letter?! I had to leave Europe just
to come back to read Krechinsky's letters? Do you know,
I hate that person. He is Cain! He killed his brother
Abel!

ATUYEVA: No, he didn't kill him. Read the letter, go on.

NELKIN (*reading*): "My dear Pyotr Konstantinovich! Only
extreme need forces me to write to you" . . . (*Stops.*)
Well, there you are: again some trick.

ATUYEVA: We thought it was a trick, but it proved to be something else . . . Go on reading.

NELKIN (*at first reads indifferently, but afterward with greater animation and emphasis*): "My dear Pyotr Konstantinovich! Only extreme need forces me to write to you. The need, however, is not mine but yours, and that is why I am writing. They are looking for a bribe from you— give it. The consequences of your refusal to do so may be dreadful. You know little about such bribes or how they are taken. If you permit me, I shall explain it to you. There are different types of bribes. For example, there is the *rural* bribe, so to speak, pastoral, arcadian. It is taken mainly in the form of agricultural products and from each according to his mug. It isn't really a bribe. Then there is the *industrial* bribe, which is taken out of profit, a contract, or an inheritance, in short out of some acquisition. It is based on the axiom "love your neighbor as you do yourself"; he acquired something—let's divide it up. But this is still not a bribe. There is the *criminal* or *snare* bribe. It is taken until there is nothing left to take, until a person is stripped bare! It follows the examples and principles of Stenka Razin* and Nightingale the Robber†. It is carried out under the cover and shade of a dense forest of laws, with the help and by means of the snares, wolf pits, and rods of justice set everywhere throughout the field of human endeavor. And into these pits will fall the old and the young, the rich and the poor, without any regard for sex, or age, or profession, or wisdom or ignorance . . . Now it is just a *snare* bribe that they want to take from you. And it is into such a wolf pit of legal procedure that they are now driving your daughter. Pay them off! . . . They want to take money from you—give it to them! Give it to them —they'll only skin you! . . . The case that was initiated by the report of the district supervisor concerning my apparent resistance to police authority, my threat to kill him on the spot, and my deception with your solitaire, is taking a dangerous turn for you. The whole

---

* A popular seventeenth-century revolutionary leader.
† A figure in Russian folk literature.

scheme was revealed to me yesterday. Yesterday it was proposed to me that I give certain evidence regarding the honor of your daughter. You're surprised. But imagine—I refused to do it! I answered that perhaps I happened to get the best of some little merchant on the verge of bankruptcy anyway or some landowner mischievously squandering his inheritance, but I never laid a hand on anyone's children, murdered anyone in his sleep, or caught young girls on the rod of legal procedure. What can be done? Everyone has his own logic. I am not defending mine but, as you can see, there are worse. Best regards,

Mikhail Krechinsky"

ATUYEVA: And do you suppose Pyotr Konstantinych followed his instructions?

NELKIN (*returning the letter*): Naturally he didn't believe him.

ATUYEVA (*putting the letter away in a desk drawer*): Of course. Aha, he says, it's a new trick: you got someone down, give it to him twice as hard. So he didn't take his word for it. People in the right, he says, don't give; the ones who are in the wrong do. I nearly took his side. After all, you know how he is—he says to me, Well, I suppose you and Krechinsky see eye to eye, eh? But what can they do to her? I'm the father here, he says, and my voice is the first one they'll listen to. But it turns out that his was the last they'd listen to because, they say, he wouldn't get his own child in wrong.

NELKIN: But I still can't understand how it happened.

ATUYEVA: Very simple. Since Krechinsky was out of the picture they dragged in Rasplyuev. And he testified the way they wanted. Well, you see, he says, there was a love affair between them, that it was arranged by him, that he carried little notes back and forth and even brought the woman disguised to Krechinsky but that he doesn't know who the woman was . . . In the beginning it was all very quiet. We left for the country and didn't know anything about it. First they summoned one of our people, then another. Then it turns out they went through the whole house examining, interrogating . . . Well, you can imagine the confusion.

NELKIN: They really wanted to confuse everything.

ATUYEVA: That's the way it was because the investigation was about Lidochka, not Krechinsky, because he had only the shirt on his back left. Anyway, they didn't get anything special out of our people until one thief, the cook Petrushka, a good-for-nothing, showed up. Pyotr Konstantinych tried twice to put him in the army. This fellow steps up and says, I'm a witness! The next thing we know they're summoning Lidochka, why we had no idea. The cook meanwhile is as stubborn as they come! Finally, Pyotr Konstantinych gives in and says, Let them ask her whatever they want; she didn't do anything bad.

NELKIN: Of course.

ATUYEVA: Well, there was nothing to be done. We came back from the country. When Pyotr Konstantinych found out that they wanted to confront her with witnesses, with Petrushka, with Rasplyuev, with Krechinsky, as soon as he found out what these confrontations were about, that's when the first blow struck him. That's when he learned that Krechinsky was telling the truth in his letter. He began running around everywhere. He got a hold of his lawyer, gave him money, and they worked out some arrangement . . . I'll tell you, though, that as soon as he gave the money, the case was lost. Things got even worse. No sooner do you give money for one thing, than you have to give more for something else. Now everything was lost. You give the money and then they say they never got it. Pyotr Konstantinych goes to the lawyer's and the lawyer tells him he paid off. Don't believe them, they're all thieves, and the lawyer keeps half for himself. Then they start asking me questions. What kind of questions? Didn't Krechinsky come calling on the young lady at night? Didn't the young lady have a child . . .

NELKIN (*throwing up his arms*): My God!

ATUYEVA: So I spit in their faces and called them antichrists. That's how it was! I tell you, you have no idea what was going on. The investigation lasted for eight months— eight months of such tortures you can't even find the words to describe them.

NELKIN: Wasn't there anyone you could turn to? You could have asked . . .

ATUYEVA: There wasn't anyone to turn to—that was just our misfortune. You can imagine the stories that circulated through the city, the opinions and the gossip. I just can't tell you. Lidochka, they said, was connected with him and wanted to run away with him, and the two of them were trying to rob her father—that's the sort of thing people were saying. It was impossible to show yourself anywhere. Afterward it went to court, and then even further. What went on, I really don't know. The case kept getting bigger and bigger, like this (*makes a gesture with her hands*). They dragged us from one office to another, and that's how it's been for five years now.

NELKIN (*walking around the room*): What a calamity. It's like a fire in the middle of the night . . .

ATUYEVA: Exactly, a fire. And now what? They've ruined us completely, got the girl all confused, torn her to pieces, and now they're getting ready for some new torture. We've been here for five months, and our money's running out. We've had to sell the place at Golovkovo.

NELKIN: You've sold Golovkovo?

ATUYEVA: Streshnevo's been put up for mortgage.

NELKIN (*with horror in his voice*): What's going to happen?

ATUYEVA: I myself have no idea what's going to happen.

NELKIN: Where is the case at now?

ATUYEVA: The case? Just lying.

NELKIN: What do you mean "just lying"?

ATUYEVA: Lying like a rock—that's all! And what are we doing? We're sitting here, like in a hole somewhere. We don't know anyone. Nothing but darkness on all sides. We can't go anywhere, we can't ask anyone for help, we have nobody to turn to. The other day, for example, some clever fellow comes to us. Pyotr Konstantinych, he says, your case is just lying now, right? Right, just lying. And it should be going somewhere. Yes . . . it should, he says, be going somewhere. Well, they're just waiting, it seems.

NELKIN: Waiting? For what?

ATUYEVA: What they usually wait for . . . (*Makes a gesture with her hands.*) Money.

NELKIN: So that's it!

ATUYEVA: And Pyotr Konstantinych isn't throwing his money around. This man says to him: Pyotr Konstantinych,

I'm honest! I live only for my honor: Give me twenty
thousand in silver, and I'll end the case for you! The
old man jumps up, scalds himself with hot tea, and
says: What did you say—twenty thousand? Twenty
thousand what? Then he started figuring. The other
shrugs his shoulders, says good-bye, and goes his way . . .
Once this middleman comes, a German in spectacles
and shrewd as they make them. I'll settle the case for
you, he says, but you'll have to pay me three thousand
in silver for it. And so sensibly he talked. No, he says,
I'm not after your money. Pay me only when the whole
business is finished and for now just give me a pledge
of three hundred rubles silver. There's one important
person, he says, and this person is very punctual, and
this person has a sweetheart who'll do anything you want.
I'll take you to her and just for a nice bracelet you'll
see how much help she'll be. At this point Lidochka
got up. There's pride for you. Why should my father
bring down shame on his gray head, she says. Then the
old man himself got stubborn. What's this, he says,
anyone off the street's going to come and take three
hundred rubles silver from me? So there was no agreement.

NELKIN: What can they agree about?

ATUYEVA: Next comes a fine fellow, but Pyotr Konstantinych
doesn't like him. What a person, though. Completely
comme-il-faut, but no position, it seems. He wants to
tell a lot of people about us and he says—you just wait
and see.

NELKIN: Was that that Tarelkin who was with you yesterday
evening when I arrived?

ATUYEVA: That's the one.

NELKIN: Is he after Lydia Petrovna?

ATUYEVA: Maybe. Anyway, I don't see anything wrong in it.
He's very . . . attentive . . . and knows everything and
everyone. Like when he sits by the window; he knows
everyone who goes by. There's so and so, he says, and
there goes so and so. What's the matter? I don't see
anything wrong in it. And then there's even a marker
who came.

NELKIN: Marker?

ATUYEVA: You know, the one that keeps score when they play billiards.

NELKIN: What on earth can such a person do for you?

ATUYEVA: Here's what: this marker, my dear, is perhaps the best billiard player in the whole city.

NELKIN: I still don't see . . .

ATUYEVA: Wait a moment. He happens to play billiards with one important, one very important person, but with whom—he didn't say. Only Tarelkin said who he was. And this important person plays billiards because the doctors ordered him to. He suffers, you see, from hemorrhoids . . . his stomach is out of order—you understand?

NELKIN: I understand.

ATUYEVA: Now when they play, this marker tells him all kinds of little stories and this way can raise some important issue when he wants. There are a number of people who've made out very well on account of this marker.

NELKIN: Anna Antonovna, it just doesn't smell right to me.

ATUYEVA: Here you get back yesterday from abroad and right away it doesn't smell right to you. Wait till you're a little older—then you'll be able to stand the smell of any kind of nonsense.

NELKIN (sighing): Maybe, it's just that . . . But I'd prefer to hear about Lydia Petrovna. She's gotten very thin. How large her eyes have become, and how soft. Do you know, she's unusually lovely.

ATUYEVA: What's lovely when the eyes bulge out from thinness?

NELKIN: Does she cough?

ATUYEVA: Yes. We did see the doctor about it, but it's nothing, he says.

NELKIN: How does she bear it all?

ATUYEVA: I wonder myself. And she's changed so, I just can't understand it. She doesn't want to make any petitions; she doesn't want to say a word about the case— and mind you, not a word about it to her. Just like it didn't exist. She stopped seeing her friends; she just follows her father around and doesn't let anyone get near him! To church she goes on foot, and that's just plain silly, I tell you. Even in grief, and God knows how

unhappy she is, to drag herself to church on shank's
mare . . .

NELKIN: But if she wants it that way—let her be.

ATUYEVA: I let her—but it's silly. When the case first began
we had a lawyer here, a very clever fellow—but a beast—
he robbed Pyotr Konstantinych of three thousand.

NELKIN: Smart lawyer.

ATUYEVA: Smart, I'll tell you how smart. He says, Lydia
Petrovna, you have to file a petition. All right. So he
wrote out the petition for her, and took care of everything the way he was supposed to, and it was all so clear
and detailed. He brought it; we all sat down and started
reading it. At first she listened to everything—but then
suddenly she began trembling. She covered her face with
her hands and started sobbing . . .

NELKIN (*wiping his own tears*): The poor thing—she's a
martyr.

ATUYEVA: I look and what do I see? The old man took heart
and agreed with her! The two of them! Well, I made a
sign to the lawyer and we stopped discussing the matter.
I went over to her and said, What are you doing, you
little fool, they're going to condemn you, don't you
see? And she says, very excited, Me?!!! No, not me,
she says! . . . Do you understand? Well, when I saw we
were just making things worse I let her alone and from
then on swore that I wouldn't say even the slightest
word about the case.

NELKIN: And does she say anything about Krechinsky?

ATUYEVA: Never! Just as though he never existed.

NELKIN (*taking Atuyeva by the hand*): She loves him!!! Does
she know about his letter?

ATUYEVA: Not a thing. We haven't told her.

NELKIN (*thinking*): You know what?

ATUYEVA: What?

NELKIN: Give up everything; sell everything; show her the
letter; go abroad, and let her get married there to
Krechinsky.

ATUYEVA: To Krechinsky? Cross yourself! What kind of a
mate is he for her now? He's a lost man.

NELKIN: Lost where others are concerned, but for her—found.

ATUYEVA: Some find! No, that won't do . . . But, in my
opinion, this Tarelkin—why wouldn't he be good for

her? After all, he's a collegiate councillor, in the government service, with connections, and that means something in the world.

NELKIN: Granted, Anna Antonovna, but look at him—he's not really a human being.

ATUYEVA: Why isn't he a human being?

NELKIN: He's a dust rag, a crumpled piece of official paper. He's made out of paper: his forehead is pasteboard, his brain is made out of papier-mâché—and you call that a human being?! That's a particular species of reptile that inhabits only the Petersburg Swamp!

SCENE 2

The same. Lidochka enters dressed in plaid, with a hat on and carrying a small handbag and a loaf of Russian Orthodox communion bread.

LIDOCHKA: Oh, Vladimir Dmitrich! How are you? (*She squeezes his hand.*)

NELKIN (*bowing*): How are you, Lydia Petrovna?

LIDOCHKA: How happy I am! —Have you had tea yet? Come, let's drink some together, and you'll tell father all about your travels. Hello, Auntie. (*Goes up to Atuyeva and kisses her on the forehead.*) Has father gotten up yet?

ATUYEVA: He's up.

LIDOCHKA: I hurried so . . . I was afraid to be late—it was time to serve him tea—he likes everything to be ready. (*She quickly removes her hat, and puts down the handbag and bread.*)

ATUYEVA: Tishka! Hey, Tishka! (*Tishka enters.*) Prepare the tea.

LIDOCHKA: Auntie—you know I set a place for him myself. (*To Tishka.*) You don't have to, Tikhon, just bring over the samovar . . . (*Tishka leaves.*)

ATUYEVA: My you're acting stubbornly, darling!

LIDOCHKA (*preparing the tea*): Auntie, I've already asked you several times—leave me alone. If it's my desire . . .

ATUYEVA: Well, young lady, do as you wish.

LIDOCHKA: Vladimir Dmitrich, bring the table and the large

chair over here to the window. (*They carry the table
and move the chair.*) That's it . . . and the pillow . . .
(*Nelkin hands her a pillow.*) That's fine—now the tea.
(*She spreads out a tablecloth, then prepares the tea.
Tishka, meanwhile, sets the samovar down.*) Wait a
moment. Yesterday he wanted some cracknels—would
you have a look there in my bag . . . (*Nelkin hands her
the cracknels. She brews the tea.*)

ATUYEVA: Did you buy those cracknels yourself, dear?

LIDOCHKA (*brewing the tea*): Yes, Auntie (*smiling*), myself.

ATUYEVA (*to Nelkin*): You see! She buys cracknels in the
market by herself! Just to spite me . . .

NELKIN (*appeasing her*): The thought of it!

SCENE 3

*The same and Muromsky who emerges from his study dressed
in a robe.*

MUROMSKY (*to Lidochka*): Hello, my little friend. (*Kisses
her. Sees Nelkin.*) Well, now . . . here already are you?
Thank you—come let's embrace, dear fellow! (*They
embrace.*)

NELKIN: How are you feeling, Pyotr Konstantinych?

MUROMSKY: So-so. You appeared by surprise yesterday, eh?
Did you come by ship?

NELKIN: Yes, by ship.

MUROMSKY: Well, tell us now, where were you, what did you
see?

LIDOCHKA (*going up to her father*): No! If you please, Papa—
(*leads him to the tea table*) first sit down, otherwise
your tea will get cold—that's right, over here (*sits him
down*). Here are pillows. All right now?

MUROMSKY (*sitting down and looking at his daughter*): All
right, my angel, all right!

LIDOCHKA: Like this—I'll sit right next to you . . . (*sits
down*). And you, Vladimir Dmitrich, opposite us. (*Nelkin seats himself.*) Now tell us—but mind, only the
pleasant things. (*She pours the tea.*) Papa, I think the
tea is excellent; I chose it myself.

MUROMSKY: Thank you. And you know, I'm just now in the

mood for tea, too. (*Drinks.*) I was already waiting in
my room. Wasn't that my Lidushechka who just came
in, I thought? I listened—she just began to sing . . . my
little songbird, you (*kisses her*), my little dove . . .
(*Drinks tea.*) Wonderful tea, Lidushechka, wonderful.

LIDOCHKA: Then I'm very glad. (*Muromsky looks for something.*) Ah . . . here it is! (*She hands him the communion bread.*)

MUROMSKY: There we are . . . Thank you, darling. (*To Nelkin.*) Say the prayer, young man. Living among all those
heathens I guess it's been some time since you've said it.
(*Gives him the bread.*)

NELKIN (*reciting*): O zdr . . . *avii* . . . *ra* . . . *ba* . . . *bo* . . .
zhiia . . . *Pe* . . . *tra* . . .

MUROMSKY: Would you believe that she's been carrying this
around for me since morning mass? (*Breaks the bread
and gives half to Nelkin.*)

LIDOCHKA (*pouring more tea*): Why, Papa, every day at early
mass I take a part of it for your health and pray God
that He keeps you healthy and happy for me . . . God is
merciful; He hears my prayers and will keep you under
His protection. And now here you are drinking tea,
knowing that your Lidochka has already prayed to God
for you. (*Kisses him.*)

ATUYEVA: I see you're passing out communion bread just like
all our poor little country squires.

LIDOCHKA: I can't explain to you, Auntie, why in the next
world there aren't poor people, or rich people, or country
squires.

MUROMSKY: That's enough nagging her, Anna Antonovna.
After all, it's not that she's doing anything bad. (*To
Nelkin.*) Do you know that just an hour or so in her
company in the morning and I feel refreshed, and if it
weren't for her I think I would have passed out long
ago. Well, has she changed any, do you think?

NELKIN: Not at all.

MUROMSKY: Not really—just a little thinner.

NELKIN: Yes—a bit. You know, Lidochka, it seems to me that
you've gotten fairer somehow, brighter. There's a kind
of tranquillity in your face, just as though God's grace
descended to you.

LIDOCHKA: That's enough—what you're saying is sinful . . . tell Papa instead what you saw, where you were.

MUROMSKY: Really now, do tell us where you were.

NELKIN: Well, I crept about a lot, looked around a lot, saw a lot . . . and learned a few things.

LIDOCHKA: Don't believe it, Papa, until you make him tell you about Paris and what he did there. Why did he stay so long there?

NELKIN (*laughing*): Well, what *did* I do, Lydia Petrovna? I got there, then settled down modestly *au quartier Latin*.

MUROMSKY: What did you say?

NELKIN: The Latin Quarter.

MUROMSKY: That's where all the girlies talk Latin, eh?

NELKIN (*not hearing him*): I visited the Sorbonne . . .

MUROMSKY: And who's that?

NELKIN: The university there.

MUROMSKY: Sorbonne, you said? (*Making a threatening gesture at him with his finger.*) Come now, young man, the truth: Isn't she some actress or other?

NELKIN: For heaven's sake!

MUROMSKY: All right, all right. Well, you've gotten kind of important looking—all decked out nice, handsomer.

TISHKA (*entering*): Pyotr Konstantinych! Ivan Sidorov has arrived.

ATUYEVA: So he's here!

MUROMSKY: Barely made it—call him in.

SCENE 4

The same and Ivan Sidorov, dressed for traveling.

MUROMSKY: Hello! What took you so long?

RAZUVAYEV (*catches sight of an icon and says a prayer, then bows to all present, one after the other*): How are you, Pyotr Konstantinovich (*bows*), how are you, Anna Antonovna (*bows*), and how are you, Miss (*bows*).

LIDOCHKA: How are you, Ivan Sidorov?

RAZUVAYEV: Permit me to kiss your hand, Miss. (*Goes up to her and kisses her hand. She in turn gives him a kiss on the forehead.*) Our kind young miss.

LIDOCHKA: And how is Marya Illinishna, well I hope?

RAZUVAYEV: What can I say? Yes, she's well, thank God. You seem to have thinned out some, though.

MUROMSKY: And how are our affairs going?

RAZUVAYEV: Well, thank God. How are you feeling, Sir?

MUROMSKY: All right. What about the grain?

RAZUVAYEV: The rye's already been harvested. All the rye's been harvested. That's all I have to report, Sir.

LIDOCHKA: Let's go to Auntie's room, Vladimir Dmitrich— Papa has a lot to talk about now without us.

MUROMSKY: Yes, that's right. Be off, go on now. (*Atuyeva, Lidochka, and Nelkin leave by the door to the right.*)

SCENE 5

Muromsky and Ivan Sidorov.

MUROMSKY: Well now, did you say good-bye to all the big shots?

RAZUVAYEV: Yes I did, Sir—how could I help not saying good-bye to them? I swear, Sir, my insides just turned upside down. So cordial they are—what a howl they let out—the peasant's lot, Sir, I guess.

MUROMSKY (*sighing*): So it seems. From time immemorial we had our patrimony to back us up, but now you've got to hand it over to a tax-farmer for half price. Well, did you take care of all the payments?

RAZUVAYEV (*sighing*): Of course, Sir, and I brought with me whatever was left. (*Takes out a leather bag from his breast pocket and removes a small package from it.*) Here is the statement, Sir, would you care to check it?

MUROMSKY (*drawing a key out of his pocket*): No, just put everything in the bureau; we'll go over it all some time this evening . . . (*Ivan Sidorov locks the money in the bureau.*)

MUROMSKY: But what can I do?! They've simply swallowed me up, swallowed me up! God in heaven! (*Crosses himself and sighs.*)

RAZUVAYEV (*also sighing*): Everything is in the hands of the Lord, Sir, in the hands of the Lord!

MUROMSKY: What are we to do now, Ivan? I'm beside myself —I can't put my mind to anything.

RAZUVAYEV: The Lord will show you what to do, and if not, He'll do it Himself. You just have faith and be calm.

MUROMSKY (*sighing*): My God in heaven! I've worked, I've toiled and troubled, I've taken care of everything I could; I've raised a lovely daughter whom I just have to settle a good dowry on and marry off to someone decent—and then what happens? The carrion descend, the thieves rush in, they set fire to my home, pilfer my property—and here I am sitting on the smoldering ruins, helpless, fingering the coals . . .

RAZUVAYEV: Don't ruin yourself, Sir, for God's sake don't ruin yourself—everything is in the hands of the Lord! I've been through plenty in my own time, and how I have! But this is something different—my heavens, what a misfortune! It seems like they've closed in on all sides, but God has just to move a finger and you see, out comes the sun shining . . .

MUROMSKY: God grant it!

RAZUVAYEV: Once upon a time this happened to me: I was young and working as a merchant's shop assistant. We used to buy hides, lard—we even used to buy and sell cattle. Then the owner passed away—what can you do? So I thought, All right, I'll go into business myself, I'll become a boss. I had some money scraped together, not much though. I found someone to come in with me, and people helped out a bit. Off we went then to the big yearly fair near Kursk. My companion and I go about the fair a whole day. Then a second day—but we don't find anything good for us—everything's more than we can manage, and you know, Sir, to make any profit you've got to have the goods right in your hands. We went around and around—and finally we wind up buying mats. Ninety rubles the hundred; we bought as much as there was. We took the goods, payed out half the money, and agreed to give the rest before the fair ended. Usually, the mats are just used for covering things. Anyway, we're living. The weather is dry, it's hot, and we're out of patience. Not a cloud in the sky. But we're living . . . We can't get rid of a single mat! We begin to worry! The fair's coming to an end; my comrade goes and gets himself dead drunk! . . . All morning long I pray . . . all night long I pray . . . nothing does any good! . . . The

fifth of June is the holiday of Our Lady of Korennaya
. . . A religious procession . . . crowds of people . . . they
carry the miraculous Korennaya icon of Our Lady . . .
Mother of God! Help us!! The procession passes by,
coming out of Old Oskol. A swarm of people the likes
of which I never saw before!! Then I almost fall flat
on my face—one of the merchant Khrennikov's fellows
comes running up. — Do you have any mats, he asks. —
We have. — How much? — A hundred rubles a hundred. — Is that so? — That's so. — Have you gone
crazy? — That'll be the day! — You cross yourself! —
I've crossed myself plenty! You've lived pretty well, eh—
eaten, drunk, slept soundly, eh? Well, I had to knock
out half a yard of land for myself with my belly . . . He
hemmed and hawed, but finally gave me what I asked.
By evening that day we sold out everything we had . . .
That's what I mean, see—everything is in the hands of
the Lord! God sees man's labor and his misfortune—oh,
He sees, He sees it all.

MUROMSKY: Yes, that's so . . . only now, Ivan, it's really
going very badly for me. Here I am, five months already;
I'm on my last legs, and there's been absolutely no
progress with the case!

RAZUVAYEV: Of course, they're waiting. You know for what.
You've come here? All right—pay! Why did you push
yourself in here, Sir?

MUROMSKY: The magistrates advised me to.

RAZUVAYEV: Wolves they are. Oh, of all people to listen to!
What can they do to you?

MUROMSKY: What do you mean "what"? They can condemn
my daughter, condemn my flesh and blood, take away
her honor.

RAZUVAYEV: It can't be, Sir, that anyone can deprive an honest
person of his honor. A person's honor stays with him.

MUROMSKY: You don't understand it, my friend. I'm talking
about her reputation in the world.

RAZUVAYEV (*shaking his head*): Oh, my God—the world—
What do you care about the world? The world's a
Babylonian harlot . . . she's just got you drunk from her
own chalice. Who commands in this world of yours—
temptation; who rules it—women. You carted your
women around with you wherever you went, Sir, and

now they've taken to traveling separately. They go
running around to balls and all kinds of gatherings—
their shoulders naked, their bosoms naked, they forget
their shame and excite men's lust, and the eyes of lust
are red and wild. But you judge yourself, Sir: what can
one expect of the world? If a woman shows what should
be private to everyone in the square, she hasn't any
shame at all, and a shameless woman's everybody's property—you know it yourself . . . Forgive me, Sir, I'm just
telling the truth. It hurts me to look on all this wild
living. What are your women good for? They don't busy
themselves with any fancywork or any honest labor. They
leave empty houses and cold ovens behind while they
go chasing all over the city striking up a friendship with
every passerby. Just look at them running together like
imbeciles. But whose fault is it? Yours, Sir. You don't
keep to the commandments; you've forgotten the commandments. The home—that's a big thing. In our home
they pray, but your home's become a tavern, forgive me
for saying it. Anyone wants to eat and drink—come
here! Anyone who's good at making idle talk, or can
dance well—come over here! Cymbals and dances—
Sodom and Gomorrah!

MUROMSKY: No, Ivan, you don't understand.

RAZUVAYEV: Maybe according to you I don't understand. You
know how fond of you I am, Sir. You took me in and
gave me shelter. I'll never forget your kindness or your
family. I'm ready to go through fire and water for you.
I'd even go to the idol of Baal for you.

MUROMSKY: Thank you, thank you . . . What's this idol of
Baal, by the way?

RAZUVAYEV: A gilded idol, Sir, an official you have to bow
down to!

MUROMSKY: Yes, you have to bow down . . . You see, even
I haven't escaped it . . .

RAZUVAYEV: Everyone has his turn, Sir. My fate, too, couldn't
get out of its clutches. (*Turns his head from side to
side.*)

MUROMSKY: When was that?

RAZUVAYEV: Just about twenty years ago it was. I was sent
here by the village community—on what business that's
beside the point, but it was honest, as honest as the

day is long. We pooled all our money, as much as each could afford—everyone pitched in, even orphans and widows. Here Sidorych, they said, take it and go look for protection for us. Well, Sir, it was to this very city I came. In the Scriptures even it's written about it: the sea flows there . . . the great and wide sea . . . there are reptiles there without number! . . . Animals large and small! . . . Ships sail past . . . That's exactly how it is.

MUROMSKY: Just so.

RAZUVAYEV: As soon as I arrived in this city, I went right away to one such big animal. His name was Anton Trofimych Krek—what a fine scoundrel that one was!

MUROMSKY: Who sent you to him?

RAZUVAYEV: The matter itself did, Sir. I come in to him— the place he lives in! What a roof, what doors—my God! He receives me. I make a bow and then say, Your Excellency, Sir, defend us! And there he sits, like some kind of animal, stern and thickset. He starts a conversation with me, his eyes all the while burning right into me. I talked a good bit, but trying to avoid those eyes of his. A lot I got off my chest, Sir, really I got a lot off my chest—so to say: two thirds of what I had on my mind but that amounted to so much you'd hardly believe it. He took note of that—after all, he was an old hand at this sort of thing. When I finish, how he starts roaring at me. Peasant, he shouts, peasant! . . . What are you doing, you peasant? Who do you take me for?—eh? . . . I even got down on my knees. —Do you know, you goat's beard you, what I'm going to do with you?—I'm going to put you, he says, where the vultures won't even find your bones . . . Kneeling, I plead with him, Don't ruin me! Call the guards, he shouts, call the guards . . . and already heads for a bell . . . Well, I see there's nothing to be done. So I get up. After all, I've already got everything off my chest. I unbutton my coat. Have a look, go ahead, I say. That quieted him down some. Well, he says, on your way now, but hereafter remember: I don't like this sort of thing! . . . So I left I did, Sir, and believe me, my forehead was covered with sweat and it was running all the way down through my side-whiskers, and

even down from my nose. I raised up my sinner's hands
—O my God, I cried! How you have led me into temptation. To the idol of Baal I brought the ruble earned
by work, the widow's alms, the orphan's kopeck, and on
my knees I had to implore him: Golden idol, I beg you,
accept the humble gift I bring before you.

MUROMSKY: And did he accept it?

RAZUVAYEV: He accepted it, Sir, he accepted it.

MUROMSKY: And he took care of the matter?

RAZUVAYEV: And he took care of the matter. As easy as you
like—one wave of his hand and the authorities who were
troubling us just fell away.

MUROMSKY: You mean just like that?

RAZUVAYEV: I'm telling you the truth. But what's strange
about it? After all, they're all his own army. He's the
one who let them loose in the first place.

MUROMSKY: Perhaps.

RAZUVAYEV: Believe God, it's so. Have you heard, Sir, the
rumor that's going around the folk?

MUROMSKY: What rumor?

RAZUVAYEV: That the antichrist has been born.

MUROMSKY: What are you saying?

RAZUVAYEV: The truth, Sir . . . an old sage told it to me. He
used to travel to far-off lands, Sir, to where our faith had
its beginnings. In these places, he says, they know truly
that this antichrist hasn't just been born but has been
living for a long time. You see, Sir, the man who told
me this is a reliable person, well along in years.

MUROMSKY: Can it be possible?

RAZUVAYEV: And how. You see, Sir, this antichrist is in the
government service. During the day he takes the form
of a state councillor, and he even has a ribbon for thirty
years of unblemished service. And he himself has fathered
an abundant and predatory race, and all these big and
small officials, this race of antichrists, has surrounded
our whole Christian land, and all our griefs, labors, and
pains come from this antichrist of an actual state councillor, and our famines and plagues from his offspring. You
can see, Sir, doomsday is already close (*a noise is heard.
A voice is raised and lowered*), and now just a re-
hearsal is taking place . . . (*Behind the door noises and
voices are again audible.*)

MUROMSKY: What kind of tumult is that? Did someone come in? Let's go to my study. (*They leave in the direction of Muromsky's study.*)

SCENE 6

Behind the door noise and voices can be heard. Somewhat disheveled, in a coat with a huge collar fastened up to the ears, Tarelkin rushes in and bangs the door after him.

TARELKIN (*listening attentively*): Scoundrel! . . . Chasing me like a hound . . . to a strange place . . . What's this? (*Someone tries to force the door, but Tarelkin holds it.*)

VOICE (*behind the door*): Never mind, I'll get you yet. I'll get you yet . . .

TARELKIN (*locking the door*): What a torture!

TISHKA (*entering from the side door*): The gentleman asks you to come out to him, Sir.

TARELKIN (*perplexed*): Tell him I don't have the time—I'm too busy.

TISHKA: They say for you to come out, and if you don't, the gentleman says he'll come in by force if he has to.

TARELKIN: So what? Don't you let him in, that's all. (*Tishka leaves.*) That's what they call the gift of heaven; life! I've got nothing against it. Give me life, heaven, but at the same time give me the means to exist.

TISHKA (*coming in*): They're asking for you again, Sir.

TARELKIN (*clenching his fists*): Oh-h-h! Tell him to go away!

TISHKA: I've already told him.

TARELKIN: And what does he say?

TISHKA: Even if I have to stay here till tomorrow morning, he says, I'm not going to let him go.

TARELKIN: Do you have a back staircase here?

TISHKA: We do.

TARELKIN: What does he mean he's not going to let me go?! Well, you go and tell him that for me. (*Tishka goes out.*)

VOICE (*behind the door*): Listen: wherever I meet you, I'll take you by the collar and . . .

TARELKIN: All right, all right.

VOICE: I'll get you even at the bottom of a garbage pit to
tell you what you are: a pig . . . (*Goes away.*)
TARELKIN: Oh, anathema . . . and in a strange place yet . . .
(*Listens attentively.*) Did he really leave? . . . He left!
. . . What a creature! He calls someone else a pig—and
he's satisfied. And off he goes, he's had his fill. Pfaugh!
. . . (*Recovering.*) These creditors have worn me out;
my life has been poisoned. I don't have any peace at
home, and on the street—there's no place for me either!!
Here's the kind of arrangement I've worked out (*raises
his collar above his ears*) . . . I call it a covered wagon
. . . and this is how I peek out of my hiding place
(*peeks out*) . . . Just let someone imagine how it must
be living in such a hiding place!! (*Folds back his collar,
removes the "wagon," and heaves a sigh.*) Ah, ah, ahhh!
(*Goes into hallway.*)

SCENE 7

Muromsky enters, followed by Ivan Sidorov.

MUROMSKY (*looking around*): Who's here? (*Tarelkin comes
in.*) Oh, it's you, Kandid Kastorovich.
TARELKIN: Yes, it's me. On my way to work, I thought I'd
drop by to wish you a good morning.
MUROMSKY: That's very kind of you. (*Looks around.*) Who
were you talking with so loudly?
TARELKIN: Who? (*Points to the door.*) Ah yes . . . just some
idle fellow . . . a friend of mine.
MUROMSKY: What was it all about, though?
TARELKIN (*getting confused*): Well, it was this way . . . You
know . . . A nice sort of fellow . . . We haven't seen
each other for a long time . . . Anyway . . . He got a
little angry with me; he's really a very strange person . . .
began scolding me in a nasty way, and that's how it
ended.
MUROMSKY: Is that so?
TARELKIN (*regaining his composure*): Exactly. You know—
he's very fond of me, but we don't see each other often
and so he gets anxious. I'll get you, he says, at the
bottom of . . . (*searches for the word*) how was it? . . .

of the sea, he says—you so-and-so, you. That's the way
he put it.

MUROMSKY: That's not good.

TARELKIN: It's bad! With us Russians this quickness with
swearwords deserves pity. In this respect we have to
give foreigners their due. They'll tell you what they
want, they will, but not just in so many words, but
we Russians just bang you on the head the way bears
do. May I trouble you, Sir, for a little coffee?

MUROMSKY: My pleasure. (*Goes to the door. Tarelkin precedes him, leans up against the door and gives an order
to Tishka.*)

RAZUVAYEV (*leading Muromsky to a side*): Who is this person, Sir?

MUROMSKY: A local official, collegiate councillor Kandid Kastorych Tarelkin . . .

RAZUVAYEV: I understand, Sir, a local swindler.

MUROMSKY: Tsk, tsk, tsk . . . Shame on you! (*Points to
Tarelkin's uniform and ribbons.*) You see?!

RAZUVAYEV: They're different everywhere. Where does he
work?

MUROMSKY: Where my case is being handled, with Maksim
Kuzmich Varravin.

RAZUVAYEV: And he struck up an acquaintance with you himself?

MUROMSKY: Himself, himself.

RAZUVAYEV: He was sent to.

MUROMSKY: Really?

RAZUVAYEV: Without a doubt. But don't take my word for it;
best of all, you ask him yourself.

MUROMSKY: Now how can I ask him?

RAZUVAYEV: Just ask him.

MUROMSKY: That's it! Devil knows what to ask him. You do
it, you're better with words.

RAZUVAYEV (*grinning*): It just takes a little shrewdness—if
you please. (*Goes up to Tarelkin and bows.*) My dear
Sir, Kandid Kastorych, if you would permit me, Sir, just
to ask you a little question.

TARELKIN: What is it?

RAZUVAYEV: Forgive me, Sir, Your Excellency, we simple
people . . .

TARELKIN (*looking at him directly and assuming a dignified air*): No matter, my friend, go ahead and speak; I love the simple people . . .

RAZUVAYEV: Thank you so much for your kindness, Excellency. (*Lowers his voice.*) This case of ours, Sir, is it with your office?

TARELKIN (*similarly lowering his voice*): Our office.

RAZUVAYEV: And the head of it is His Excellency, Maksim Kuzmich, isn't that so?

TARELKIN: He's the head, I'm the arms, and the body's something else.

RAZUVAYEV: I understand, Sir; God be with it, with the body.

TARELKIN (*aside*): He's not dumb.

RAZUVAYEV: And the head and arms together can do everything?

TARELKIN: Everything.

RAZUVAYEV: And how can they be seen?

TARELKIN: Whenever you wish.

RAZUVAYEV (*looking him straight in the eyes*): That's just what we'd like.

TARELKIN (*aside*): Not dumb at all. (*Aloud.*) Varravin's office is always open to receive.

RAZUVAYEV: Ah, so they receive, do they?

TARELKIN: And why shouldn't they receive? . . . With pleasure they receive . . . (*Tishka serves him coffee.*)

RAZUVAYEV: Thank you so much for your kindness, Sir (*bows*); I shall tell it to the master.

TARELKIN: Yes, do tell him (*savors the coffee*) . . . why we receive . . . with pleasure . . . he, he, he . . . (*Ivan Sidorov withdraws to a side.*) I love the simple Russian mind. There's no cunning in it, no craftiness. Why, here's an example of it: we never saw each other before, and look how beautifully we got along together. (*Eavesdrops.*)

RAZUVAYEV (*to Muromsky*): Well, there you are, my dear, you see—he receives!

MUROMSKY: Receives whom? What?

RAZUVAYEV: The usual. He said so himself: they receive, with pleasure, he says, they receive.

MUROMSKY: He said so himself?

RAZUVAYEV: Himself. You can thank him.

TARELKIN (*aside*): Aha! . . . There's a wise owl for you! I'd be the first to hang the Order of St. Stanislav around his neck. (*Puts down his cup.*) Pyotr Konstantinovich! It seems that you're busy now, and it's time for me to report for work. All the best.

MUROMSKY (*approaching him*): My dear Kandid Kastorych. How grateful I am to you for your . . . disposition . . . toward us. (*Extends his hand to him.*)

TARELKIN (*bowing in a quite casual manner and crowding Muromsky slightly*): Think nothing of it; I'm always ready to do what I can for you. (*Takes him by the hand with both hands.*)

MUROMSKY (*pressing his hands*): For your . . . interest . . . in this . . .

TARELKIN (*aside*): Phew! Choke on it, you numbskull. (*Leaves through the middle door.*) My compliments!

RAZUVAYEV (*quickly approaching Muromsky*): Not that way, Sir.

MUROMSKY (*vexed*): Then How?

RAZUVAYEV: You've got to pay him off now.

MUROMSKY (*startled*): Oh-h-h-h . . . What are you saying?

RAZUVAYEV (*running up to the door, shouting*): Your Excellency! . . . (*Takes a piece of paper from the table and wraps up some money in it.*)

MUROMSKY (*quickly going up to Ivan Sidorov*): What are you doing? What are you doing?

RAZUVAYEV: What other way is there, Sir? You want to go riding, but you won't grease the wheels! . . . (*Shouts.*) Your Excellency!! —Kandid Kastorovich . . . (*Goes to the door.*)

TARELKIN (*coming in again*): What is it? Were you calling me?

RAZUVAYEV (*collides with him and quietly hands him the package*): You dropped a little note, Excellency.

TARELKIN (*surprised*): No. What note?

RAZUVAYEV (*softly*): Just so, Sir—dropped it. I picked it up this minute.

TARELKIN (*feeling about his pockets*): Not at all, my good man; I have no idea what note you're talking about.

MUROMSKY (*bewildered*): Oh, God in heaven—he's going to cause a scene . . .

RAZUVAYEV (*looking Tarelkin hard in the eyes*): What are you upset about, Sir? You dropped it, we picked it up, and (*with emphasis*) please take it!

TARELKIN (*recollecting*): Ah—yes, yes, why of course! (*Takes
the package and advances quickly to the forestage.*)
Ohhh, there's a real shrewd bird if ever there was one!
Now I don't know whether to hang the Stanislav on him,
or him on the Stanislav. (*Puts the money in his pocket.*)
Well, with this one we can do business . . . (*Bows on all
sides and goes out. Ivan Sidorov accompanies him.
Muromsky stands dumbstruck.*)

TARELKIN and RAZUVAYEV (*bowing to each other and speaking
at the same time, their voices merging*):

I thank you, my good man, I thank you. Your servant.
My compliments, my compliments.

Begging your pardon, Sir, the obligation is ours. We
are always prepared to fulfill it. Our esteem, Sir; we are
always prepared to fulfill our obligation.

SCENE 8

Muromsky and Ivan Sidorov.

RAZUVAYEV (*closing the door after Tarelkin*): You didn't pay
attention to me, Sir, when I was saying you had to
show him your gratitude.

MUROMSKY: But how could you take such a chance? Another
one might have given it to you right in the face.

RAZUVAYEV: In the face? Why should he give it to me in the
face for my kindness?

MUROMSKY: After all, he's no little magistrate—but someone
who counts for something.

RAZUVAYEV: O my God! So that's how you understand it:
They count for something.

MUROMSKY: Obviously, someone who counts for something:
a collegiate councillor, he handles cases.

RAZUVAYEV: I see. And his lacquered boots, you saw them?

MUROMSKY: I saw them.

RAZUVAYEV: And the fine English cloth, and the Dutch
collar, and the first-class driver; and the theaters to suit
their taste, and the actresses at their beck and call . . .
yet they don't have any family estates, right, no patri-
monies, eh?

MUROMSKY: Yes.

RAZUVAYEV: Then what do they live on?

MUROMSKY: What do they live on? . . . What do they live on?! . . . Well now, they also get their government salary.

RAZUVAYEV: A government salary, Sir, hardly suffices for those things; a government salary doesn't permit anything like that. An honest person takes care of his wife with it, or gives his mother a piece of bread, but rest assured he doesn't pamper his belly on that kind of money. No! For that he needs more. That's why to such a person, who has to have as much as three people, you're no more than a taxable item, Sir.

MUROMSKY (*annoyed*): Then according to you they all take bribes.

RAZUVAYEV: Depending on their power.

MUROMSKY: Nonetheless, distinguished lords don't take them; you can't convince me they do . . .

RAZUVAYEV: But why would they have to? What reason would they have to?

MUROMSKY: Then it's to them I'll go.

RAZUVAYEV: Go ahead.

MUROMSKY: This prince, they say—he's supposed to be a fair man, impartial, and the kind of person who says everyone's equal before me.

RAZUVAYEV: Just like flies before a swatter. Whether it's a small fly or a big one—it's all the same.

MUROMSKY: Well, I'll soon see.

RAZUVAYEV: You won't see anything, Sir. You'll stand before him with your case; it's worn you down and got you under its heel, while there he is, standing before you in all his splendor, with his ribbons and decorations, in all his power, with all his ranks and titles, and looking at you like he was gazing down from heaven . . . What is there to see here? In my opinion, going to the big people is like beating air. And if the little ones are hooked and dragged in—then you have to give.

MUROMSKY: Give, give, give! That's all I hear! —The money isn't all mine that I can distribute it so freely; besides, it's not money I got sinfully, indecently, money that was stolen!

RAZUVAYEV: I know, Sir, I know. But what can be done?! If we give, we can go away; we can begin getting busy

again—harrowing and sowing. The Lord will help us—
we'll recover everything we lost.

MUROMSKY (*dejectedly*): I don't know to whom to give. How
much to give.

RAZUVAYEV: Whom else, if not to this Varravin person—
after all, the case is in his hands now. You heard yourself: he's the head, and the Tarelkin who was here is
the arms.

MUROMSKY: Then, it's to him I have to go?

RAZUVAYEV: To him, Sir, to him. Only when you're with him,
be careful. At first he'll put on airs, but afterward he'll
come down, and it's where he lands that'll tell how
things are. Don't oppose him and don't start any arguments. This neo-Centaur rules us; the power is his, not
ours.

MUROMSKY: Then when should I go to him?

RAZUVAYEV: Even tomorrow's good. I'll first stop by Kandid
Kastorych's; he's your man now—let him go ahead and
arrange the matter (*takes his hat and wishes to leave*)
because without that you can't shove your nose in.

MUROMSKY: But hold on, wait a moment . . . Don't you
know tomorrow's a holiday, tomorrow they don't even
do business in the stores.

RAZUVAYEV (*bowing*): No, Sir, in the stores there's no business, but in government bureaus it makes no difference,
business goes on as usual. (*Goes out.*)

CURTAIN

ACT TWO

(*The reception room of a government bureau. Desks and officials all around. At the front of the stage a desk with papers,
behind which Tarelkin is seated. Farther to the rear, other
desks. The door on the right leads to the director's private
office; the door on the left, to the entrance hall. Facing the
audience, a door leading to other offices of the bureau, which*

*are open. More desks and officials can be seen. Some of them
are writing, others conversing.*

Scene 1

*Tarelkin, Chibisov, Ibisov, Shilo, Omega, Gerts, Sherts,
Shmerts, and other officials.*

TARELKIN *(sitting at his desk and singing an aria from
Elisir*)*: Ci-e-lo-si-pu-o-mo-sir . . .

IBISOV *(from another desk)*: Tarelkin, were you at the Italian
opera last evening?

TARELKIN *(nodding his head and singing merrily)*: Si-si-si-si-
non-ci-e-do.

IBISOV: What luck! Was Maksim Kuzmich there too?

TARELKIN *(as before)*: Si-si-si-non-ci-e-eee—damn, again it
didn't come out right!

IBISOV: Since Salvi used to make a mess of the aria in Moscow, my compliments. No matter what you say, though,
Mario still has a long way to go to catch up to him.

TARELKIN *(singing and waving his hand)*: Si-si-non-cie- . . .

IBISOV: Yes, a long way to go.

TARELKIN *(stopping)*: Oh, shut up.

IBISOV: I have my own opinion.

TARELKIN: What is your opinion? Do you have that many
feelings?

IBISOV: I have five senses.

TARELKIN: But for this you need a sixth. *(The officials laugh.)*

SHILO *(from his place)*: For poverty's sake, add a seventh,
so that he shouldn't conduct his affairs the way he does.

TARELKIN *(casting a glance at him over a shoulder)*: What
affairs?

SHILO: The Muromsky one, to take any example. For five
years it's been dragging on! Five months alone it's sitting
in this department. With tears they're begging us, Have
mercy on us, gentlemen!

CHIBISOV: What case is that?

IBISOV: You remember, about the girl. About the illicit relationship between some landowner's daughter and a
district secretary. It's coming up for discussion.

* A reference to a comic opera by Donizetti.

SHERTS (*secretly, in Shilo's ear*): A ticklish matter in the extreme. Maksim Kuzmich is reviewing it himself.

SHMERTS (*striking the same pose, from the other side*): Tarelkin is putting together the report on it.

SHILO (*loudly*): Kandid Kastorych, have you drawn up the report on the Muromsky case yet?

TARELKIN (*singing and keeping time*): No I haven't . . . haven't . . . haven't-t-t . . . (*Ibisov also picks up the melody. They sing in chorus. Tarelkin stops.*) Where's it from?

IBISOV: Wait a moment . . . from the *Huguenots**?

TARELKIN: Right.

SHILO: It's just plain nonsense!

TARELKIN: The *Huguenots*, you mean?

SHILO: No, not those Huguenots, but our own half-baked ones. This assault on the Muromskys is completely without foundation. The entire intrigue of the girl with Krechinsky is nothing more than supposition.

IBISOV: Well, just don't say so.

SHILO: I've seen the file.

IBISOV: And I'm telling you that there was a scheme, and that she was getting ready to run away with him. I have the clearest picture of the whole thing; they took some diamonds, too. You know the prince has a governess and their governess told her everything.

SHILO: It so happens they had no governess.

IBISOV: There was, Kasyan Kasyanovich, there was.

SHILO (*impatiently*): But it's evident from the file, my dear Sir, that there was not.

TARELKIN: Tell it to them there—you won't be contradicted. I think you're ill; you ought to go take the waters— cure yourself . . . (*Yawns.*) Just imagine, gentlemen: last evening, Maksim Kuzmich and I were sitting in a box; there I was looking everyone over with my opera glasses, and what do you think? In the second circle, above the dress circle, who do I see but Oranzhensky!

IBISOV: Is that why his house is higher than the second circle?

SHILO: He's nothing but a crook and a robber.

TARELKIN: How's this, old fellow, everyone's a crook and robber to you? Aren't you afraid they'll break your neck?

---

* A reference to the opera by Giacomo Meyerbeer.

SHILO: I don't have a neck, Sir, but I do have a head, so I'm not really afraid. The person who's got a neck but not a head, that's the one who's got something to worry about.

TARELKIN: My, what a museum of natural history!

SHILO: But did you notice that in the museum there are animals whose entire body consists of a neck; they're called reptiles.

TARELKIN (*going away and aside*): Dog.

SCENE 2

Maksim Kuzmich Varravin, with papers in hand, appears from the side door on the right. Silence settles on the entire office; everyone sits down and takes himself to his work. Maksim Kuzmich approaches a desk, distributes some papers, makes some comments and, finally, reaches the place where Tarelkin is working.

TARELKIN (*getting up*): Your Excellency—here is the case. (*Maksim Kuzmich sits down in Tarelkin's seat, opens the file Tarelkin gives him, and leafs through it. Tarelkin points things out to him. The conversation between them is conducted in half-tones.*)

VARRAVIN: Well?

TARELKIN (*quietly*): A messenger from the Muromskys . . . Everything's all set! (*Leafs through the file.*)

VARRAVIN: So slow . . . (*Leafs through the file.*)

TARELKIN (*reporting in soft voice*): What can be done? A real torture; he loves his daughter and he loves his money, too. One day he wants one thing, the next day something else . . .

VARRAVIN: It ought to be done through a third party.

TARELKIN: It won't work out. He says either himself or nothing.

VARRAVIN: Mind you!

TARELKIN: A third party, he says, I don't want. He'll just steal.

VARRAVIN: So he knows that alphabet, does he?

TARELKIN: He knows it. He's been through the whole routine. As his manager told me. My God, what they didn't do to him. First, he paid off through a third party; the

third party snatched half of it for himself. Then he
started to handle it himself, directly. It was even worse.
Whoever he gives it to gets sick; then someone new
crops up to take his place—and delivers another judgment. And now something else has happened . . .

VARRAVIN: What is it?

TARELKIN (*bethinking himself*): Ah, here it is! (*Leafs through
the file, points out something to Varravin and continues
talking quietly.*) Please have a look: concerning the question of the illicit relationship between the daughter and
Krechinsky a certain artist has turned up and confused
(*speaks loudly*) the decision. Taking this and that into
consideration, he says, and on the other hand consider-
ing this and that, I recommend that (*quietly*) the medical board be invited, he says, to arrange a medical
examination . . . he, he, he.

VARRAVIN: Of whom?

TARELKIN (*relishing it*): Of her, of course!

VARRAVIN: The daughter! Ha, ha, ha! Well now! (*Both laugh
softly.*)

TARELKIN: Well, you've got what you wanted!

VARRAVIN: Nonsense! . . . How is it possible?

TARELKIN: Why not? It's only an opinion, after all. Nobody's
responsible for an opinion. Most certainly not! And
as regards the court decision itself—why, nobody can
be held accountable for that either!

VARRAVIN: There's nothing about it in the file.

TARELKIN: I know there isn't. To prevent any agreement, he's
had to pay off once, and to keep it out of the file, twice.

VARRAVIN: So?

TARELKIN: So—divide it up! There's enough to go around for
everyone.

VARRAVIN (*shaking his head*): Shhhh . . . !

TARELKIN: For heaven's sake! That's nothing! . . . He'd give
everything he had.

VARRAVIN: How much have we got now?

TARELKIN: Don't expect a fortune! So far . . . (*thinks*) ten
thousand . . .

VARRAVIN: For such a case! He only has one daughter! She's
his whole life. Ask thirty!

TARELKIN: No!

VARRAVIN: He can raise it.

TARELKIN: Where?

VARRAVIN: He'll lose his daughter.

TARELKIN: Take the shirt off his back.

VARRAVIN: He'll mortgage his estate.

TARELKIN: It's already mortgaged.

VARRAVIN: So he'll sell it.

TARELKIN: It's already been sold.

VARRAVIN (*anxiously*): Can't be!

TARELKIN: The truth.

VARRAVIN: If that's so, then how are they getting along?

TARELKIN: You know the kind of people they are: with their last ounce of strength they'd hang on!

VARRAVIN (*in a complaining tone*): And how is he now?

TARELKIN: After selling his estate and borrowing, he's good for maybe twenty-five thousand.

VARRAVIN: Nothing for it then—twenty-five thousand it will have to be.

TARELKIN: He has to live too, doesn't he; he does have debts.

VARRAVIN: Debts? They'll wait.

TARELKIN: They're already waiting, Your Excellency, but not debts. You see, here I am, sitting here in my uniform (*points to a desk*), and over there (*indicates the entrance hall*) they're already coming to call. But a private person—what about him? The private person is—nothing, a zero! Ha!

VARRAVIN: Nothing less than twenty thousand or the case won't be concluded. But make it as fast as you can. (*Gets up.*)

TARELKIN: Everything's ready. They're all set.

VARRAVIN: Now pay attention: the prince is going somewhere to a meeting right now and I'll let the clerks have the rest of the day off on the occasion of the holiday. Consequently, in an hour I'll receive him here myself. (*Rises.*)

TARELKIN (*loudly*). As you wish, Your Excellency.

VARRAVIN (*loudly*): Now please go and draw up the summons. (*Goes off in the direction of the study.*)

(*At just that moment the doors of the study swing apart and the prince appears. The doorman Paramonov precedes him. The first gust of an impending storm breezes through the entire bureau. The entire mass of clerks leave their places and bow undulatingly to the measure*

of the prince's movement through the chamber. Maksim
Kuzmich runs behind him with short steps and swaying
somewhat so that the arc of his gait suggests obedience
and its swiftness—devotion. At the exit he bows directly
at the prince's back as the latter leaves, then locks the
doors after him and again assumes the bearing and pace
of a head of department. The clerks return to their
seats.)

VARRAVIN (*stopping in the middle of the chamber and looking at a wall clock*): Gentlemen! Today is a holiday—
you're free to leave. Until tomorrow. (*Bows and leaves
in the direction of the study.*)

SCENE 3

*Noise. The clerks get up and quickly collect their papers.
Throughout this scene the chambers of the bureau gradually
empty. With their hats in hand, Tarelkin, Chibisov, Ibisov,
Gerts, Sherts, Shmerts, the clerk Omega, and Shilo make up
a group at the front of the stage.*

IBISOV: Kandid Kastorych, we're all going together (*winking*)
you know where . . .

TARELKIN: Leave me out, I'm afraid; I have a case still to
work on.

THE VOICE OF VARRAVIN (*from offstage*): Tarelkin!!

TARELKIN (*turning on his heels*): Here!! (*Rushes off in the
direction of the study.*)

IBISOV: Aha! What a fellow our Kandid is!

OMEGA: Yes! He's blossomed like a rose! No money, no name,
and he's already copped himself a Stanislav.

SHERTS: Already wormed his way into the collegiate council-
lors.

SHMERTS: Getting a double salary.

OMEGA: Amazing how he's made out.

CHIBISOV: He was born under a lucky star, gentlemen.

OMEGA: It's just like they say: Better to be born lucky than
wise.

SHILO: That's a stupid saying, in my opinion. It depends on
the country you're in. In England, for example, they
say: Better to be born a merchant than wise; in Italy,

better to be born a singer than wise; in France, better
to be born a fighter than wise . . .

SHMERTS: And in Russia?

SHILO: In Russia? You see yourselves (*pointing to the door
Tarelkin left through*), better to be born a scoundrel
than wise . . .

CHIBISOV (*smiling ironically*): You've had a hard time of it,
old fellow, eh?

SHILO: A hard time, yes.

IBISOV: And you've passed through quite a few offices.

SHILO: They rejected me in two; now I'm in the third.

CHIBISOV: And?

SHILO: They'll get rid of me too.

IBISOV: Then what will you do?

SHILO: I want to work for a merchant.

CHIBISOV: A shop assistant, trading in tallow candles.

SHILO: Tallow candles, but not tallow cases.

CHIBISOV (*taking Ibisov under the arm*): Let's get away from
here, my dear fellow. (*Quietly.*) I'd hang him with
pleasure.

IBISOV: And I'd buy the rope. (*They go out.*)

OMEGA (*approaching Shilo and taking him by the arm*):
Kasyan Kasyanovich, don't annoy them; they'll make
trouble for you. Spit on them!

SHILO: I tried to! (*Hiccoughs.*) There isn't enough saliva . . .

OMEGA: Where are you going now?

SHILO: Where? (*Hiccoughs.*) To my tropical apartment.

OMEGA: Tropical? Why tropical?

SHILO: Because it's not (*hiccoughs*) heated.

OMEGA: Wouldn't you rather go with me? We'll have dinner
together.

SHILO: I want to! . . . You know, I have dinner every other
day, but I want to every day.

OMEGA: Wonderful! . . . What do you like best?

SHILO: Ha . . . everything! Just so long as there's no bones . . .
I tried to . . . (*Hiccoughs.*) I'll be lucky if I can get
anything down. (*They laugh, take one another under
the arm, and go out.*)

SCENE 4

TARELKIN (*emerging from the study, displaying a currency bill, which he holds between two fingers*): My Benefactor! . . . Here's what he was going to make me so happy with; not even enough to pay a coach driver's salary. (*Shoves the bill angrily into his purse.*) You know what they say about the race of bureaucrats: why was this nettlesome race ever born? What good is it? They drink tea with their bits of lump sugar, for a walk go to some café, have dinner for twenty-five kopeks silver and that's it—they're already filled, they don't need any more. But me? An aristocrat? It's no cheap café for dinner for me—when I have dinner out, then it's Palkin's; for just another pair of gloves I have to give out three rubles—and what do I get now—a noose to put my head in! My life is nothing but debts; I'm being killed off by debts . . . My God, when will this punishment end? But now I see—here I can expect nothing, nothing at all! The rascal—he'll pick me bare like some linden; he'll pick me bare, like he's picked all the others. If I could just hide in some nook and cranny somewhere, maybe somewhere in the country— just give me the power and the opportunity and I'd become such a bribe taker, such a grafter I'd take the hide right off a corpse. You're damned right I would— because I'd have to! But what's surprising, though, is that I have neither the power nor the opportunity. (*Becomes pensive.*)

SCENE 5

Varravin emerges from the study; Tarelkin.

VARRAVIN: What's this, you haven't prepared the summons yet?

TARELKIN: This minute; I have it right here. (*Sits down and starts to write.*) By the way, Excellency, another pest's cropped up.

VARRAVIN: Who's that?

TARELKIN: That fellow Shilo who got permission to transfer here not long ago. We ought to get rid of him; he gets in my way.

VARRAVIN: What do you have anything to do with him for?

TARELKIN: If you please, Sir—he's a troublemaker; he won't admit anything. Runs around the whole bureau shouting his head off about the case. Well, what can I do? (*Leaves in the direction of the entrance hall.*)

VARRAVIN (*alone; arranges chairs, piles papers and sits down at Tarelkin's desk*): Amazing, what times these are! If someone's smart, then he's such a scoundrel you've got to get rid of him right away; or else he's rubbish, like old rags, good for nothing. (*Tarelkin reenters.*) One has to admit, even you've become handsome! Well, what are you good for? All frayed and worn out—it's impossible to make a person out of any one of you. I remember once when a real person—Anton Trofimych Krek—was with us. Now there was a man for you! Solid build, broad shouldered, clumsy, what they call poorly cut, but strongly sewn. He never had much to say, but when he did he hit the nail on the head each time. He got along pretty well; you couldn't even tell there was ever anything the matter with him, except once when he got an attack of apoplexy as he was coming out of a bath. But all he did was twist his mouth and make a face like this (*grimaces*) and that was that!

TARELKIN: I heard a great deal about him, Your Excellency.

VARRAVIN: You did, eh? But what kind of officials are you nowadays? Some kind of worms—all thin and sick, creaking and coughing, rotten and falling apart. You shake hands with any one of them and you get hold of a wet rag. No, Sir, it was different in our day. When someone like Anton Trofimych shook hands, he'd extend all five fingers so; you'd have something to think about. As soon as he stuck his hand out, he'd be the first to grab hold and shake—like he was opening the door of a coach to let someone in. That's how he did things— go compare yourself to him. He'd get up at four in the morning, huff into his fists, and take his seat. He could work like an ox, he could. He wasn't afraid of anyone, and accomplished the impossible. A tidy little fortune

he left behind, too: a big place on an island, let alone
cash and God knows what else. But what kind of people
are you? Fine gentlemen, with dainty little gloves, hanging around theaters, joking and carrying on, expecting
money to crawl into your pockets on its own strength
. . . No, my dear fellow, it doesn't come without money.
Then they have the nerve to say: You gave me my rank,
but you didn't, they say, give me my fortune.

TARELKIN: I'm not of that mind, Excellency.

VARRAVIN: I know what mind you're of before you do.
Fortune?! What, do you think I got mine for nothing?
Well? I got it by my own sweat and blood! Anton Trofimych Krek took me raw and started kneading me . . .
and he kneaded me a long time, damn his soul. From
his hands I drank from the cup of sorrow. I suffered
everything, I had scruples about nothing. I lived in the
pantry, filled pipes, and even did errands—yes, Sir! And
just as he hung the Order of St. Anna around my neck,
so he'd shove a quarter of every take-in into a file case
for me and just give me a look with his eyes—without
any words being exchanged.

PARAMONOV (*entering*): Your Excellency, a petitioner wishes
to see you.

VARRAVIN: Show him in. (*Paramonov goes out.*) You be on
your way too, Tarelkin, there's no need to eavesdrop!
(*Tarelkin also leaves; Varravin surrounds himself with
piles of papers.*)

SCENE 6

Varravin, buried in papers, is writing as Muromsky enters.

MUROMSKY: Allow me to introduce myself—Captain Muromsky, a landowner from Yaroslav district.

VARRAVIN (*continuing to write*): A pleasure. (*Silence.*)

MUROMSKY (*waiting a while*): Having heard of your fairness,
I have come to ask your assistance in a matter.

VARRAVIN (*pointing to a chair while continuing to write*):
Have a seat. (*Muromsky sits down. Silence.*) I doubt
that there is any way I may be of advantage to you.

MUROMSKY: Your favorable opinion is always advantageous.

VARRAVIN (*writing*): You are mistaken. In our department the routine of work is so arranged that one's personal opinion or intervention count for nothing. (*Turning around to Muromsky and putting away his papers.*) In any case . . . what is it that you're asking?

MUROMSKY (*very softly*): You doubtless know about the case involving the theft of a solitaire from me by the district secretary Krechinsky.

VARRAVIN (*softer still*): It is under our review but has been inactive for a while. I am afraid that that is something we can do little about. We have so many cases, there is hardly sufficient strength to handle them all. From all corners of our Fatherland there flow in to us the petitions, complaints and, as it were, wails of our oppressed fellowmen. Cases far more difficult and complicated than yours. Our attention, drawn to thousands of quarters at one and the same time, completely vanishes, and we become like the Titans who perished beneath the weight of the mountains with which they were struggling. (*Straightens himself with obvious satisfaction.*)

MUROMSKY: That is the very reason why I am trying to win your attention, Sir.

VARRAVIN: I shall do what I can, my dear man.

MUROMSKY: The case is actually a simple one, but it's become so tangled up because of all the legal procedures that I can't even explain it to you in an orderly way . . .

VARRAVIN: As best you can.

MUROMSKY: You see, Sir, my daughter developed an infatuation for this Krechinsky and although I was opposed to it—I finally agreed to let them get married. That was my mistake! (*Sighs.*)

VARRAVIN (*also sighing*): I can believe it . . .

MUROMSKY: Because he needed money badly, Krechinsky took a solitaire of my daughter's on the pretext of wanting to show it to friends of his, and like a trusting child and on account of her great infatuation for him, she let him take it . . . (*Sighs.*)

VARRAVIN (*also sighing*): I see . . .

MUROMSKY: Almost as soon as he got his hands on it Krechinsky arranged a fake pawn with it with Bek the pawnbroker, so that he had the chance to return the diamond to my daughter the same day. The result was that just

like innocent babes we didn't have the slightest suspicion
of anything . . . (*Sighs.*)

VARRAVIN: Go on . . .

MUROMSKY: It just so happened that at that moment someone
I know quite well warned me about what happened.
Right after that along came the pawnbroker himself
who now had in his possession a fake diamond, not the
original solitaire that Krechinsky pawned when he first
went to him. In no time, the whole matter was out in
the open. There you are—the whole story, that's what
this case is all about. And believe me, such openness
and naturalness on our part throughout the investigation that followed has met nothing but all kinds of
suspicions.

VARRAVIN: I believe you, my good man, I believe you . . .
However, you omitted certain circumstances of the case.

MUROMSKY: I swear by everything that's holy . . .

VARRAVIN: According to the facts of the investigation the
position of your case remains entangled and, I may say,
two-sided. On the one hand, it seems completely clear
and natural, and on the other hand—completely unclear
and unnatural.

MUROMSKY (*spreading his hands*): In what way unclear and
unnatural, Your Excellency?

VARRAVIN: In the first place, I ask myself the question: Is it
possible that your daughter would have given so valuable
an object to a stranger without any receipt or certifica-
tion? After all, there are women—I know some like that
myself—who wouldn't even trust their husbands with
something like that.

MUROMSKY: She couldn't have imagined anything, Your Excellency.

VARRAVIN (*continuing*): In the second place: For what secret
reason did your daughter give the diamond back to the
pawnbroker Bek for a second time and with her own
hands, thus depriving you of it again and making herself
appear to be a party to the crime?

MUROMSKY: She wanted to save him.

VARRAVIN: Whom? The criminal? The law forbids that!

MUROMSKY: Yes, but he was her fiancé.

VARRAVIN: Even so . . . The way I see it, she should have

been terrified of him (*makes a gesture*) instead of coming to his rescue. You will agree, won't you, that you paid the pawnbroker Bek money only on account of this collusion of your daughter with Krechinsky. This is a fact, after all. What have you got to say?

MUROMSKY: Let's suppose that it is a fact, but I'm not asking for that money.

VARRAVIN: You're not asking for it? But what about the law? It is unmoved by pleas! . . . And it is asking.

MUROMSKY: But even the law takes inexperience into account. After all, she is a child.

VARRAVIN: According to the birth certificate she was nineteen.

MUROMSKY: Yes, that's right.

VARRAVIN: Therefore legally an adult.

MUROMSKY: Legally? God forbid! Just because a young girl helps her fiancé because she feels sorry for him. She'd have given her blood for him. You must take into consideration her attachment to him and her infatuation!

VARRAVIN (*smiling*): There, you've gone and caught yourself now!

MUROMSKY (*anxiously*): Where? . . . How? . . . I didn't say anything.

VARRAVIN: You did . . . But don't upset yourself—you'll always say what we need. (*Slyly.*) Infatuation, you say —well, I assure you, it has been taken into due consideration by us. And now we wish to determine by law the degree of this infatuation.

MUROMSKY (*becoming confused*): Forgive me . . . I . . . I don't quite follow you.

VARRAVIN: About what? Don't you know about the testimony of two witnesses regarding this infatuation? To be blunt about it, that between your daughter and Krechinsky there existed an illicit relationship!

MUROMSKY (*with evident suffering*): Have mercy! I beg you! It's nothing but slander, a trick of some kind . . . they were paid off . . . these two witnesses aren't worth a damn.

VARRAVIN: Sworn testimonies, Sir. That means something! And now there appears as though by Fate itself, the fact of your own acknowledgment.

MUROMSKY (*passionately*): Never!

VARRAVIN: When your daughter returned the solitaire to the pawnbroker she said, It was my mistake! . . . Do you hear! (*Raises a finger.*) My mistake!!

MUROMSKY: No, she didn't say, My mistake! (*Beats his chest.*) I swear to God she didn't say it! She said, It was a mistake . . . that is, everything that happened was done by mistake.

VARRAVIN: I believe you, but the matter does seem odd: All the witnesses who were at the scene at the time pleaded ignorance, with the exception of four. These four are divided in turn into two groups: two against and two for. Witness Rasplyuev and police official Lapa testified that your daughter used the possessive pronoun "my" . . .

MUROMSKY (*interrupting*): She did not use it! She did not use it! Even if you cut me to pieces, I still say—she did not use it!

VARRAVIN: As you wish. You, Sir, and Madam Atuyeva both affirmed in your testimonies that she said, It was a mistake, apparently omitting the possessive pronoun "my" . . . Now I ask you: Where is the truth? (*Turns around as if looking for the truth.*) Where is it? Where? What darkness! . . . What night! . . . And in the midst of this night what two-sidedness!

MUROMSKY (*ironically*): Darkness . . . In the midst of the darkness, in the midst of the night two-sidedness . . . (*Shrugs his shoulders.*) I guess I've become old—but I just don't understand!

VARRAVIN (*vexed*): You'll get it soon enough. (*Firmly.*) In the eyes of the law, Sir, the testimonies of the first two witnesses carry full force. The testimony of Madam Atuyeva, as an aunt and governess, does not carry full force, and your personal testimony, I am afraid, none whatsoever.

MUROMSKY: Why so cruel?

VARRAVIN: Because, Sir, you were brought to trial for false testimony about the Tyrolean breed bullock you received as a present from the accused! Remember!

MUROMSKY: I remember. (*Shakes his head.*) Therefore, according to your law, the word of that cheat Rasplyuev means more than mine. Your law is cruel, Your Excellency.

VARRAVIN (*smiling*): Forgive me, but we have no intention

of changing it just for you. Anyway . . . it's time to
finish; I brought up these facts merely to show you the
two-sidedness and shakiness of your case. That is why
the whole thing could go one way or the other . . .
this way, or that way . . .

MUROMSKY (*ironically*): I see, either this way (*making a
swinging gesture with his hand*) or that way, eh?

VARRAVIN: Yes! This way, or that way. It's as though the law
in all its power to punish the guilty raised its sword
up (*raises his hand and advances on Muromsky, who
moves backward*), and was asking, Where am I to strike,
Varravin?!

MUROMSKY (*frightened*): Merciful God in heaven!

VARRAVIN: That, Sir, is what is known as the Scales of Justice.
The Goddess of Justice, you know, Themis, is symbolized
by the scales and sword!

MUROMSKY: Hm . . . Scales and sword . . . Well, with the
sword, of course, she cuts, but on the scales?

VARRAVIN (*suggestingly*): On the scales, the barbarian, she
bargains.

MUROMSKY: Ahhh . . . I understand . . .

VARRAVIN: You see (*ironically*), and you were just saying, I've
become old . . . I just don't understand . . .

MUROMSKY: Now I no longer know whether or not I should
present my opposing arguments.

VARRAVIN: My dearest fellow, why go to the bother? When
I was young, I enjoyed arguing, but that's all past now;
I've come to know life and living. You recall how it
used to be in the old days—simple, sincere. Those were
the days! There's something very appropriate about them
in a poem:

> Where the heart is free and open,
> Bared, as in the days of yore . . .

MUROMSKY (*animatedly*): Free and open?! . . . Bared?! . . .
(*Aside.*) There it is! . . . He's coming down to business
now. (*Aloud.*) What exactly do you mean by "bared"?

VARRAVIN: Just that in the old days people didn't argue back
and forth. They'd talk things over nice and easy, explain
themselves in a free and open way, and then settle
matters by baring them right to the core! (*Makes a
gesture.*)

MUROMSKY (*with dread in his voice*): Baring them right to the core!

VARRAVIN: Yes, right to the core!

MUROMSKY (*aside*): Here is the antichrist, an actual state councillor. (*Aloud.*) Ah, Your Excellency! Our fore-fathers! Our benefactors! In the old days we lived in grand halls, and government officials in ordinary rooms. Now we're the ones who are living in ordinary rooms, while the officials are in the grand halls.

VARRAVIN: Well, tell me now: How much do you think an official in the old days would have taken for such a case?

MUROMSKY (*stirring*): To tell the truth, I don't know. When it comes to such negotiations, I have no experience.

VARRAVIN: Take a guess, just for a joke.

MUROMSKY: But really, Excellency, I have no experience in these matters.

VARRAVIN: Oh, for heaven's sake (*persistently*)—go on, take a guess.

MUROMSKY (*undecided*): I would have taken, let's say, three thousand or so.

VARRAVIN (*in his ear*): Thirty thousand! (*Turns about and walks away.*)

MUROMSKY (*trembling*): What?! What was it you said?

VARRAVIN: You heard me: An official would have taken thirty thousand and not a kopeck less. And, mind you—in silver he'd have taken it, not in paper notes.

MUROMSKY: In silver!!! God in heaven—why that's a hun-dred thousand—a fortune!!! A person's whole life! —A hundred thousand . . . But, if I may say so, why would he have taken so much? The case is really a simple one.

VARRAVIN: On the contrary.

MUROMSKY: If there were a lot of land at issue or a plant of some kind—let's say an iron foundry—but what we are talking about? Only one opinion, that's all—nothing —just air.

VARRAVIN: Let's suppose that it's nothing but air—but this air has already exhausted you. And people in the old days, Sir, did not decide matters that way . . . People in the old days used to say: the first good in life is my own peace of mind.

MUROMSKY (*with particular softness*): Yes, that is so, Your

Excellency . . . But not a hundred thousand, Your
Excellency!

VARRAVIN (*also softly*): Agreed! . . . Agreed! . . . Time
changes everything; people nowadays have become softer.

MUROMSKY (*with curiosity*): May I ask how much softer?

VARRAVIN (*looking at him straight in the eyes*): Philosophers
say that they have become . . . let's see . . . yes—twenty
percent softer.

MUROMSKY (*quickly reckoning aside*): Ten kopecks—three
thousand . . .

VARRAVIN (*continuing*): There is more spiritual warmth now,
they say . . .

MUROMSKY (*as before*): Yes, ten kopecks—three thousand
more . . . six thousand off . . .

VARRAVIN: Compassion for the needs of one's fellowman—all
this has developed and become stronger.

MUROMSKY (*as before*): That makes twenty-four thousand in
silver.

VARRAVIN: That's exactly what they mean when they speak of
progress.

MUROMSKY (*aloud*): Out of honor, Your Excellency, an old-
time official wouldn't have taken it.

VARRAVIN (*tenderly*): He would have taken it, my dear
fellow, he would have taken it . . .

MUROMSKY (*firmly*): No, he would not have taken it.

VARRAVIN (*dryly*): As you like. (*Collects his papers from the
desk.*)

MUROMSKY (*softer*): To tell the truth . . . for that . . . I
would have supposed . . . ten thousand.

VARRAVIN (*bowing and in a sharp tone*): Would you please
forgive me, I have a number of important official matters
to attend to. (*Goes to the study.*)

SCENE 7

Muromsky alone.

MUROMSKY (*falling into thought*): Twenty-four thousand
silver—let's see—that makes eighty-four thousand in
paper! Where will I get it? God knows, I don't have

it . . . What else is there for me to do but sell Streshnevo? The ashes of my father—the property of his father before him . . . my daughter's inheritance . . . No! I won't give it up! . . . I'm getting away from here! I'll see whoever I can! I'll open doors with my head if I have to; I'll tell the whole truth! (*Becomes calmer.*) I'll tell everything briefly, in an orderly way; I'll take Lidochka along with me. People aren't stones, after all; God is on the side of the just! (*Leaves quickly.*)

SCENE 8

Varravin emerges from one door, Tarelkin from another.

TARELKIN: How obstinate, Your Excellency! Well, I never expected such ignorance from him.

VARRAVIN (*annoyed*): Ignorance, and how! He even dared propose a third of what I had in mind.

TARELKIN: Nevertheless, maybe you should just take it and forget about it.

VARRAVIN: Out of the question, I said.

TARELKIN: Now he wants to go.

VARRAVIN: Where to?

TARELKIN: I don't know. People, he says, aren't stones; God is on the side of the just.

VARRAVIN (*figuring*): I imagine he's going to throw himself at the prince.

TARELKIN: There's no other way but to the prince.

VARRAVIN (*thinking*): How do you have the case arranged now? Is everything the way it should be?

TARELKIN: In perfect order.

VARRAVIN: Do you have the different possible verdicts prepared?

TARELKIN: All set. Following your instructions, I gave this particular attention and even exchanged correspondence with the old man about it.

VARRAVIN: Well, what about the old man?

TARELKIN: He divided them into three groups.

VARRAVIN: Go on.

TARELKIN: The first is for release: The girl would be acquitted and freed of any court action.

VARRAVIN: Go on.

TARELKIN: The second—the girl would be held under suspicion regarding the love affair. The third—the case would be turned over to a new investigation and the determination of new decisions not dependent on the previous.

VARRAVIN: That's just fine! Excellent solutions! Now that you've opened up three roads for me, I just have to lead the department head to them, then turn him whichever way I want!

TARELKIN: Besides these three main judgments, there were also some others suggested.

VARRAVIN: Let there be.

TARELKIN: And one judgment according to the new formula.

VARRAVIN: Which one is that?

TARELKIN: That it is not un-like-ly.

VARRAVIN: Ah—yes! In what sense?

TARELKIN: I'll explain: regarding the illicit relationship between the Muromsky girl and Krechinsky the question was carried further, namely, that in the light of the intimacy of the parties and the secrecy of their relations (*raising a finger*) it is not un-like-ly . . . that a child might yet appear . . .

VARRAVIN: Yes, I suppose it is possible.

TARELKIN: Quite possible, and it would be ticklish for the old man, no matter where—like jabbing him with a pin and making him jump.

VARRAVIN (*musing*): Hm . . . making him jump . . . that's good! Well, then, let him go to the prince if he wants. It would be good, though, if we could see to it that he got there early in the morning, while the prince was making his rounds and while he was having his usual soda water . . .

TARELKIN: That's possible, Your Excellency.

VARRAVIN: So's he'd fall right into the soda water!

TARELKIN: Right into the soda water he'll fall!

VARRAVIN: And if he falls in, then he'll inevitably drown there . . . As soon as the prince starts shouting at him in his usual manner, he'll be back to us soon enough.

TARELKIN: He will be, Excellency, he definitely will be back here again.

VARRAVIN: See to it then. (*Starts to go out.*)

TARELKIN (*assuming an imploring pose*): Your Excellency.

VARRAVIN (*flaring up*): What? Again?

TARELKIN (*as before*): I don't have the energy!

VARRAVIN: You're laughable!

TARELKIN: If you please (*pointing to his throat*), I'll just sit like this-s-s.

VARRAVIN: Now what is it you're trying to show me? Is that supposed to be something new; you'll sit just like this-s-s (*making the same gesture*) for a whole century.

TARELKIN: Be merciful, save me this one little time; for God's sake, don't let me die of starvation! I'm utterly lost; my life has become just bitterness; they're even hounding me in the streets, like a rabbit . . .

VARRAVIN: Who's hounding you?

TARELKIN: Who? — Creditors. I owe everyone money, including even the street cleaner. No sooner do I step out onto the street, when who do I come face to face with —who?—a creditor! I've already tried hiding all over the place: in this alley, and that alley, in a store, in a shop, once I hopped into a café; but all I'm doing is compromising myself. And my tailor—a German to boot —went completely mad! I gave my cook the strictest orders: Anyone comes, I'm not home and that's that— even if they burst . . . But so help me God, the other day the tailor comes barging in by force. I heard how they started breaking the doors in, and I've got this closet, so there was nothing else I could do—I crawled in behind it, crouched down, and just sat there . . . Then what do you think happened? He finds where I'm hiding, comes up to the closet, and gives a good spit behind it —right smack in my face!

VARRAVIN: Well!

TARELKIN: Well, so he spit. Ha! What can you do? The rascal then goes into the hall and without saying a single word lets the cook have it in the face . . . Now I ask you, Excellency, I ask you, why did he have to do that to her?

VARRAVIN (*collecting his papers from the desk*): How is it possible?

TARELKIN: You judge yourself, Your Excellency, how is it possible. All I can say is: what kind of an existence is it? Everyone talks to you with loathing in his voice. Begging your pardon, Sir, the first thing everyone strives

for is respect; think what you want about me, but show
me respect to my face.

VARRAVIN (*going to the study*): Why of course, I quite agree
with you, he must show you respect.

TARELKIN (*following him*): Yes! You'll show me respect yet,
you rascal.

CURTAIN

ACT THREE

(*The Muromsky apartment. Morning. Stage decoration as in
the first act; a desk with papers on it in the middle of the
room.*)

SCENE 1

*Lidochka is sitting behind the tambours. Ivan Sidorov comes
out of the study and hurriedly fingers the papers on the table.*

LIDOCHKA: What are you looking for, Sidorych?

RAZUVAYEV: Ah, there it is, Ma'am, the petition the clerk
copied. Over there (*pointing to the study*) Kandid
Kastorych and I turned the study upside down looking
for it.

LIDOCHKA: Here you are. (*Gets up and hands him the paper.*)
What are you doing?

RAZUVAYEV: Kandid Kastorych and I are holding counsel,
Ma'am; your Papa is going to the prince with this petition. They're now discussing how one should talk to
this person.

LIDOCHKA: Oh, Ivan Sidorov, somehow I have the feeling that
this all won't turn out well . . . Well, did Papa see that
official?

RAZUVAYEV: He did, Ma'am.

LIDOCHKA: And what happened?

RAZUVAYEV: They didn't come to any agreement. Speaking truthfully, how could they come to any agreement? They don't just want to take from you—but rob the last hair off your head. The whole country's destitute—because of their robbing and stealing. Take anyone: he gets a thousand from the tsar, spends five, but still wants to get more—so how can there be any agreement? Why, near our estate once, Ma'am, there was one little judge who picked up a million with the most incredible robbing and stealing. He bought himself an estate of five hundred souls, and set up two factories. And you know what? He now has an income of fifty thousand rubles a year and has already become a great lord. Judge for yourself, young lady, what this world of temptation of ours is like if just one scoundrel like this gets away with what he's doing.

LIDOCHKA: Yes, the world is terrible.

RAZUVAYEV: Nowadays, you know, they don't stop at taking just their wages or what someone gives them besides out of gratitude for some favor or other—let them have this, it's not that we're arguing about—but instead they just wait for the chance to grab whatever they can so as to have plenty for themselves and enough left over to leave their brats. Well, as a result, the robbing and stealing have become enormous. They all sit in their places like hunters or trappers and lie in wait to snare God's creatures in their traps. As soon as one falls in, right away they tangle him up in this net (*indicates the petition he has in his hand*)—then they're happy.

LIDOCHKA: In this net! . . . Oh, Sidorych, what an ache I have in my heart.

RAZUVAYEV: How can you help it, my dear. We've had three invasions in our country—the Tartars attacked it, the French discovered it, and now the bureaucrats have covered it from top to bottom. And what has our country done? It's sad to watch—our country's become ill to the very marrow of its bones, it's become rotten through and through! It's been sold out in the courts, drunk away in the taverns, and now it's lying on a great plain soiled and dirty, covered with cheap bast matting, weak from drunkenness.

LIDOCHKA: How right you are. Sometimes I think the best

thing would be for me to die, everything would end then—and those nets of theirs would be disentangled.

RAZUVAYEV: You make God angry when you talk like that, young lady. God sends misfortune, He sends strength, and He sends patience.

LIDOCHKA: No, Sidorych, I can tell already—my strength is weak, my patience is exhausted, and I'm worn out! The only thing I pray God for now is to take my sinful soul . . . Look, if I die, bury me quietly, without any tumult; don't ask anyone to the funeral, just weep for me yourselves . . . which means more to me than . . . (*She begins to cry.*)

MUROMSKY (*from the study*): Ivan Sidorov; do you hear me —Ivan Sidorov!

RAZUVAYEV (*hastening*): Forgive me, Ma'am. Coming, coming! (*Runs to the study.*)

SCENE 2

LIDOCHKA (*alone*): I'd want only one thing—for him to come, for him to come and cry over me. He did really love me . . . in his own way . . . No! He didn't love me. Why couldn't he come and say to me that he needs money! My God—money! When I was giving my whole being to him . . . and was so happy that I was giving . . . (*Cries and coughs at the same time.*) I hope I have consumption—but no, it's no use, nothing helps, I don't have any consumption at all. Yet how good it would be to die . . . to bless everyone . . . That's really what's good about death, that anyone—a child or a beggar—can bless anyone he wants because he's going off to the next world . . . I'd even bless him . . . I'd say to him: With all my sufferings, with my consumption . . . with this blood which has been flowing for four years from my wounded bosom, I have atoned for everything that's happened, and because I have atoned—I bless you . . . I'd extend my hand to him. He'd throw himself on it, and a whole stream of tears would run through him and would irrigate his soul like a dry steppe drenched by a warm shower! . . . But my hand is cold now . . . A twilight has quietly crept up around me, and already

I hear sadly the words of the Bible: "Now, Master, art Thou freeing Thy servant from this world." I'd tell him once again . . . You . . . *Michel* . . . forgive me . . . you see over there (*cries bitterly*) . . . in a far-off distant place which I can't even imagine to myself, I shall be praying . . . for you . . . for your heart. (*Weeps.*)

Scene 3

Muromsky enters from his study wearing a dress coat with various ribbons on it. He is followed by Ivan Sidorov, holding, in addition to his hat and gloves, the petition rolled up and tied around with a small ribbon. Finally, Atuyeva and Tarelkin, lost in conversation.

muromsky: Lida, oh, Lida—where are you?

lidochka (*regaining her composure*): I'm here, Papa dear.

muromsky: Good-bye, darling. Hello? What's been going on? You've been crying, haven't you?

lidochka: Who, I? — No, Papa. Why are you dressed up so formally?

muromsky: Oh-h-h-h, it's nothing, dear, I just have to go somewhere.

lidochka: Go somewhere? Where?

muromsky: Well, we've decided to go to the prince, to ask his help, to present him this petition here.

lidochka: Wait just a moment. (*Goes to her room.*)

tarelkin (*turning to Muromsky*): Pyotr Konstantinovich, I beg you not to delay—any longer. I'm telling you again for I don't know which time: he's free now, there's nobody with him, and it would be easier for you to explain all these circumstances to him when he's at his leisure.

atuyeva: That makes sense—there's no pleasure talking about such a matter, let alone when there are other people around.

tarelkin: Exactly. After all, I am here to advise you.
(*Lidochka comes in.*)

muromsky: And what are you doing, may I ask?

lidochka: I'm going with you.

TARELKIN (*aside*): Oh, the damn goat! She'll spoil everything!

MUROMSKY (*to Tarelkin*): She'll come along with me then.

TARELKIN: Out of the question, completely out of the question. (*To Muromsky, meaningfully.*) They don't approve of that sort of thing.

ATUYEVA: Well, my dear, you see—they say you can't.

MUROMSKY: You're liable to catch cold, darling . . .

LIDOCHKA: No, Papa, I won't catch cold (*with determination*) —and besides, you know I never let you go anywhere without me.

MUROMSKY: Yes, my angel . . .

LIDOCHKA: I'll only ride along with you in the carriage; after all, Papa, who'd prevent me from being in the carriage with you.

TARELKIN: Yes, but remember you can't go up to the prince's.

LIDOCHKA (*looking at Tarelkin*): Don't worry—I won't!

TARELKIN: Well, in that case, it's all right. Let's be off, come now.

(*Muromsky takes his hat and the paper and goes out with Lidochka. Atuyeva and Ivan Sidorov accompany them to the door.*)

SCENE 4

Tarelkin and Atuyeva, returning.

ATUYEVA: Well, there you are—almost had to force them to go. Thank you, Kandid Kastorych! . . . It's true after all: A person lives, lives, and can't ever decide anything. I do feel better somehow, now that they're on their way. (*Ivan Sidorov comes in.*) And you? What do you think?

TARELKIN: I don't think anything, Ma'am.

ATUYEVA: What I meant was, do you think they'll be successful? Huh?

TARELKIN: Not in the least.

ATUYEVA: What do you mean, not in the least?

TARELKIN: That's what I suppose.

ATUYEVA: You mean to say one can't really explain one's case to such a person? If that's it, I'll go explain to him myself.

TARELKIN: Explain you can.

ATUYEVA: Then rest assured; I'll put down all the ins and outs of the case in the petition, down to the last detail.

TARELKIN: And you can put down all the ins and outs of the case, down to the last detail.

ATUYEVA: I can't submit the petition.

TARELKIN: On the contrary; there are even special days set aside for receiving them.

ATUYEVA: You see then—you yourself say, there are special days for receiving. I've made up my mind; I'm going myself.

TARELKIN: Let's say you do go. They show you into a chamber, where there are already some thirty petitioners there ahead of you. You sit down on the edge of a chair and wait . . .

ATUYEVA: Why on the *edge* of a chair? I'll sit down on the whole chair.

TARELKIN: That's what you think; you won't sit on the whole chair, mark my words.

ATUYEVA: Oh yes I will. I'm not just some housekeeper. My father crossed the Alps with Suvorov.

TARELKIN: Let's suppose even that he crossed them with Hannibal, you still won't sit in the whole chair for the simple reason that you have—a case! . . . The prince himself will come out, the officials behind him. He'll put his hands behind his dress coat like this (*flings his arms back in a wide motion*) and then say, What is it you wish?

ATUYEVA: Then right then and there I'll tell him just what's on my mind.

TARELKIN (*maintaining his pose*): Let's suppose so.

ATUYEVA: I'll give him such a talking to, the blood will rush to his head.

TARELKIN: I doubt that; His Excellency suffers from hemorrhoids, and gets a bad taste from such conversations—to the point where even his teeth ache. You just think you'll be an exception, but in the final analysis it'll all be the same. Five hundred petitioners—and each sounds the same.

ATUYEVA (*with emotion*): The same and not the same.

TARELKIN: And what if he asks you just as excitedly (*imitating her tone*), Do you have a petition?

ATUYEVA: Then I'll hand him a petition.

TARELKIN: He'll accept it, and right away hand it over to a clerk. Then he'll bow to you (*bows*) and assure you that everything will be all right, and the same to the next one on down the line, and there are a good fifty he has to go through, each of whom has a petition until there are enough of them to fill a cart, let alone what comes in by mail. He has all kinds of matters to arrange. Then there may be a meeting at one; two committees to preside over; a dinner party to attend down by the river; an opera in the evening; a ball afterward, and he already has on his mind God knows how much (*makes a gesture*), so that he'll simply hand over your petition along with all the others to a secretary. And he'll say to him, Look them over and make a report . . . you understand . . . And then the secretary will turn over everything to be checked—to me.

RAZUVAYEV (*quietly to Atuyeva*): And Thy rival shall surrender Thee unto a judge.

TARELKIN: And then I'll hand it over to my section head.

RAZUVAYEV: And the judge shall deliver Thee unto a servant . . .

TARELKIN: And there you are . . .

RAZUVAYEV (*shaking his head, quietly to Atuyeva*): And Thou shalt not leave there until Thou hast given up Thy last kopeck.

ATUYEVA (*throwing up her hands*): I don't understand!!

TARELKIN: The secretary, you know, also has power. And I, after all, I have power too, and my section head—he's another one to be reckoned with!

ATUYEVA: So be it—I have to run from one to the other— from the prince to your section head.

TARELKIN: Why make so much trouble for yourself—actually it would be enough if you just saw my section head.

ATUYEVA: Come now! I don't believe it!

TARELKIN: If you please, we'll figure it out for you. (*To Ivan Sidorov.*) Let's have the counting board, please. (*Ivan Sidorov hands him the abacus.*)

TARELKIN (*striking a pose and putting his hand on the abacus*): Our country, my gracious lady, counts two capitals and forty-nine provinces . . .

Scene 5

Muromsky and Lidochka come in.

TARELKIN (*leaving his place as soon as he sees them*): Well? What happened?

MUROMSKY (*throwing up his hands in obvious distress*): Nothing—he is not receiving.

TARELKIN: What do you mean "not receiving" when I tell you he's receiving.

MUROMSKY: The doorman told us.

TARELKIN: Did you slip the doorman anything?

MUROMSKY: Of course I did.

TARELKIN: And he says he's not receiving?

MUROMSKY: He says he's not receiving.

TARELKIN (*rubbing his forehead*): That's strange. How much did you slip him?

MUROMSKY: A fifty-kopeck piece.

TARELKIN (*pounding on the accounts*): Why, no wonder he isn't receiving. Now I ask you, did you ever hear of giving a doorman like that just fifty kopecks?

MUROMSKY (*annoyed*): Then how much are you supposed to give a doorman like that?

TARELKIN: A five- or ten-ruble piece.

MUROMSKY (*in anguish*): Thirty-five rubles!

TARELKIN: You're reckoning in terms of paper money.

MUROMSKY: After all, that is how I collect my rents.

TARELKIN (*vexed*): Allow me: nobody is asking you if you're collecting rents or how you collect them—in paper notes, copper, or even animal skins, the way it was done in the old days. Understand this—you have a case to settle, isn't that so? What did you come here for?

MUROMSKY: You know why.

TARELKIN: And you want to leave as fast as you can?

MUROMSKY: Another ten days wearing myself out here this way, and I'll be ready for the grave.

TARELKIN: That won't help; nobody's interested in your death.

LIDOCHKA (*frightened*): Oh, my God! —What are you . . .

TARELKIN (*to Lidochka*): I beg you, Ma'am—let's not speak about that. (*He takes Muromsky by the hand and leads him to a window.*) Have a look, are there many people on the Nevsky now?

MUROMSKY: Many.

TARELKIN: Which of them cares whether or not you die from your troubles?

MUROMSKY (*looking out the window and shaking his head*): Yes, nobody cares about me . . .

TARELKIN: Go on, make a test: shout out the window that you're giving away money. Well, what do you think would happen? (*Roars with laughter.*)

MUROMSKY (*aside*): Failed, damn you.

RAZUVAYEV: He's telling the truth.

TARELKIN (*spiritually*): You see—as simple as two times two. (*To Atuyeva.*) What is a day worth to you?

ATUYEVA: About twenty rubles.

TARELKIN (*forcefully*): And don't you think a messenger like that knows a day is worth twenty to you? Eh? He knows, the rascal, he knows. Well, if you give him ten then, you still have ten left in your pocket. That's the way everything is here, after all.

RAZUVAYEV: He's telling the truth.

TARELKIN (*continuing*): Here nothing is ever taken for nothing, nothing is ever taken by force or trickery— never. Here everything is done on good will and even, speaking fairly, by halves. Let's say you've got a case worth, oh, two hundred rubles, well—give a hundred and keep a hundred for yourself.

MUROMSKY (*to Atuyeva*): It seems that that's what Krechinsky had in mind when he wrote about the "industrial" bribe.

ATUYEVA: Yes, yes.

MUROMSKY (*to Tarelkin*): Just as though according to the commandment: "Love Thy neighbor as Thou lovest Thyself."

TARELKIN: Exactly—everything by halves. You'll agree yourself: it's always profitable to pay your bills at half price.

RAZUVAYEV: Profitable, Sir, profitable.

TARELKIN (*continuing*): And it's simple keeping accounts that way; everyone knows how much he has to give in his own case.

RAZUVAYEV: A clever arrangement.

MUROMSKY: Well, there's nothing we can do . . . let's be off,

Lida. (*Takes his hat, then raises his hands to God.*) My God in heaven! . . . What torment! (*They go in the direction of the door.*)

TARELKIN: On your way, Pyotr Konstantinovich, on your way while there's still time . . . or rather no, wait. (*Muromsky and Lidochka stop.*) It would be better if I took you, otherwise you wouldn't get in a second time.

MUROMSKY (*going out*): That's just fine; I'll feel somehow easier about things if you do. (*Leaves with Lidochka and Tarelkin; Atuyeva and Ivan Sidorov accompany them.*)

SCENE 6

A change of setting. A huge room. Tables and chairs along the walls. On one table a silver tray containing a pitcher of soda water and cups. To the left of the audience an entrance door; to the right, a door leading to the quarters of the Important Person; directly in front of the audience a door leading to an office.

At the center door the doorman Paramonov is sitting in a chair. He takes a pinch of snuff, blows his nose quietly and then wipes it. A heavy silence. Chibisov enters on his tiptoes, carrying papers.

CHIBISOV (*whispering*): Well, what's going on?

PARAMONOV (*shaking his head*): Nothing yet.

CHIBISOV: But it's late already.

PARAMONOV: Who knows what he's apt to do. He's still walking around and drinking his water (*points to a cup*). Not ready yet, I guess.

IBISOV (*coming in, papers in hand*): Well, Paramonych— how is it? Can I come in, huh?

PARAMONOV (*taking a pinch of snuff*): Shhhh . . .

IBISOV (*quietly*): Shhhh yourself . . . I've got an urgent matter here.

PARAMONOV: Try it.

IBISOV: What's there to try? I'm asking you, my dear fellow.

PARAMONOV: You see—there's not a soul around; he's alone, moving like a storm.

IBISOV: Not yet ready, I imagine.

PARAMONOV (*whispering, but opening his mouth wide*): Not rea-dy; I'm telling you, he's not rea-dy!!

Scene 7

Tarelkin, followed by several clerks carrying papers.

CHIBISOV and IBISOV (*waving their arms and blocking the way*): He's not ready . . . Gentlemen, not rea-dy!!

TARELKIN (*leading Paramonov to a side*): Well. How's his mood now?

PARAMONOV: Oh-h-h-h . . . a storm's brewing!

TARELKIN: Splendid!!! Listen, I'm going to let a petitioner in. Don't you bother him . . . let him say his piece . . . (*slips something into his hand*) understand?

PARAMONOV (*screwing up his eyes*): Make it good and hot for him till he gives in, eh? Come on, let's see how he takes to a nice steaming . . .

Scene 8

From the door on the right the prince appears in handsome morning dress. He moves slowly, immersed in his thoughts, and slightly rubbing his stomach. The clerks noisily crowd toward the door of the office with great commotion. Voices can be heard exclaiming: Oh! Gentlemen . . . Oh, gentlemen! Finally, the entire mass of them squeezes into the doorway. Paramonov keeps them in check.

PRINCE (*stopping in the middle of the room*): I say . . . what is that?

PARAMONOV: Clerks, Your Excellency.

PRINCE: Aha . . . and what is it they want?

PARAMONOV: They do not want to disturb Your Excellency.

PRINCE: Aha . . . excellent. (*He pours out a cup of soda water, drinks it and leaves slowly. Paramonov takes a seat.*)

SCENE 9

Muromsky comes in from the entrance door, attired in a dress coat with all his decorations and gloves. In one hand he carries the petition tied around with a small ribbon. He is obviously confused.

PARAMONOV (*showing Muromsky to a chair*): Please wait here. (*Muromsky sits down, breathing heavily and turning the petition around in his hands. Paramonov observes him askance and continues taking snuff and cleaning his nose. The prince again appears at the door; Muromsky quickly rises and bows several times.*)

PRINCE: Varravin! Varravin! (*Varravin runs in and bows; Paramonov leaves.*) And what may I ask is this?

VARRAVIN (*still in the posture of a bow*): A petitioner, Your Grace, doubtless a petitioner. Today you receive petitioners, Your Excellency.

MUROMSKY (*coming closer and interrupting Varravin*): My name . . . my name is . . . Muromsky, Your Excellen . . . Your Grace. Retired captain Muromsky.

PRINCE: Yes, I see. And what is it you wish?

MUROMSKY: My case . . . that is—not my case, but the case of the theft of a solitaire belonging to me is now under Your Grace's consideration.

PRINCE: Ah-h-h-h . . . We shall consider it.

MUROMSKY: I want, I beg Your Grace's support.

PRINCE: Aha . . . Support, my good man, I cannot give; I can only consider the case.

MUROMSKY: Consider it, Your Grace, in God's name I beg you consider it. It's an urgent matter!

PRINCE (*to Varravin*): I am surprised; I have yet to meet a petitioner who doesn't shout about an urgent matter.

MUROMSKY: A person suffering is apt to shout, Your Grace.

PRINCE (*casting a glance at Muromsky*): Perhaps. You have the petition? (*Extends his hand.*)

MUROMSKY: I do. I would just like to add, Your Grace, that I made the long trip here especially in order to explain to you personally what I have suffered through no fault of my own.

PRINCE: Explain, by all means—but only the case itself, not your sufferings. Here we do not take suffering under consideration—there's a medical board for that.

MUROMSKY: Your Grace, I have an only daughter, and five years ago we lived in Moscow; we had a circle of friends, and to make a long story short, I have the kind of home befitting my name and background. (*The prince raises his eyes to heaven and rubs his stomach.*) My daughter always conducted herself in such a way that, if I may say so, I prayed God every hour . . .

PRINCE: Prayer concerns God, Sir, not the case at hand. Would you please explain just the case! (*Silence. In obvious confusion Muromsky wipes his brow.*) Well, if you please . . . (*To Varravin.*) What the devil is this?

MUROMSKY (*confused*): Oh . . . When . . . ah . . . Now . . . but . . .

VARRAVIN: Please explain your case to His Grace.

MUROMSKY (*convulsively*): Now . . . when . . . Your Grace, I accepted Krechinsky's proposal, my daughter, already his fiancée . . . already his fiancée, you understand . . . did give him this diamond, as she understood it, only so that he might show it to some friends. No sooner does he get his hands on the stone, though, when he pawns it with the pawnbroker Bek—that is, not the same stone, but a fake one, Your Excellency, please understand, a fake one . . . Well, when I learned of this, I gave the pawnbroker Bek his money back. That is, I gave the money back to him afterward, but my daughter returned the real diamond to him at once. Well, Bek and I were square with each other and had no claims, but then in stepped the police and the next thing I knew my daughter and I found ourselves under investigation on account of the attempted swindle.

PRINCE: Swindling, you understand, Sir, is prohibited by law. Any swindle is naturally subject to investigation. But what do you have to complain about? All you and your daughter have to do is show your innocence, and you're complaining?

MUROMSKY: Why should an innocent person have to prove his innocence?

PRINCE: Even an innocent person must show his innocence,

Sir; but a guilty person will not become innocent in my
eyes—that much I promise you. Continue.

MUROMSKY: During the inquiry Krechinsky showed that the
whole thing was a mistake—but what do I care about
Krechinsky? My daughter, however, just happened to
say "It was a mistake," and one of the policemen who
was present at the time reported that what she said was
"It was my mistake," and the entire case grew out of
that. All because of the "my"! The poor girl is now under
suspicion of complicity in the crime and knowledge of
the intention of perpetrating a crime.

PRINCE (*puffing audibly*): Phewww!

VARRAVIN (*quietly to the prince*): Are you feeling bad?

PRINCE: Awful . . .

MUROMSKY (*taking heart*): So awful, Your Grace, you have
no idea! . . . To make matters worse the whole investigation has now concentrated on the presumed love affair
between my daughter and Krechinsky. Even witnesses
have been brought in: my cook Petrushka and Rasplyuev,
a tramp. The two of them slandered my daughter. The
case went to court. Well, there they turned it round and
round and finally decided to hold the Muromsky girl on
suspicion of an illicit affair. Believe me, Your Grace, it
would be better to hang her than that.

PRINCE (*utters a sigh and rubs his stomach*): Ah-h-h! . . .

VARRAVIN (*quietly to the prince*): Isn't there something I
can get you?

PRINCE: I don't know what; this hasn't happened for a long
time.

MUROMSKY (*throwing his arms wide*): From time immemorial, it hasn't happened! . . . The world has seen much
injustice, God knows, but nothing the likes of this! . . .
It's like some trick of magic: out of nothing all of a
sudden a big case develops, gets all twisted on itself and
tangles us up in this web like . . . like flies. I beg you
hear me out further. (*The prince rubs his stomach.*)

VARRAVIN (*quietly*): Perhaps some soda.

PRINCE (*pointing to a glass*): I'm already on the third; after
all, I'm not an ox!

MUROMSKY: An ox?! . . . Ah—yes! There was some talk about
an ox, but nothing to do with what we're discussing here.
Let's just say, Your Grace, that I'm fond of cattle . . .

PRINCE: Who's fond of cattle here?!!

MUROMSKY: I am—I, Your Grace.

PRINCE (to Varravin): He says he's fond of cattle.

MUROMSKY: Quite so, but could I exchange my daughter for that Tyrolean ox?! The investigators asked me what became of the ox, and to put an end to such silly trifles I answered: I ate it! . . . Such insolence! They took advantage of my temporary absence and sent people right off to my estate and discovered, of course, that the ox was alive!

PRINCE (pouring himself a glass of soda water): What on earth? He has a daughter (drinks); the daughter he apparently exchanged for an ox—that's doubtful; he ate the ox—I believe it; but the ox is still alive! (Bangs the pitcher of soda water on the table.) I don't believe it! A practical joke! I don't believe it!

MUROMSKY (excitedly): Alive!! . . . Your Grace!

PRINCE: Alive!! Ah . . . Pshaw! (Spits.)

MUROMSKY: Because of that very ox I fell into their clutches. They turned the ox over to the local authorities for special care, and delivered me to court on the charge, they say, of false testimony . . .

PRINCE: My head is spinning; I understand nothing.

MUROMSKY: And I too, Your Grace, understand nothing.

PRINCE: There you have it! . . . (Muromsky throws up his hands and shakes his head. They look at one another.) Is that all then?

MUROMSKY (blocking his way): Please—that was just the beginning of my troubles! When the case went to the higher court, the decision of the lower one was repealed . . .

PRINCE (obviously ill at ease): He'll wear me out, be the death of me!

MUROMSKY (persistently and louder): It repealed the decision on the grounds that it had no legal foundation, and accepted my slip of the tongue as "absentmindedness due to advanced age," for which I was grateful. But the court senate met again, at first, they said, to examine the case all over again—that is, for four years more. Then they couldn't reach a unanimous agreement. Nine different opinions were handed down about this calamitous case and from all of this, as I had the honor to

inform you, a regular whirlpool emerged and it sucked
me and my daughter into it. For five years now the
two of us have been living under the threat of court
action. We've lost our honor, our property, and we've
become worn out to the point of complete exhaustion.
I beg you have mercy on us! It's my daughter, Your
Grace! Free her from all this ridiculousness! I beg you
judge for yourself, why on earth would my daughter have
to run away and cheat me when I gave her in marriage
myself? You have children yourself, Your Grace; let
your heart be the judge; this is something for the heart
to feel.

PRINCE: Sir, we are obliged to judge—not feel.

MUROMSKY: It's impossible to judge without feeling.

PRINCE: None the less, we shall try. (*Wishes to leave.*)

MUROMSKY (*again blocking his way*): What will you try?
You're destroying an innocent girl. Think of her age! . . .
You're depriving her of the best years of her life; you're
staining her honor and you'll see (*pointing toward
heaven*) . . . you'll have to answer to God Almighty
for it!

PRINCE (*looking at the ceiling*): I imagine now you've
finished, am I correct?

MUROMSKY: No, I have not finished.

PRINCE: Well, if you'll excuse me, I have! (*Bows to Muromsky and heads in the direction of the door; Varravin also
bows and looks Muromsky straight in the eyes.*)

MUROMSKY (*follows the prince in obvious agitation*): Your
Grace! . . . Your Grace . . . permit me, permit me . . .
I beg you, give me back my daughter! (*Takes the prince
by the sleeve of his jacket.*) I implore you, save us from
this torture . . .

PRINCE (*stopping and turning around*): Save you from what?

MUROMSKY: I'm telling you: from your courts and from all
your destructive legal proceedings.

PRINCE: There is nothing I can do—that's the law.

MUROMSKY: That's what you all say—the law, the law, but
look, whose hands is it in? In the hands of an execu-
tioner, the law is—a whip!

PRINCE (*flaring up*): What right have you to make such a
judgment, tell me?

MUROMSKY: I *have* the right! And it's one that can't be taken away from me.

PRINCE (*ironically*): There you are! And what are your claims to it, my dear captain?

MUROMSKY: Here they are! (*Points to his hair.*) And my heart here (*points to his heart*); and my agonies . . . my tears . . . my weariness . . . the breaking-up of my entire family—there's my right—and there's even a higher one!!

PRINCE: A higher one yet! . . . Aren't you satisfied?

MUROMSKY: No, I'm not satisfied! I am protecting my own daughter!! . . . There's my right, there are my claims to it; can you read them?

PRINCE (*his voice trembling somewhat*): Well and good, even eloquent. But I must tell you that I do not recognize the eloquence of the petitioners who come to see me.

MUROMSKY: Why is that?

PRINCE: Because otherwise it would be impossible to distinguish the scoundrel from the honest person.

MUROMSKY: You can't distinguish?

PRINCE (*smiling slightly*): No, I cannot.

MUROMSKY (*sharply*): Then you are not fulfilling your responsibility. (*The prince flinches; Varravin sways somewhat to a side.*)

PRINCE: Ah-h-h-h—you think so?

MUROMSKY: Yes.

PRINCE (*showing a flash of anger*): And I think that with your claims even responsible people sometimes find themselves behaving like cads.

MUROMSKY (*also stunned*): Who?!!

PRINCE: Please, please—don't get angry. I see you served in the military, that you fought with Suvorov—I know, I know, so we'll pull you down a peg; we'll see from the case what kind of a person you are and how your daughter conducted herself in this innocent affair: sensibly or foolishly.

MUROMSKY (*forgetting himself*): My daughter?! . . . Sensibly! . . . (*Approaches the prince.*) Why are you humiliating us, Your Grace, why?!! Can it be because I happen to love my own child when you don't see your own for weeks on end?

PRINCE: What did you say?

MUROMSKY: Or because they busted my head here (*points to his head*) with a rifle butt at Borodino when I, a simple army captain, took a Frenchman right on top of my chest, while a French nannie was fondling you at the time in her arms?!

PRINCE (*advancing on Muromsky*): Forgive me—have you gone out of your mind?

VARRAVIN (*restraining him*): Your Grace, Your Grace, be merciful—he has a head wound, he was wounded in the head . . .

MUROMSKY: No, Mister Official, I was wounded in the heart! I am protecting my own daughter, my honorable daughter, handed over to the public slander of a court, hear me?! I'm not to blame because your bureaucratic heart loves an Anna or Stanislav but has no love for children.

PRINCE: Do you know that I can have you turned over to the police for this?

MUROMSKY: I don't want to know anything. The blood inside me is speaking, and blood doesn't ask what it can say and what it can't. I'm not some Petersburg dollie you've got here; I don't know anything about your official's schooling and behavior. I'm talking the truth; it's crawling along my throat, so you listen to me! You have no truth! Your courts are the justice of Pilate! Your legal procedure—worse than that of the Jews in Christ's time! Your judges no longer conduct business—those were the happy days—but plunder! They catch a father by his heart with the hook of justice and pull . . . and pull . . . and shake him: give, give . . . and it's his blood, his blood that comes pouring out of him. What are they torturing me for? For five years now I've been experiencing a suffering words can't describe . . .

PRINCE: If that's the case: hey there, doorman!!

VARRAVIN (*restraining the prince*): For God's sake . . . Your Grace . . . You see . . . (*Points to Muromsky's head.*) (*The doorman enters.*)

MUROMSKY (*not noticing anything*): Let the doorman hear me too; let him go to a tavern, to a grocery store, yes even to a house of ill repute and let him tell—yes even there—that he found at least one landowner in Russia whom the courts tortured to the point where truth gushed out of his mouth along with his blood and brea . . . (*he becomes dizzy and begins swaying on his feet*) breath!!

PRINCE (*beside himself, shouting*): Hey, doorman! . . . Take him out of here . . . Drag him away if you have to, drag him away . . .

MUROMSKY: Don't upset yourself, Your Grace—I'm going myself. (*Goes out, unsteady on his feet. Paramonov accompanies him to the door.*)

SCENE 10

The same, with the exception of Muromsky. The prince remains motionless for several minutes, following Muromsky with his eyes. Varravin, behind him, appears in utter astonishment.

PRINCE (*after a short silence*): What kind of a person is that?! (*Pause. Points to the door through which Muromsky left with a forceful gesture.*) Why, that's rebellion! What people! And we talk about the provinces! Why even in the provinces they don't talk like that. He must be insane, mad . . .

VARRAVIN: You see yourself.

PRINCE: He ought to be taken away and locked up. Why did you keep on holding me back? . . . Fine receiving days! Just let in anyone right off the street. His Excellency is right when he says that one of these days a fight's going to break out here . . . (*Suddenly pulls himself together and walks out.*)

SCENE 11

VARRAVIN (*alone*): Well . . . there's an attorney for you! Read the law to him he did! . . . Put him right in his place. The justice of Pilate . . . Jewish legal procedure . . . ah, Jewish . . . go on, pay up . . . We won't go chasing after words. (*Falling into thought.*) Only . . . what if some sort of disagreement came out of all this? Maybe he irritated His Grace too much? . . . Now the

prince is going to go running around. Give me the file
on the case, he'll say. What kind of a case is it if the
petitioner somehow crawled out of his own skin? He'll
turn it round and round; the craziest whim will come
into his head and he'll say to me, You, Varravin, carry
it out!

SCENE 12

Varravin and the prince.

PRINCE (*stopping at the door*): Hey! Maksim Kuzmich! . . .
    Hey . . .
VARRAVIN: What is it, Your Grace? (*The prince makes an
    affirmative sign.*) Really?
PRINCE: Yes! (*Comes in.*)
VARRAVIN: And I was afraid all the time that he upset you.
PRINCE: No, my dear, on the contrary, not in the least; it
    all turned out for the best.
VARRAVIN: For the best! How fortunate!
PRINCE: Fortunate indeed! Yesterday, you know, I must have
    downed a gallon of soda water in the club, and nothing
    happened.
VARRAVIN: You'll have to report this to the doctor, Your
    Grace.
PRINCE: Most certainly. Next time he'll prescribe me soda
    in the evening, and in the morning a petitioner. (*Roars
    with laughter.*)
VARRAVIN (*also smiling*): Very good, very, very good.
PRINCE: Joking aside for the moment, tell me what is this
    case all about? They supported him in the court there,
    didn't they? They're a responsible bunch, after all.
VARRAVIN: Certainly, but once in a while, they're not above
    a little extortion either. But Your Grace knows that
    their decisions have no validity without your personal
    review. So let them do what they want—they won't
    cause any harm.
PRINCE: Cause me any harm? I should say they won't! . . .
    So he's mad, is he, this Muromsky? Wounded in the
    head at Borodino?

VARRAVIN: In the head; the wound's an old one. But you can
see the effects in his incoherent speech and bitterness.

PRINCE: Precisely. You perceived it quite well: incoherent
speech and bitterness. But I'd like to see the file on
the case for myself; do you have it ready?

VARRAVIN: Ready, Your Grace.

PRINCE: Then give me a brief outline of it.

VARRAVIN: To begin with, Muromsky himself—you've already
seen the kind of person he is. Very well off. One daughter. You can imagine how he brought her up, being the
sort he is.

PRINCE: I can just imagine.

VARRAVIN: Well, some dandy, a certain Krechinsky, good-
looking, big broad shoulders, wormed his way into the
girl's good graces.

PRINCE: Ah, yes—I saw him in the club once in a while; he's
a gambler.

VARRAVIN: And consequently you can easily imagine what the
results were.

PRINCE: I can indeed: the father half-witted, the girl frivolous.

VARRAVIN: After the obvious results, Krechinsky helped himself to some diamonds and pawned them; the pawnbroker he duped in the most unusual way.

PRINCE: Yes. I heard about it in the club.

VARRAVIN: The matter went to the police, and the police
official's report led in turn to the subsequent investigation. The same police official, note also, was himself
present during a most terrible scene: Krechinsky almost
killed him, for he's unusually strong and has the most
violent temper.

PRINCE: The old captain joined in the fight too, did he?

VARRAVIN: Well, that's the type he is; besides, he's a boaster.
Nobody lays a hand on my daughter, he says.

PRINCE: There you are.

VARRAVIN: I'm a great lord I am, he says . . .

PRINCE: A captain?

VARRAVIN: At this point, another circumstance arose: The
girl, we saw, was passionately in love with Krechinsky.
Well, judge yourself, Your Grace—in such a relationship a girl like that will give herself soul and body . . .

PRINCE: I can imagine! . . .

VARRAVIN: At the very moment the catastrophe occurred, she threw herself at the police official in utter despair and, sobbing, declared "It was my mistake"!

PRINCE: Ah-h-h-h! The policeman pointed that out in his report.

VARRAVIN: He did indeed. You can understand yourself, Your Grace, what the word "mistake" means to a girl like that brought up on all kinds of French novels!

PRINCE: How well I know—*une faute*. Well, I can see the case is self-evident; there's nothing I have to read really.

VARRAVIN: And the father, you see, when he heard his daughter say what she did grabbed hold of her—he was completely beside himself then—in order to run away, as he put it, from all that shame. So he dragged her off after him.

PRINCE: The stubborn fool dragged her from their own house? Where to?

VARRAVIN: Not from their own house, Your Grace; everything happened in Krechinsky's apartment.

PRINCE: At the young man's, eh?! Getting worse by the minute. The father doubtless discovered them, as they say, *en flagrant délit*, he, he, he . . .

VARRAVIN: Probably. But it was the father, according to his own words, who brought her to Krechinsky's in the first place.

PRINCE (*astonished*): The father! That can't be!

VARRAVIN: Please have a look at the file.

PRINCE: Then the man really is a fool . . . He ought to be put away, and as regards the young man and the girl— they deserve the strictest punishment, the strictest! . . . The whole episode reeks of the greatest immorality. Please permit me to select the most essential facts of the case and then render my decision—and I assure you, it will not be a light one.

VARRAVIN: Incidentally, Your Grace, I should again point out that there is no juridical evidence for the rendering of a formal verdict to this case.

PRINCE: What do I care about such nonsense? Juridical evidence. Tell me now: when the investigation was in progress was any attention directed to the results?

VARRAVIN: What results, Your Grace?

PRINCE: What results?! The results that usually obtain when some broad-shouldered charmer and a tender female come together.

VARRAVIN: Ah . . . I understand, Your Grace.

PRINCE: Haven't your investigators looked into this yet?

VARRAVIN (*recollecting*): In the file on the case there is mention of the fact that the Muromsky wetnurse, Semyonova, refused to give testimony.

PRINCE: Refused? Why wasn't she compelled to?

VARRAVIN: It's forbidden by law.

PRINCE: Forbidden?

VARRAVIN: That's correct, Your Grace, forbidden.

PRINCE: Oh, well . . . there's nothing to be done in that case. Nevertheless, if there is a child, then we have to discover where it is, right? Well, where is it? (*Silence.*) A second crime apparently is involved here, eh?! (*Raises his eyebrows in a meaningful way.*) Then please be so kind as to enter in my assessment that the question of the wetnurse's refusal to speak has not yet been elucidated, and that the entire case . . . (*thinks*) the entire case should be directed (*with determination*) to reinvestigation (*waves his hand*) and to the strictest . . . the strictest . . .

VARRAVIN (*aside*): My God—he'll spoil everything! (*Out loud.*) Your Grace, I beg you take into consideration the fact that the case has already been going on for five years.

PRINCE (*stopping momentarily*): Five years . . . ten if need be! I must have the truth . . .

VARRAVIN: Then you yourself, Your Grace, must take responsibility for the delay in the processing of the case.

PRINCE (*casting a stern glance at Varravin*): Why have you begun badgering me? . . . (*Shakes a finger at him.*) No, no, no . . . I said reinvestigation, and I meant it! Not another word on the subject, hear?! . . . (*Sternly.*) Draw up my assessment, and at once. (*Looks at his watch.*) My heavens, what's this? Twelve o'clock, and I have a conference and then a committee meeting. Give me some of the papers I have to sign, but not all of them, and be quick about it!

VARRAVIN: As you wish; I'll fetch only the most important.

PRINCE: Yes, yes . . . Hey, doorman! (*Paramonov comes*

running in.) My carriage! —Get rid of all petitioners!
I can't be bothered with them now—I'm busy. (*The
prince and Paramonov leave through different doors.*)

SCENE 13

Varravin alone, then Tarelkin.

VARRAVIN (*annoyed*): Reinvestigation? What's the sense of
that?! And you, he says, write. Nowadays everyone does
exactly as he pleases, each his own way; it's simply
chaos, I say, a babble of tongues (*shaking his head*).
The world's coming to an end. (*Sighs.*) Ah . . . the
case is messed up (*opening the door to the office*).
Tarelkin! (*Tarelkin comes in.*) The Muromsky case is
messed up.

TARELKIN (*with fear in his voice*): How?

VARRAVIN: The old man blabbed so much to the prince that
all his talk worked better than the soda water. He's
kicked up his heels and off he goes prancing around.
He ordered the whole case to be reinvestigated. Write
out a form.

TARELKIN: But what's to be done with Muromsky?

VARRAVIN: The prince gave an order—and you know his
temper.

TARELKIN: But the case was always in your hands.

VARRAVIN: There's no approaching him further on the matter.
Once he gave me such a look that I backed down—hell
with you, I thought.

TARELKIN: Wouldn't it have been better then to agree to
Muromsky's first proposition?

VARRAVIN: I said it was out of the question. The case will
just have to be reinvestigated.

TARELKIN: He'll die. You'll see, he'll die soon. And the
daughter, I promise you, won't budge an inch. She's
got her principles; you'll see, she won't budge.

VARRAVIN and TARELKIN (*together*): Tsk, tsk . . . oh . . .
(*They groan. Silence.*)

TARELKIN: Then it means he'll return home with all his
money.

VARRAVIN: So he will.

TARELKIN: The thought is unbearable! . . . So many years
. . . of cares . . . and troubles; (*aside*) tomorrow my
creditors'll grab me by the collar. (*Aloud.*) It's just unbearable.

VARRAVIN (*thinking*): A hot-tempered person—is dangerous.
If we take money from him, but do nothing about his
case, I grant you he'll cause a scandal. There's none of
the humility in him that all the other petitioners have.
When the ordinary petitioner comes, why he's just like
a tame sheep—you can do with him what you want.
But with him, it's different. The prince even wanted to
have him taken to the police—he took him for a madman.

TARELKIN: Is that so? . . . For a madman. Hm. Your Excellency!—if he is mad then . . . (*They look knowingly
at one another.*) Why this is even better than a tame
sheep . . .

VARRAVIN (*thinking*): Hm—yes.

TARELKIN: Nobody'd believe what he had to say, even if he
shouted his head off . . .

VARRAVIN (*to himself*): There is a way of handling such
cases . . . anyway it's worth trying! (*Thinks.*)

TARELKIN: But, Your Excellency, he'll be leaving . . .

VARRAVIN (*making up his mind*): Good! . . . Let him! . . .
(*To Tarelkin.*) Sit down at once and write up the decision to turn the case over to reinvestigation.

TARELKIN: At once, Sir. (*Sits down and quickly begins
writing.*)

VARRAVIN: Write carefully. His Grace likes it that way . . .
Begin in the usual style, then go on like this: "and then
taking into consideration first . . ."

TARELKIN (*writing*). First . . .

VARRAVIN: And list those fourteen points about the suspicions
regarding the love affair—you know—from private opinion . . .

TARELKIN: I know Excellency. After all, the old man made
them up.

VARRAVIN: Yes, so he did. Then go on to say (*dictates*):
"and to enjoin the investigating commission to determine the causes of the refusal to give testimony of the
nurse Semyonova, and if necessary, to proceed, according to the law, to a medical examination of the accused."

TARELKIN (*writing*): Of the accused.

VARRAVIN (*gathering up his papers*): And submit the paper immediately for copying, so that it'll be ready for the report tomorrow, hear?

TARELKIN (*continuing to write*): Yes, Sir.

VARRAVIN (*coming closer to him and in a low voice*): Meanwhile, tomorrow morning have that confidant of Muromsky's, Sidorov, come to see you; then hit him smack in the face with this business about the medical examination! . . . See here, greybeard, tell him, here's what's threatening them! Give it to him good: life or death! Money! . . . Twenty-five thousand rubles if one. And have him bring the money right away! No delays and no shilly-shallying . . . (*Goes in the direction of the office.*)

TARELKIN (*aside*): How about that! (*Thinks.*) —We're drawing up the report; the case is going to be reinvestigated; we can't come to terms with the authorities —but give money! (*Writes diligently.*) I don't understand . . .

VARRAVIN (*opening the door leading to the main office*): Gentlemen! The papers for His Grace's signature, but mind—just the most urgent ones and as fast as possible.

TARELKIN (*stops writing and thinks*): I don't understand . . . (*Makes a gesture with his hand.*) But as long as there's a chance for money . . . (*Diligently occupies himself with writing for the rest of the scene.*)

SCENE 14

Tumult. A crowd of clerks come in with piles of paper which they have to hold above their heads, because of the cramped quarters, and in so doing block Varravin's path. The entire scene is played rapidly.

CHIBISOV (*handing over the papers to Varravin*): Three committee papers, Your Excellency, and three very urgent matters—absolutely necessary.

VARRAVIN (*rapidly leafing through them*): Hm-m-m-m yes, I know . . . Good. (*Takes them in hand.*)

IBISOV (*handing him papers*): As you ordered, Sir—absolutely urgent.

VARRAVIN (*leafing through them*): Hm-m-m-m . . . Good, hm-m-m-m . . . (*Takes them in hand.*)

GERTS (*quickly*): Your Excellency, I have some very urgent papers.

VARRAVIN: The most urgent?

GERTS (*arranging the papers for him*): The most urgent.

SHERTS (*also arranging papers*): The most urgent, Your Excellency.

ALL THE CLERKS (*bumping into each other with piles of papers*): The most urgent.

VARRAVIN (*shouting*): Quiet! What's going on here? Stop, I say! (*Stamps his feet.*) I'm not accepting a single paper more, and that's final!

SHMERTS (*spinning out of the office and dumping a whole pile of papers on Varravin*): The most urgent, Your Excellency!

VARRAVIN: Oh-h-h-h!! . . . (*Disappears under the papers and shouts at the top of his lungs.*) Stop!! . . . You're trying to kill me! . . . (*Chibisov and Ibisov rush to him and hold him up. Dumb scene.*)

CURTAIN

ACT FOUR

The Muromsky apartment. Morning.

SCENE 1

Lidochka is sitting by the window behind lace frames; Nelkin is beside her. Atuyeva is in the other corner of the room. Silence. Muromsky comes in in a dressing gown, observes everyone, then begins wandering about the room.

MUROMSKY (*stopping in front of Atuyeva*): Well . . . what
   are you thinking?

ATUYEVA: I'm not thinking anything; I'm just wondering
   why we came here.

MUROMSKY (*throwing his arms up*): But you already know
   why . . . there's nothing doing, I simply couldn't bear
   it any longer.

ATUYEVA: Now think of something yourself.

MUROMSKY: Didn't you come to some kind of understanding
   among yourselves?

ATUYEVA: What kind of understanding? She purposely isn't
   saying a word to me, and that's the end of it.

MUROMSKY: I sent Ivan Sidorov to call on Tarelkin.

ATUYEVA: Why send him? After what happened, they'll
   show him the door and that'll be the end of that.

MUROMSKY (*confused*): What . . . am I to do now?

ATUYEVA: I don't know.

MUROMSKY (*suffering*): Sister, I beg you, don't torture me . . .
   I feel really like I'm in a fog . . . a fog. (*Makes a
   gesture.*)

ATUYEVA: There's a child for you. Gets into trouble, then
   goes around asking for advice. You'd have done better
   to think of your daughter instead of getting yourself
   worked up to such a fever. (*Lidochka and Nelkin
   quickly get up from their seats.*)

LIDOCHKA: Auntie, leave father alone! What are you blaming
   him for! What you're saying isn't true; father did the
   best he could.

MUROMSKY: What did I do, my dear? I myself don't know
   how it happened.

LIDOCHKA: Believe me, Papa—everything happens for the best
   even if you yourself don't know it. Please don't think
   about me, but think about what's more important than
   me—your honor, and what's more important than your
   honor, your honesty, then act as you see fit. I said a long
   time ago: give up all the deals, the secret comings and
   goings, and stop bowing your honest head before a
   dishonest body. It will be much better that way!

NELKIN: Look about you—are there only a few honest people
   suffering? Are there only a few of them rotting in prisons,
   languishing in the courts? Must all of them submit to
   force, and lick the boots of oppression? Don't we have

within us enough honesty in order to wear with pride
the rags of outward honor which was torn to shreds by
that old jester—the law, all decked out in embroidery
and ribbons and wearing around its neck the sack of
Judas!

ATUYEVA: What kind of a tragedy is it you're making out of
the whole thing? You're just spouting empty words and
phrases out of French novels.

LIDOCHKA: No, Auntie, they're not just empty words and
phrases, but the voice of a clean conscience which, believe me, is more powerful than all the tumult of the
soulless crowd, which from this moment on I am re-
nouncing forever, forever, do you hear? . . . Let me
wander the whole world, poor but honest . . . and I'll
always tell everyone I come across that my father did
the right thing.

MUROMSKY (crying and taking her into his embrace): My
dear friend, my dear child!

LIDOCHKA (kissing her father and holding him in her arms):
Don't cry, Papa, don't eat your heart out over me;
you see how calm I am about everything. I know that
the cause of all our trouble isn't in me, in my heart,
and such trouble doesn't dishonor us or bring us down
but instead . . . raises us up even higher than before . . .
and to such a height where nothing can bother us anymore . . .

MUROMSKY: Then what do you want, my darling? How is
it all going to end?

LIDOCHKA (emotionally): I want an end to humiliations, an
end to bowing and scraping before others . . . I want to
see you strong and proud in the face of adversity.

MUROMSKY: But they're going to convict you.

LIDOCHKA: Let them.

MUROMSKY: What will happen to you?

LIDOCHKA: Everything's already happened to me—there's
nothing more that can happen to me!

MUROMSKY: Then you think we should go back to the country?

NELKIN: No! You should go and demand the truth!

ATUYEVA: Just as I said—novels and empty words. Now think
what you're saying, Sir. Where is there truth in the
world? Where are you going to find it?

NELKIN: Well, if there really is no truth anywhere in the
world let *it* be ashamed and not me . . .

SCENE 2

*Ivan Sidorov comes in, puts his hat on a table and remains
standing at the door.*

MUROMSKY: There he is now. (*Goes over to him.*) Well,
what have you to say for yourself?

RAZUVAYEV: I was there, and I saw.

MUROMSKY: Whom?

RAZUVAYEV: Kandid Kastorych.

MUROMSKY: And what happened?

RAZUVAYEV: If you please, Sir (*leads him to a side*), it doesn't
look good at all.

MUROMSKY (*anxiously*): What do you mean. (*To Nelkin.*)
Come over here a moment, Vladimir Dmitrich. (*Nelkin
draws closer.*)

RAZUVAYEV: You see, Sirs: the prince got angry something
awful and now they're turning the whole case over again
to a new investigation and this time they're going to
be even stricter than before.

MUROMSKY (*his voice trembling*): Merciful God . . .

NELKIN: You're absolutely certain?

RAZUVAYEV: He gave it to me in black and white: they're
drawing up the report now, he says.

NELKIN: Well, let them investigate all over again if they
want—there's nothing to be done, let them go ahead.

RAZUVAYEV: But do you know how they'll go at it this time?
(*Atuyeva approaches Ivan Sidorov; Lidochka remains
alone to a side and weeps.*)

NELKIN: I don't know what you mean. Thank God, the agony's
all over with.

RAZUVAYEV: Not yet, it isn't. It's a kind of poison, isn't it?
He says they're going to take whatever steps necessary
to discover the truth . . .

NELKIN: Maybe.

RAZUVAYEV (*continuing and jabbing a finger to make his
point*): . . . And he says, if circumstances demand they're

going to call in a medical board to conduct a medical examination.

ATUYEVA and MUROMSKY (*together*): My God!!

NELKIN: What do you mean? I don't understand!

RAZUVAYEV: It's Lydia Petrovna they want to examine!

NELKIN (*the cry escaping him*): Oh!! This is hell itself!! . . . Pyotr Konstantinovich (*gesturing with his hands*)— give them whatever they want, give them everything!

RAZUVAYEV: Just a moment, gentlemen—don't get excited. In my opinion, they can't do it; there's no law says they can.

NELKIN: Ha, ha, ha—the law . . . What did he begin to talk about, what rot . . . (*To Muromsky.*) There's nothing more you can do: give them what they want!! . . . What are you fighting for any more? Give them everything!!

LIDOCHKA (*going up to him*): What do you mean? Tell me, I don't understand.

MUROMSKY (*embarrassed*): Oh well, my dear . . .

NELKIN (*interrupting him*): Stop! Not another word more! Nobody . . . nobody here can tell you.

LIDOCHKA: We were just saying . . .

NELKIN (*completely beside himself*): No-o-o-o, this isn't the time for that now! . . . Now . . . they've gone beyond all bounds; the conscience has become deaf, reason blind. You're in a dark forest! . . . The thieves have descended on you, and they're holding a knife above you —oh, no! . . . (*Covers his face with his hands.*) A hundred knives!!! Give them everything, Pyotr Konstantinovich, everything—down to your last shirt, your last thread, down to your bare skin, if you have to!!!

MUROMSKY (*taking money from a bureau*): Here it is . . . (*Puts it on the table.*) All lost—that pack of devils!

NELKIN (*to Razuvayev*): How much did they say?

RAZUVAYEV: Thirty thousand.

ATUYEVA: What do you mean, thirty? They said twenty before, didn't they?

RAZUVAYEV (*shrugging his shoulders*): He banged a fist on the table: life or death . . . Thirty thousand, he says, or nothing!

NELKIN: When are you supposed to take it to them?

RAZUVAYEV: I have to be there at four . . .

NELKIN (*to Muromsky*): How much have you got there?

MUROMSKY: Twenty.

NELKIN (*groping in his pockets*): What's there to be done? What's there to be done?

MUROMSKY (*throwing up his hands*): I don't know, I just don't know. (*General silence.*)

LIDOCHKA: Vladimir Dmitrich—I have some diamonds . . . worth about three thousand.

NELKIN: Get them! (*Lidochka goes out.*)

ATUYEVA: Wait a moment, I also have some things . . . Just a moment. (*Leaves quickly.*)

LIDOCHKA (*carrying several jewelry boxes and putting them on the table*): Here they are . . . but please, Mama's ring is here too—that I won't give up.

MUROMSKY (*taking out the ring and giving it to his daughter*): Here it is! I gave it to her as a present, God bless her memory . . . when she . . . made me a present (*sobs*) of you . . . (*Lidochka throws herself on his neck and the two of them cry.*)

ATUYEVA (*also carrying jewelry boxes and other things and putting them on the table*): Here . . . everything . . . God be with them . . . after all it was for her I kept them. (*All crowd around the table and busily take to going over everything spread out on it.*)

MUROMSKY: Let's see . . . is there much here? . . . Is there enough to make up thirty thousand? . . . Here's twenty; these things are worth another three anyway, that makes twenty-three; sister's things come to about two more, that's twenty-five; that still leaves five missing. (*Silence.*)

NELKIN (*burrowing in his pockets*): Oh, my God! . . . It's all been for nothing . . . Where can we get the money? (*Thinks.*) Who knows me here? . . . Nobody, nobody at all!

RAZUVAYEV (*during the above conversation he moves to a side, extracts a purse from his inside breast pocket, withdraws some tickets from it and approaches Muromsky*): How much did you say you were still missing, Sir?

MUROMSKY (*throwing up his hands*): Five thousand!

RAZUVAYEV (*handing the tickets to him*): Here you are, Sir; now it ought to be just right.

MUROMSKY: What's this? Pawn tickets! Where did they come from?

RAZUVAYEV: From the heart, Pyotr Konstantinovich, from the
   heart.

MUROMSKY (*examining the tickets*): They're not familiar to
   me . . .

RAZUVAYEV: Familiar, unfamiliar—what difference does it
   make as long as they mean money; they're only burning
   a hole in my pocket this way.

MUROMSKY: Then it's your money you're giving. (*All turn
   toward Ivan Sidorov.*)

RAZUVAYEV: That's right. We're simple people we are, Sir;
   if it's already come to pooling money—then you give
   as much as the heart can raise. Here's everything mine
   raised—whatever there was to raise, it raised.

MUROMSKY (*moved*): You are a good person . . . a fine
   person . . .

LIDOCHKA (*quickly going over to Ivan Sidorov*): Ivan Sidorov!
   Take me in your arms!

RAZUVAYEV (*embracing her*): Our good . . . honest . . .
   young lady . . .

LIDOCHKA (*quietly, to Muromsky*): You should give him a
   receipt.

MUROMSKY: Yes, you're quite right, my dear. (*Lidochka sits
   down and writes; Muromsky, Ivan Sidorov and Atuyeva
   count the money.*)

NELKIN (*remaining alone in the middle of the room*): My
   God! And what about me? . . . I have nothing . . .
   nothing at all I can lay my hands on!

LIDOCHKA: Vladimir Dmitrich! It's sinful for you to talk like
   that.

RAZUVAYEV (*continuing to count the money*): Don't give it
   a thought, Sir—you'll make it up later on.

NELKIN: Make it up later on? When? To whom?

RAZUVAYEV: You'll see, mark my words; right now I'm giving
   for you, but the time will come when you'll give for me.

NELKIN (*surprised*): Give me your hand, Sidorych—I'll make
   it up to you yet, I promise. (*Shakes his hand.*)

RAZUVAYEV (*quietly, to Lidochka*): Miss, that's not necessary . . . not necessary at all.

LIDOCHKA: What isn't necessary, Sidorych?

RAZUVAYEV: That little piece of paper you're writing out.

LIDOCHKA: But that's your receipt.

RAZUVAYEV: I know, Miss, but why waste the paper—Christ be with it, with the receipt.

LIDOCHKA: It's the proper thing to do.

RAZUVAYEV: No, not really, it isn't, Miss. If you asked me for the money, then I'd say yes, it would be proper, but you didn't ask me for the money, now did you? So why bother making out receipts? Whether I gave one ruble or a thousand, it's all the same, isn't it? Tear the paper up, Miss, please, otherwise I'll be insulted. (*Lidochka tears up the receipt.*) That's the way; it's like we say—the Lord giveth, and the Lord taketh away —blessed be the name of the Lord. (*Turning to Muromsky.*) Well there, Sir, we've ended on a good word. Let's be on our way with it now! (*He helps Muromsky collect the money and other things on the table.*)

MUROMSKY (*moving weakly and in evident confusion*): Lord . . . Lord . . . Thy will . . .

RAZUVAYEV: Don't fret, Sir, don't fret . . . you'll see, the Lord God will return everything—just remember what I'm telling you, He'll return everything.

MUROMSKY: But Ivanushka . . . it's not money we've robbed people of . . .

RAZUVAYEV: I know, Sir, I know . . . But God will return it all, just have faith . . .

MUROMSKY: But you just see to it that you get the money due you in Streshnevo . . . do you hear?

RAZUVAYEV: I hear, Sir; I'll get it.

MUROMSKY: Sell the Belkov forest if you have to.

RAZUVAYEV: We'll see when we're there, Sir; right now I have to rush off to Kandid Kastorych and let him know that you'll be there at four o'clock.

MUROMSKY: All right, all right . . . (*After wrapping up all the things he intends taking with him, he points to them.*) What do you think—they're diamonds after all; should I take them to him just like this?

RAZUVAYEV: Of course not. You'll stop on the way at a jeweler's and leave them with him. Ten kopecks maybe, but he won't take off any more.

MUROMSKY: You leave with me at least; you know, I don't see . . . too well . . . all of a sudden . . . and something seems to have gotten dark in my head . . . (*Rubs his head.*)

LIDOCHKA (*taking him by the hand*): Papa! What's the matter with you? . . . Papa!

MUROMSKY: It's nothing, my dear . . . I, nothing . . . (*Gets ready to go.*)

LIDOCHKA: My darling . . . (*helps him*) don't get upset . . . for God's sake, don't get upset . . . please, at least for my sake . . . (*Embraces him.*) Ivan Sidorov will help.

MUROMSKY: Yes, he'll help . . .

RAZUVAYEV: Yes, Miss, of course I will. (*Takes the things, his hat, and opens the door for them. Lidochka takes her father under the arm and leads him out; Atuyeva supports him from the other side. They leave.*)

SCENE 3

NELKIN (*alone. Watches them leave, and covers his face with his hands, afterward quickly advancing downstage*): My God! . . . (*Strikes himself on the chest.*) Your heart is empty—what are you striking yourself for? . . . What good are you, you useless pendulum, swinging aimlessly, of no advantage to anyone? (*Points to the place where Ivan Sidorov was sitting.*) A simple peasant yet useful and noble, but I?! . . . Vengeance! I'll nourish in my heart a great vengeance against every insult, against every lawlessness! . . . No, I won't keep it inside me— I'll shout it instead to the whole world! . . . I'll heat a branding iron in its coals and press it straight against the forehead of lawlessness!! (*Moves to leave.*)

SCENE 4

Nelkin; Lidochka runs in.

LIDOCHKA: Vladimir Dmitrich . . . Vladimir Dmitrich, you're still here?

NELKIN (*rushing at her*): Here! Here! —What is it?

LIDOCHA: Let me have my drops . . .

NELKIN: What's the matter? What happened?!!! (*Looks for the drops.*)

LIDOCHKA: Nothing, nothing at all happened—it's just that I'm so afraid! —He's very weak.

NELKIN (*handing her the drops*): Here they are! —There's nothing to be afraid of; God will look after him— there's nothing to be afraid of.

LIDOCHKA (*leaving*): Don't go away, please! Don't leave us . . .

NELKIN: God is with you! . . . Leave you? But what can I do for you? You see the kind of person I am, what my fate is! Just like now—of what use am I to you at all?

LIDOCHKA: Do you think money is the only thing that's necessary? You love us, don't you? Isn't that the truth?

NELKIN: Oh, the truth! I swear it—the pure, holy truth! . . . I'm filled with this love, I'm burning with it, it's the only thing that keeps me alive . . . (*Lidochka stretches out a hand to him; he covers it with kisses. They leave together.*)

CURTAIN

ACT FIVE

A room in the government bureau. The door to the private study is open.

SCENE 1

TARELKIN (*alone. Stands at the front of the stage sunk in thought and looking at his watch*): A few minutes more and he'll come rushing in with a full cart. I have to admit—I thought he bit off more than he could chew, asking thirty thousand! . . . He got away with it though! Muromsky gave in! But when you come down to it, it's all my doing, mine, not his, as God is my witness! (*Also deep in thought Varravin crosses the entire stage from*

one end to the other, stops and looks intently at Tarel-
kin for a few minutes, then withdraws again.) By everything that's fair then, half of the loot belongs to me! . . .
And if he doesn't give it to me . . . Well, he'll give it
to me all right, if I have to rip his guts open . . . What
do you need in such circumstances? Character—yes;
character, and nothing more. (*Rubs his hands together.*)
Fifteen thousand! . . . Why I'm rich! When you think
about it, it's really strange: I was poor, so poor in fact
I didn't even have that bag beggars go around with—
or even the old trousers that'd be even worse off than
me—when all of a sudden I have a fortune. I'm rich.
What a word that is, so weighty, just like it was all
padded—rich. Splendid! No, no matter what you say,
I regard this as the law of nature. Precisely—the law
of nature, because there are numerous examples of
someone being poor, not having anything at all to his
name, and all of a sudden becoming rich . . . (*Varravin
again crosses the stage, stops a short while, then withdraws.*) He'll get mad all right! And how he'll get mad,
mad as the devil—but I'll put in for retirement—why
shouldn't I? Why do I have to hang around here any
more? . . . I've seen everything I cared to, tried everything I cared to . . . I plucked flowers along the banks
of the Moika, and wove garlands along the banks of
the Fontanka—I tasted all the sweets of the Neva! The
flowers had the same thorns the god Leviathan harm-
lessly trampled underfoot. And here's what remained of
the garlands (*raises the wig he has on and reveals a
completely bald head*); from the sweets of the Neva I
had to have false teeth made up! God keep this splendor.
I'll hop off to Mother Moscow—a nice peaceful town;
I'll rent me a flat at the Assumption in Cemetery Hills,
in Death Lane, at the home of the merchant Coffin
and I'll sleep it out till the Second Coming. (*Varravin
again appears and noise is heard in the hallway; Tarelkin
rushes over to him.*) Your Excellency! It's him! . . .
Him!!! . . . He's come!

VARRAVIN (*very calmly*): So what? Receive him, detain him,
then come and report to me.

TARELKIN: Yes, Sir.

VARRAVIN: And see to it that the sergeant-at-arms comes here
right away, as I ordered! (*Goes out in the direction of
the private study.*)

TARELKIN (*dashes to his desk, sits down, and begins leafing
through papers*): What the hell does he need the
sergeant-at-arms for? Why on earth does he have to
have that animal? . . . I don't understand . . .

SCENE 2

*Muromsky comes in, somewhat bent over, breathing hard,
a side pocket stuffed tight. Tarelkin buries himself in his
papers but follows him with his eyes over the edge of the
papers.*

MUROMSKY (*approaching Tarelkin*): Kandid Kastorych—ah,
Kandid Kastorych—it's me!

TARELKIN: Oh, my heavens—I was so busy I didn't notice
you.

MUROMSKY: Everyone's so busy . . . May I?

TARELKIN: I'm terribly busy right now—wait a little while . . .
over there if you don't mind . . . (*Points to a chair.
Muromsky sits down slowly and looks all around. Tarelkin buries himself in his papers. Silence.*)

MUROMSKY: Forgive me, my dear fellow—can I have a little
glass of water? I don't feel too well; my throat's all
parched and I'm awfully thirsty.

TARELKIN: Why, by all means, at once . . . (*Gets up; aside*)
Right before the operation, it's always water they want.
(*Goes out.*)

MUROMSKY (*alone*): So this is how it all has to end! My God
in heaven! Everything . . . everything . . . even the
diamonds!! It's all happening just the way Krechinsky
prophesied . . .

TARELKIN (*coming in with a glass of water*): What do you
say, Pyotr Konstantinovich? Don't we take good care
of you here?

MUROMSKY (*drinking and wiping his face*): Thank you,
thank you.

TARELKIN (*gathering his papers into one pile*): I'll go right

away with the report and I'll say that you're here. You'll
see, it won't be long now (*whispering in his ear*), he'll
take care of everything—be calm.

MUROMSKY: Good, good.

TARELKIN: Just have a look at the mountain of cases he has
to take care of. (*Shakes the papers in his hands.*) You
see? (*Goes to Varravin's study.*)

SCENE 3

MUROMSKY (*alone, in a weak voice*): My God, (*looks all
around*) just like Daniel in the lions' den . . . A wolf-pit,
that's what this place is. (*Takes a billfold out of a pocket
and extracts a piece of paper from it.*) Aha, just the way
he prophesied it . . . (*reads distinctly and with emphasis*) . . . "there is the criminal or the snare bribe. It is
taken until there is nothing left to take, until a person is
stripped bare" . . . (*looks around himself*) stripped bare
. . . "It follows the examples and principles of Stenka
Razin and Nightingale the Robber. It is carried out under
the cover and shade of a dense forest of laws . . .
(*observes the bookcases standing along the walls and
reads*) code of laws . . . code of laws" . . . yes! . . .
(*continues*) "with the help and by means of the snares,
wolf-pits and rods of justice, and into these pits (*again
looks around*) will fall the old and the young, the rich
and the poor, without any regard for sex, or age, or
profession, or wisdom, or ignorance" . . .

TARELKIN (*leaving Varravin's study with more papers in
hand*): Please. (*Muromsky folds the piece of paper he
has been reading, puts it back in his billfold, and drags
off slowly in the direction of the study.*)

TARELKIN (*alone*): He still insists on the sergeant-at-arms?!
What does he have in mind to do? . . . (*Thinks.*) I
must be stupid, I guess, but I just don't understand it . . .
but still I have to go and call him. (*Goes in the direction of the center door.*)
(*For a minute or two the stage remains empty. A heavy
silence.*)

SCENE 4

Tarelkin comes in, followed by the sergeant-at-arms, Zhivets.

TARELKIN (*continuing their conversation*): I don't know, I tell you, I don't know. Maksim Kuzmich was saying that His Excellency wishes to do it in an economical way.

ZHIVETS: I have no objections! I'm not all all against economy! As His Excellency wishes. (*Turns in the direction of the study.*)

TARELKIN (*blocking his path*): No, no—wait a while.

ZHIVETS: For what?

TARELKIN: There's a petitioner there.

ZHIVETS: Oh, in that case! That's got nothing to do with me . . . (*Begins walking around the room.*) And really, Kandid Kastorych, my friend, from all these contracts there's nothing but trouble; believe me, nothing but trouble . . .

TARELKIN (*keeping an eye on the study all the time*): You're quite right, quite right.

ZHIVETS: And how I am! These people just look like contractors on the outside, but they're really Judases, not worth a damn . . . That's just the way it is, take my word for it!

TARELKIN (*as before*): I believe you, you're absolutely right.

ZHIVETS: They don't let you live! And that's because it's this way with them: each contractor has his own place, and the next one doesn't shove himself in there. This is where you are, one says to the others, and this is where I am. They've got all these places of theirs neatly sorted out, they have. Fine. Well, I come along and take a look, because it's my job to, and what do I see? —Padding figures, stealing right and left. Now is that good, I ask you? And what do you think they do then? Send me in a dozen peaches on a tray or raspberries for a holiday table. Well, you be the judge—I served in the army, what's a raspberry to me? I've got children, after all, what good's a raspberry to me? . . . Aren't I a mammal, after all?

TARELKIN (*goes toward the study and stops directly opposite Zhivets*): A mammal? . . . Yes, of course you're a mammal. (*Passes by him.*)

ZHIVETS (*insulted*): I? . . . A mammal! —Then you're a pig!

TARELKIN (*approaching the door of the study*): Your Excellency! —Sergeant-at-arms Zhivets.

VARRAVIN (*from the study*): Excellent. (*Taking leave of Muromsky at the door.*) Rest assured—I shall review your case with my fullest attention (*bows*), with my fullest attention. (*Goes back into the study.*)

SCENE 5

Muromsky, Tarelkin, and Zhivets.

TARELKIN (*quietly, to Muromsky*): Well, how did it go?

MUROMSKY: He gave his word.

TARELKIN: You explained everything to him, did you?

MUROMSKY: Yes, I explained . . .

TARELKIN: You submitted everything?

MUROMSKY: As expected.

TARELKIN: Then be calm—everything will be all right (*bows*), all right.

MUROMSKY (*also bowing*): Please God. (*Moves downstage.*) I feel like a big weight's been taken off my shoulders . . . all I want is to see her, my little darling, happy and peaceful again, just that . . . (*Shakes his head.*) My God! Human blindness! . . . I saved and saved, everything for her—and now look where it's gone . . . He took everything I had, right down to the last . . . Now, it's all theirs! . . . To hell with the lot of them—it's all their fault anyway. (*Leaves slowly.*)

ZHIVETS (*to Tarelkin*): Can I go in now?

TARELKIN (*in high spirits*): Now you can, go ahead. (*Zhivets directs himself toward the study.*)

SCENE 6

Varravin emerges from the study and collides with the sergeant-at-arms. Tarelkin and Zhivets.

VARRAVIN: What are you doing here?

ZHIVETS: You had me summoned.

VARRAVIN: Ah—yes; wait a moment. Hey! Doorman!

TARELKIN (*running to the door*): Hey! Doorman! Paramonov!
(*Paramonov comes in.*)

VARRAVIN (*holding a package in his hands*): Give this back
to the petitioner who just left, and be quick about it!
(*Paramonov runs after Muromsky.*)

TARELKIN (*alarmed*): Your Excellency! Maksim Kuzmich!
What are you doing? (*Varravin stares at Tarelkin and
remains motionless; Zhivets observes the two of them;
Muromsky and Paramonov appear at the door.*)

SCENE 7

Varravin, Tarelkin, Zhivets, Muromsky, and Paramonov.

MUROMSKY (*to Paramonov*): You . . . you're making a
mistake, friend . . . you couldn't mean me.

PARAMONOV (*pressing close to Muromsky*): His Excellency
has given his order!

MUROMSKY (*softly*): But not for me, not for me . . .

PARAMONOV: Perhaps, but His Excellency . . .

MUROMSKY: You're making a mistake, my friend . . .

VARRAVIN (*interrupting Muromsky*): If you please! I have
to see you a moment.

MUROMSKY (*astonished*): Me?!

VARRAVIN: Yes, you! You left this package with money in it
in my study (*shows him the package*), isn't that so?

MUROMSKY (*trembling*): I? . . . No . . . Oh, wait, yes, I
did! . . . I left it . . . that is—maybe I did . . . please
. . . I don't know . . . what is it you want?

VARRAVIN: I want to announce your crime here and now,
like this, in front of witnesses.

MUROMSKY: What is all this? (*Looks around.*) A trap?!

VARRAVIN: You wanted to buy me off, didn't you?

MUROMSKY (*utterly confused*): I'm afraid there's some misunderstanding here . . . forgive me . . . I'm sorry! I was
doing just what he told me. (*Points to Tarelkin.*)

TARELKIN (*also confused*): What are you doing? What's
going on here? . . . Your Excellency! I swear by every-

thing that's holy, that I never did anything of the sort, never! I never even saw him before . . .

VARRAVIN (*paying no attention to Tarelkin*): I want you to understand that I do not take money! (*Throws the package on the floor in front of Muromsky.*) Take it! And get out of here and take that *foul* case of yours with you!

MUROMSKY: I'm not here about any *foul* case—if you please . . . (*Advancing on Tarelkin*). What is this? Huh? How could you . . .

TARELKIN (*losing control of himself*): I beg your pardon! What are you trying to mix me up for? Your Excellency! What does he want from me?

VARRAVIN (*interrupting him*): Either you take the money or I'll order the sergeant-at-arms here to. (*Zhivets makes a start for the money; Varravin holds him by the arm; Muromsky picks up the package.*) I could prosecute you to the fullest extent of the law for this, but because of your age, I'll let you go. Go on, get out of here! (*Points to the door.*)

MUROMSKY (*feeling about the package, then running downstage*): What is this? What is this?—Where's all the money? . . . (*Opens the package and quickly examines the money. Varravin stands on the right, Tarelkin on the left. Zhivets is behind Muromsky. All look at the latter with intense interest.*)

VARRAVIN: Please leave or I'll have you removed.

ZHIVETS and TARELKIN (*exchanging glances*): Ah-h-h-h! —That's it!

MUROMSKY (*forgetting himself, forcefully*): Where is the money, I say?! It's not here! (*Gropes around the package.*) It's not . . . it's not! You took it!!! Help!! . . . Good people! . . . Help me!! . . . (*Turning to Tarelkin.*) Hel . . . (*Stops, then turns to Zhivets.*) Help . . . Oh-h-h-h! (*Strikes himself on the head.*) A trap!!! (*The others move in closer around him.*)

VARRAVIN: Get out of here, I tell you! I have the power . . .

MUROMSKY (*taking himself by the head, completely beside himself*): Robbery . . . The Muromsky woods! . . . Robbery . . .

VARRAVIN (*his voice trembling*): Get hold of yourself, what's the matter with you? —Get hold of yourself . . .

MUROMSKY: What's happening? . . . Eh? . . . (*Coming to.*)
Here . . . here . . . they just rob and cheat you! . . .
(*Raises his head.*) I'll say it out loud—rob and cheat!!!

VARRAVIN (*to Tarelkin*): What's the matter with him? He's
subject to fits, it seems.

TARELKIN (*beside himself*): I know nothing, nothing, nothing.
Don't confuse me, Maksim Kuzmich, for God's sake,
don't confuse me . . . I know nothing.

MUROMSKY: Who are you here (*looking around*) —you're
all one gang, all in it together . . . (*Suddenly draws himself up straight.*) Wait!!! (*To Zhivets.*) Take me to the
tsar!

ZHIVETS and TARELKIN (*blocking his path, waving their arms
and trying to calm him down*): Sh-h-h-h . . . calm yourself . . . old fellow . . . calm yourself . . . What's the
matter with you? Sh-h-h-h . . .

MUROMSKY (*pushing forward strenuously*): I demand . . .
take me to my tsar! . . . Call the guards! . . . the police!
. . . Through the streets! . . . Without a hat on! . . .
We're all accomplices! . . . We're thieves!!! (*Grabs
Varravin by the arm and pulls him.*) Let's go!!

VARRAVIN (*tearing himself away*): What's the matter with
you? . . . What are you doing?

MUROMSKY (*pulling him*): Let's go!!! . . . We're oath-
breakers . . . put us in chains! Police!! . . . Chain us
together (*his voice falters*) . . . To the tsar!! . . . I'll
say to him . . . Father! . . . Father of us all . . . Your
gracious, benevolent . . . Sovereign!! . . . (*Gets dizzy.*)
Your . . . your . . . your gra . . . (*Staggers. Tarelkin
supports him.*)

TARELKIN: Pyotr Konstantinovich, old man, Pyotr Konstantinovich—don't get upset, we'll fix everything . . .

MUROMSKY (*forcing himself to speak*): Your . . . Your . . .
High . . . (*Throws the package of money at Varravin
and falls into Tarelkin's arms. The money scatters across
the floor. Silence. Varravin observes Muromsky. Zhivets
moves to retrieve the money.*)

VARRAVIN (*pushing Zhivets back*): If you please . . .

ZHIVETS (*thrusting himself toward the money*): No, allow
me, Your Excellency—it's my duty.

VARRAVIN (*grabbing up the money*): If you please!

ZHIVETS (*also snatching the package*): If *you* please!!

MUROMSKY (*tears off a decoration and his necktie and hurls them at Varravin*): Oh-h-h-h . . . (*Loses consciousness in Tarelkin's arms.*)

VARRAVIN (*excitedly pulling the package to himself*): Allow me, I'm telling you! I'm ordering you, as your superior here!

ZHIVETS (*also pulling the package*): My duty . . . (*They stand near each other at the front of the stage, their voices hissing.*)

TARELKIN (*holding Muromsky in his arms, plaintively*): Gentlemen, gentlemen—for Christ's sake . . . (*Puts Muromsky in a chair.*)

VARRAVIN (*tearing the package to himself*): Come now . . .

ZHIVETS (*the same*): Come on . . .

VARRAVIN: I have to count it.

ZHIVETS (*pointing to his pocket*): Count here instead . . .

VARRAVIN: How dare you?

ZHIVETS: Dare nothing . . . I won't give it up! I have authority here too.

VARRAVIN: Will you keep quiet about it?

ZHIVETS: Why? (*Sticks his hand in the money and pulls out a batch of notes.*)

VARRAVIN: What do you think you're doing?

ZHIVETS: I'll keep quiet. —What did you think? (*Shoves the money into his pocket.*) That's it. Fine!

TARELKIN (*after stretching Muromsky out on some chairs, he runs over to Varravin and Zhivets; they move apart*): Well, gentlemen, what's this all about? What's going on?

VARRAVIN (*straightening out the package, he throws it on the floor; to Zhivets*): Please stand here—and don't move from your place.

ZHIVETS (*fastening all the buttons on his jacket*): Yes, Your Excellency; I give my word, I won't.

VARRAVIN (*to Tarelkin*): And you send immediately for the police—and tell them that there's a petitioner here who's not in full possession of all his faculties. Understand me? . . . They should take the petitioner from the sergeant-at-arms and have the money delivered to his place of residence.

TARELKIN (*pleadingly*): Your Excellency . . .

VARRAVIN (*shaking his head and shouting*): Delivered to his place of residence . . .

TARELKIN (*to Zhivets*): Ivan Andreich!

ZHIVETS: Who did you say was a mammal, my dear fellow?

PARAMONOV (*running in*): Your Excellency. His Excellency and His Grace are coming!

TARELKIN (*moving slightly into a sitting position*): —My God! The Day of Judgment!!

VARRAVIN (*threateningly*): Keep quiet!! (*Rushes to meet the Important Persons.*)

ZHIVETS (*straightening out his uniform, talking in a drawling manner*): Yes, Sir, I do know my duty . . .

SCENE 8

The Important Person and the prince come in.

IMP. PERS. (*catching sight of Muromsky*): What is tha-a-at? Come now, what's happened here?

VARRAVIN (*spreading his arms wide*): A most unusual occurrence, Your Excellency. He came here, judging by everything, a petitioner. He began explaining what it was he wanted in rather a strange way, not completely coherent. I received him as my duty requires and suddenly—no sooner does he leave me when I discover he left behind for me this envelope with money here. The sergeant-at-arms happened to come by just then and we dispatched the doorman to return the package to the petitioner. When I began to rebuke him for his attempted bribery, admittedly somewhat sharply . . .

IMP. PERS. (*interrupting him*): It was a waste of time.

VARRAVIN: What was there to do, Your Excellency—he couldn't take it.

IMP. PERS. (*impatiently*): A waste of time!!

VARRAVIN: Your Excellency! Spare me . . . such an insult . . . Thirty years I've been serving! Nobody ever called me a bribe-taker . . . (*Strikes himself on the chest.*)

PRINCE: Your Excellency, I understand his position and, in my opinion, this petitioner should be dealt with most severely . . . (*Approaches Muromsky and runs his eyes over him.*)

IMP. PERS.: Go on, please.

VARRAVIN (*straightening himself*): This very moment, right here, in the presence of officials, he caused a dreadful scene . . .

PRINCE: Yes-s-s—it's the same captain who came to see me.

VARRAVIN: The same, Your Grace.

PRINCE: It's just as you were saying. Your Excellency, when he came in to me it was the same thing—he made a lot of fuss.

IMP. PERS.: What on earth is the matter with him?

PRINCE: He's probably just another of those rowdies we used to have in the old days . . . Besides, he was wounded in the head at Borodino. The wound is an old one, so he has this incoherence of speech, you know, and . . . and . . . (*looks at Varravin*) and . . .

VARRAVIN: And ill temper, Your Grace.

PRINCE: Ah, yes—and ill temper.

IMP. PERS.: What do the doormen do around here? Why do they let in everyone right off the street? Doorman!! (*A doorman comes running in.*) What are you doing? Well? (*The doorman remains silent.*)

VARRAVIN: A clear case of negligence, Your Excellency.

IMP. PERS.: Negligence—and you know I do not tolerate negligence.

VARRAVIN: May I say, however, Sir, that it was really impossible to notice anything strange when he first came in.

IMP. PERS.: But it's his job to notice.

VARRAVIN: On the surface he looks respectable enough.

IMP. PERS.: I repeat, it's up to him to keep his eyes open!!

VARRAVIN: It was a day for receiving petitions, Sir.

IMP. PERS.: But it's . . . Oh, what's the use . . . You've tied my hands with these receiving days of yours . . . Well, anyway, please spare me such scenes. (*Silence.*) Take him away.

VARRAVIN (*to Tarelkin*): Take the petitioner away! Doorman! (*Indicates Muromsky with his eyes. Tarelkin and Paramonov lift him up.*)

MUROMSKY (*opening his eyes*): Your . . . your . . . your . . . (*beats his chest*) your . . .

IMP. PERS.: He's clearly not himself! (*To Tarelkin.*) Doesn't he smell of something?

TARELKIN (*sniffing Muromsky*): Yes, he does smell, Your Excellency.

IMP. PERS.: Of what?

TARELKIN (*confused*): I can't . . . can't say . . .

IMP. PERS. (*impatiently*): Of what, I'm asking you?!!

TARELKIN: Uh-h-h-h (*confused*) . . . of fish . . .

ZHIVETS (*quickly turning about from behind Varravin, approaching Muromsky and sniffing him*): Of spirits, Your Excellency.

IMP. PERS.: Yes, that's it. (*Gestures with his hand.*) Carry him out.

ZHIVETS (*quietly passing Tarelkin*): Now who'd you say was a mammal? (*Stops again at the package of money. Muromsky, in the meantime, is removed.*)

VARRAVIN: Your Excellency! Would you be so kind as to interrogate the sergeant-at-arms here, as an eyewitness to this unusual occurrence.

IMP. PERS.: I see no occurrence here whatsoever! —A man got loose of his chains, came here and made a fuss; so what? (*To Zhivets.*) Were you here at the time?

ZHIVETS (*straight as a ramrod*): Yes, Your Excellency, as my duty requires.

IMP. PERS.: I know. Well, were you here when the disturbance took place?

ZHIVETS: According to my duty, I must always remain within sight.

IMP. PERS. (*impatiently*): I know!! I'm asking you—how it all happened.

ZHIVETS: It happened here, in the office. His Excellency ordered me to go out and call the petitioner. After rebuking him for attempting to bribe him by giving him money, he returned it, threw it right on the floor. I was standing here, doing my duty, and I'm keeping watch over the money just as the law commands on force of oath.

IMP. PERS.: Duty, again! (*To Varravin.*) Quite a zealous person, it seems.

VARRAVIN: Quite, Your Excellency, quite.

IMP. PERS.: That's very good.

ZHIVETS: When I served in the army, I was more accustomed to carry out the wishes of my superiors than my own.

IMP. PERS. (*interrupting him*): Fine, fine. That will do.

VARRAVIN: Regarding the incident itself, what is the next course of action?

IMP. PERS.: The usual—according to form; have him draw up a report.

PRINCE: And shouldn't an investigation also be made, Your Excellency?

IMP. PERS.: And an investigation too, perhaps—according to form.

PRINCE: And he should be dealt with as sternly as the law permits. (*The Important Person and the Prince wish to leave.*)

VARRAVIN (*detaining them*): Your Excellency! Your Grace! But the money. What must be done?

IMP. PERS.: Oh, the money . . . Well, take it and submit it together with the report.

VARRAVIN: No, Your Excellency, I have no intention of putting even a finger to it. Would you please be so kind as to have it counted and then sealed—I have no idea myself how much there is there. That way at least I and my subordinates will remain entirely beyond reproach.

IMP. PERS.: Yes, that's quite right. That's the sort of thing I like. (*To the Prince.*) Tactfully.

PRINCE: Tactfully.

IMP. PERS. (*to Zhivets*): Count it. (*Zhivets counts the money.*) And you Prince, would you please take it and have it filed. (*Leaves in the direction of the study.*)

ZHIVETS (*after counting the money, very carefully putting it back in the package, and grasping it firmly*): One thousand three hundred and fifty rubles, Your Grace.

PRINCE: All right. Bring it to me. And you (*to Varravin*) please initiate the investigation—and see to it that it's thorough, hear! (*Goes out in the direction of the study. Zhivets precedes him with the money.*)

VARRAVIN (*accompanying him*): At once, and the motion that the entire case be reinvestigated, as you ordered, is ready.

PRINCE: Well, then, everything seems to be in order. (*Goes out.*)

Scene 9

VARRAVIN (*musing*): Yes, everything in order . . . yet . . .
all these orders take my breath away . . . Hm, hm . . .
Investigation?! . . . Why, this Muromsky would raise
Cain during an investigation! Or, perhaps, by that time
he'll have cooled down somewhat. Then as calmly as
you please he could show that he actually did place the
money on the table just out of imprudence and that
State Councillor Varravin accepted it as a bribe, which
he in reality was not guilty of offering. Worse still—
what if I'm held in suspicion—is that anything to joke
about? Well, many a person I've put under suspicion.
Yet they're all well and still command respect; they live
out their lives on their estates and die good Christians,
in due repentance, surrounded by their families . . . So,
if worse comes to worse, I'll retire too to my country
place . . . it used to belong to a prince . . . I'll set up
a sugar plant maybe; I'll be a landowner, an honorable
enough profession . . . of course, not a high-ranking state
dignitary, but still respectable.

Scene 10

Varravin; Tarelkin comes in.

VARRAVIN (*going over to him in obvious agitation*): Well?
. . . What's going on over there?
TARELKIN (*removing his coat, drily and casually*): Over where,
Your Excellency?
VARRAVIN: You know where—at the Muromsky's.
TARELKIN (*as before*): Over there? . . . Oh, nothing . . .
VARRAVIN: Is anything happening?
TARELKIN: Nothing's happened? . . . It's already happened!
VARRAVIN: I've been ordered to initiate an investigation.
TARELKIN: Initiate something else—but not an investiga-
tion . . .
VARRAVIN (*not understanding him*): Are you in your right
mind?

TARELKIN (*raising a finger*): Surprised!! (*Whispers in Varravin's ear*). As though made to order.

VARRAVIN: What is?

TARELKIN (*enthusiastically*): He died!!!

VARRAVIN: Died? Who? . . . How? . . . The petitioner? . . .

TARELKIN: He didn't even make it home—he died in the carriage on the way.

VARRAVIN: Died on the way!!

TARELKIN (*making a gesture*): And nobody's the wiser . . . Case closed and that's that!

VARRAVIN: Tsk, tsk! . . . (*Pauses.*) What an extraordinary turn of events . . . (*Slowly crosses himself.*) God grant him the kingdom of heaven.

TARELKIN (*heaving a sigh*): What? God grant him the kingdom of heaven. I've nothing against that . . . But, what does a poor person like me get out of it? . . . Huh? . . . (*With a swagger.*) Well, who's work was it, who brought it all about, huh? . . . Who dragged him away from right here (*indicates the place*) on his own shoulders? You keep mentioning that in your time you had to fill people's pipes for them and go running back and forth to stores doing errands for them but did you ever have to drag around on yourself such goods, huh? . . . That's why I am asking you now to let me know how much I'm worth . . . Come on, make an estimate . . . I won't leave without it—make an estimate!

VARRAVIN (*thrown into confusion*): What are you nagging me for? How can I tell you how much you're worth?

TARELKIN (*angrily*): How? Good heavens, man! Even children know. How can you ask a question like that, especially with such an ending to the case where not only doesn't anybody know anything but even all the hooks and loops went to the bottom too? (*Saucily.*) My part in the whole thing's stretched to half now.

VARRAVIN (*flaring up*): To half? . . . (*Aside.*) I'll teach you a lesson! (*Aloud.*) Well, if it's half, so it's half . . . Say you were the one who did everything—you won't get an argument from me.

TARELKIN: No, that's not what I meant. I'm talking about the money you got.

VARRAVIN (*clenching his teeth*): Hm! Got? . . . Got from whom?

TARELKIN: From whom? From the deceased.

VARRAVIN (*smiling*): You're joking. After all, you were right there when I gave it back to him.

TARELKIN: What do you mean "gave it back"?

VARRAVIN: And I consider it a stroke of good fortune that I decided on that course of action.

TARELKIN: Great heavens! What did you say?!!!

VARRAVIN (*ironically*): I said—what luck that I didn't accept the money from the deceased . . . eh?

TARELKIN (*losing control of himself*): Didn't accept?!! . . . You didn't accept?!! Impossible! (*Throws himself on his knees.*) Your Excellency, my friend, my benefactor, my soul, please. I beg you in God's name, please—I'm poor—I'm poor—I'm doing this out of poverty—I've got debts—I'm naked—I want to eat . . .

VARRAVIN: Enough, Tarelkin. What cowardice—get up off your knees! . . . (*Helps him get up.*) —You're just compromising yourself. You be the judge: (*with a malicious smile*)—let's say I took his money, then I'd have to reproach myself the rest of my life—my conscience wouldn't give me a moment's peace.

TARELKIN (*recovering his composure*): Ah-h-h-h—so you didn't take it; ha, ha, ha. And you didn't take it because your conscience would trouble you . . . ha, ha, ha! (*Laughs loudly.*)

VARRAVIN (*clenching his teeth*): Now you're laughing—make sure you don't cry later! (*Comes up to him and whispers in his ear.*) I'll see to it that it's a nice slow death . . . understand?

TARELKIN (*pausing*): No—nothing.

VARRAVIN (*as before*): I'll extract the soul from your frail body with such an instrument that there won't even be a squeak . . . (*His eyes flash.*) Understand now?

TARELKIN (*getting frightened*): For pity's sake—what are you saying? I didn't mean anything . . .

VARRAVIN: That's better! (*To the audience, softly.*) Really. As soon as he deposited that money on the table, it was just as though someone pushed my hand . . . (*recoils in terror*). And I did not take it . . . (*Casts a sidelong glance at Tarelkin.*) It was God Himself saved me—His great mercy . . . (*Goes off in the direction of the study.*)

SCENE 11

TARELKIN (*alone; gazing for a long time all around him*):
Some case! Wonderful!! . . . Every dumbhead's got a
lesson to learn. But it shouldn't stop there—I think he's
got to be taken (*takes his hat*) and a fist shoved smack
into his asinine mug (*shoves his fist into the hat*) —you
fool, you, you were born a scarecrow and you'll die a
jester!! . . . (*Puts on the rumpled hat and turns to face
the study.*) Oh! He robbed me. He robbed everyone! . . .
I said that he'd pick me clean, clean as a linden tree—
and that he did, and how!! (*He turns around and stands
facing his coat.*) Well, what now my old friend? Huh?
Let's be off . . . let's be off again to strut our clerk's
dance through a world embroidered with poverty and
covered with tinsel. I thought this day for sure I'd be able
to drop you off in the flea market . . . But no, fate
decreed otherwise. (*Puts on his coat.*) Ah—dreams,
dreams! You just tumble into nothingness . . . (*Takes
his walking stick, pulls on his gloves, and moves downstage.*) I used to dream, when I was young . . . of taking
a drive down the Nevsky in a splendid carriage; I used
to dream, when I was adult, of grabbing myself some
rank and decoration, of hooking onto a dark, freckled
merchant-woman two girths wide and covering all the
wounds and fatigue I got in government service with
her piggish, drowsy fat. I used to dream at least here,
in this place, of getting my hands on a real piece of
change for a rainy day—but no, no, and no!! says Fate.
Why do you hold me on a leash, Fate, like some mangy
dog? Why do you set sweets and viands around me,
then torture me with hunger and cold? Why do you
thrust money, plenty, and wealth into someone else's
pocket right under my very nose? May you be damned,
in your deeds, Fate! There's no justice on earth, no
compassion: The strong oppresses the weak, the sated
consumes the hungry, the rich skins the hide off the
poor! You hateful world you, I'd like nothing better
than to take you and set you ablaze from one end to the

other, and then, putting on that miserable uniform of mine, go walking through your smoldering ruins saying, There you are, you devil's progeny you. (*He raises the collar of his coat, buttons himself up and goes out, waving his walking stick.*)

CURTAIN

THE DEATH OF TARELKIN

A COMEDY-FARCE IN THREE ACTS

To Nikolay Dmitrievich Shepelev

My dear friend:

When still young did we not live together on the heights of Albano, in the memorable Locanda Emiliana, and read Gogol to the point of exhaustion?

Did not your keen artistic sense foretell a real success for Krechinsky at a time when it was still being composed *just for the sake of a joke?* And was it not from you then that I heard the first and, as it were, *unanimous* approval?

And now, a few weeks ago, when I was preoccupied with the rapid completion of *The Death of Tarelkin,* was it not to you that I turned for advice? And was it not by your faithful instructions as an Artist that I was led to make the corrections that gave this play unity and introduced into it the Logic of Motives?

Our old friendship certainly did nothing at all unusual when it whispered that I should make this dedication to you and place at the head of this third and last play of mine your name, which is so close to me.

As ever,

A. Sukhovo-Kobylin

Moscow, February 20, 1869

To the Reader

Any impartial witness would admit, I think, that the Fate of my two previous plays could not attract me to further activity for the stage. At least that is how the events accompanying their appearance affected me—and much of what I had outlined *a la prima* died in its infancy.

My activity transferred itself to other higher spheres where, just as in the upper layers of the Atmosphere, there is more beneficial Quietude and Freedom for the Spirit.

However, in publishing my dramatic efforts, I desired, in a sense even of affirmation, to preserve the beloved number Three, as much for Reality as for Dialetics.

The Germans have a saying:

Ein Mal ist kein Mal.
Drei Mal ist Ein Mal.

We Russians say instead:

Even a house isn't built without the Trinity.

Therefore, collecting several scenes I had written some time ago based on Tarelkin's Last Monologue in *The Case*, which were just lying idle, I strengthened my heart, as they say, joined them together hastily, divided the joke into three Acts, and in such a half-reworked form present them now to the public, not without a certain timidity, begging it to approach them with indulgence.

If these scenes grant the public a few minutes of simple joyous laughter and in so doing provide an occasion to forget for a time the cares each new day brings, as the Scriptures tell us, then I shall consider myself completely gratified.

Kobylinka
October 31, 1868

CAST OF CHARACTERS

MAKSIM KUZMICH VARRAVIN

CAPTAIN POLUTATARINOV,[1] a military greatcoat with sleeves, little green eyes and crutches } one person

KANDID KASTOROVICH TARELKIN
SILA SILICH KOPYLOV } one person

ANTIOKH ELPIDIFOROVICH OKH, high-ranking police officer

IVAN ANTONOVICH RASPLYUEV, fulfilling the responsibility of a district inspector, has become more corpulent and acquired a certain bearing

CHIBISOV
IBISOV } clerks
OMEGA

FLEGONT EGORYCH POPUGAYCHIKOV,[2] a merchant

CHVANKIN,[3] a landowner

KRESTYAN KRESTYANOVICH UNMOEGLICHKEIT,[4] a doctor

LYUDMILA SPIRIDONOVNA BRANDAKHLYSTOVA, a laundress, a huge woman about forty years old

MAVRUSHA, a cook

PAKHOMOV, a yardkeeper

KACHALA[5]
SHATALA[6] } police officers of heroic proportions

VANECHKA, Rasplyuev's son; a scribe

Tarelkin's creditors:

FIRST CREDITOR
SECOND CREDITOR } of an excitable nature

THIRD CREDITOR, a leechlike person of a litigious nature

FOURTH CREDITOR, a stalwart type, with a huge moustache and the body of a crocodile

OTHER CREDITORS *ad libitum*, all of them are attired in the most fantastic array of furs and coats

CLERKS

BRANDAKHLYSTOVA'S CHILDREN

[1] A telling name meaning someone who is half Tatar.
[2] A telling name suggesting a parrot.
[3] A telling name suggesting a braggart.
[4] The doctor's last name is the German word for *impossibility*.
[5] A telling name suggesting rocking, swinging, reeling.
[6] A telling name suggesting swaying, shaking.

ACT ONE

(*A room, in the middle of which is a door leading to the entrance hall. To the right, another door leads to the kitchen and the back passage. To the left, a bed behind a screen. Everything in disorder. Tarelkin enters carrying all his personal belongings. Very preoccupied; rearranges the furniture.*)

SCENE 1

TARELKIN (*alone*): Decided! . . . I don't want to live . . . Poverty has exhausted me, my creditors have torn me to pieces, my superiors have driven me to the grave! . . . I'll die. But I'm not going to die like any old horse dies. Any fool can die according to the law of nature. Your time comes and that's that! No—I'm going to die in defiance of the law and nature. I'm going to die for my own pleasure and satisfaction; I'm going to die like nobody ever died before! . . . What's death? The end of sufferings. Well then, an end to my sufferings too! . . . What's death? The end of all accounts! I too have ended my accounts, liquidated my debts, gotten even with my supporters, freed myself of friends! . . . A coincidence: next to each other, in two separate apartments, live Tarelkin and Kopylov. Tarelkin is in debt, Kopylov is not in debt. Fate says, Die, Kopylov, and live, Tarelkin. —Why, Fate, says I; Fate, you're nothing but a turkey, that's what you are! —Better that Tarelkin die, and the fortunate Kopylov live. (*Musing.*) Decided! . . . Tarelkin has died! . . . Down with the old rags! (*Removes his toupee.*) Down with all this sham. Give me nature! —Long live nature! (*Takes out his false teeth and puts on a coat belonging to Kopylov.*) That's the way! (*Stepping back to the rear of the stage, he adjusts a pair of side whiskers, stoops, assumes the appearance of a man near sixty and then advances downstage.*) I have the honor to present: retired Aulic Councillor Sila Silich Kopylov. Here is my service record. (*Displays a service record.*) Single. No relatives, no children; I have no family: I don't owe anybody a thing—I don't want to know anybody; I'm my own master! Here is my apartment,

my belongings! . . . Oh you, all of you, forgive me! . . .
Farewell, you roaring beasts my superiors—farewell, comrades of Judas! . . . My friends, you gravediggers, you
traitors—farewell! My creditors, you thieves, you leeches,
you crocodiles . . . farewell! Tarelkin exists no longer.
Another road of life, other desires, another world, another heaven!! . . . (*Strolls about the room.*) From
theory I pass now to practice. I've just come from
Schlüsselburg; I've buried Kopylov's bones; the case is
settled; I've got the papers—it's all finished over there!
. . . Now here, in Petersburg, my own official and un-
doubted death has to be arranged. For that the police
are notified; my colleagues are invited; the windows are
veiled; a mysterious semidarkness hangs over the room;
the stuffiness and odor are unbearable . . . In the casket
lies my dummy, wrapped in wadding, dressed in my
uniform, correctly, not at all badly . . . In a serious and
dignified sort of way! However, the odor has to be increased for the sake of curious eyes. (*In high spirits,
shouts.*) Mavrusha!! Mavrusha—you robber—where are
you?

SCENE 2

Tarelkin; Mavrusha comes in.

MAVRUSHA: What do you want?
TARELKIN: Do you understand, my faithful friend Mavrusha,
    the kind of immortal game I'm playing?
MAVRUSHA: The what?
TARELKIN: No—that thick skull of yours will never under-
    stand such loftiness . . . go on and buy some more rotten
    fish.
MAVRUSHA: Some more! Don't we have enough already?
TARELKIN: No, not enough yet—now be off with you! (*Mav-
    rusha goes out. Tarelkin shouts after her.*) Make it fast!

Scene 3

Tarelkin alone.

TARELKIN (*pacing the room*): Everything the way it should be . . . yes . . . the fish has to be stuffed into my dummy so that they'll get hit with the smell like a log on the head . . . No! (*Imagines.*) It's not enough. I want my superiors to bury me at their own expense! I don't want this immortal death of mine to cost me a red cent— and so it will be! It'll all go like clockwork; it just has to be done up nicely. —Mavrusha knows her lessons; for already a month now Varravin's most private correspondence has been here (*indicates the place*), right under my jacket!! He's already discovered it's gone, is looking for it, and is furious with me. Therefore, as soon as he hears the news he'll arrive here in a rage and rush the funeral proceedings so as to start searching my apartment as quickly as possible—ha, ha, ha, ha! . . . Ohhhh! —you're the one, you robber, who drove me live into the grave! You were the cause of my death. There is no mercy for you. We're fighting to the last. You'll buy back these letters of yours at the price of blood—your own blood. Or no! At the price of your money, the money you stole—the money that's dearer to you than children, than a wife, than even yourself. Slowly, delightfully, ruble by ruble, sum by sum I'll pull this money out of you with terrible pains. And myself I'll conceal in a safe place and laugh—and it'll be sweet to laugh while you writhe and shrivel from those pains! God! What infinite sweetness there is in vengeance. What balsam it is to place vengeance on an open wound . . . (*Extracts a packet of letters from beneath his waistcoat.*) Here they are—these letters (*strokes the packet*) lie on my very heart; they keep it warm! —They're my flesh and blood! —This is the wickedest, most malicious of all Varravin's deeds, a bouquet, which could be presented to Satan himself as a token of love and esteem. (*Carefully conceals the papers beneath his waistcoat and then buttons himself up.*)

SCENE 4

Tarelkin; Mavrusha comes in.

TARELKIN (*going to meet her*): Hurry up, hurry up, Mavrusha—they'll be here soon—time is of the essence . . .
(*Takes the fish and covers his nose.*) Phew, the devil
take it! (*Goes out.*)

SCENE 5

Mavrusha alone; then Tarelkin.

MAVRUSHA: Look what he's thought up, the devil . . . Help
me, he says—then later on he'll cheat me. Did you ever
see such a rascal! (*Goes about tidying up the room.*)
TARELKIN (*coming back*): Now see to it, old girl, that you
don't start making up any stories. The best thing is not
to talk too much, understand? Just sit yourself down
and wail. Make sure you keep on repeating: "There's
nothing left at all. He lived honestly but died poor!"
Understand? "There's no money; nothing even to bury
him with. And he's already beginning to rot, that's why
there's such an awful smell here. What's there to be
done?" And then do like this with your hands. (*Makes
a gesture. Mavrusha imitates him.*) That's the way! . . .
(*Thinks.*) And to Varravin say: "The police are going
to come, and they'll confiscate all his belongings. There
were some papers left behind, and they'll grab them,
too. It's not good." Understand?
MAVRUSHA: Yes, Sir, I understand.
TARELKIN: Well then, on your way. (*A noise is heard.*) It's
them—my God, it's them. (*The initial timidity in his
voice gives way to determination.*) Well, listen now—
as soon as the stink gets the best of them, you lead them
over here so they won't spend any more time than necessary creeping around the coffin. Follow me?
MAVRUSHA: Yes, Sir, completely. (*Goes out.*)

SCENE 6

Tarelkin alone.

TARELKIN (*hiding himself behind the screen*): So . . . here
they are . . . (*Listens.*) Good luck . . . There's a lot of
them . . . They're talking . . . (*Listens.*) They're making
noise . . . (*Listens.*) What's that? . . . Heavens! . . .
(*Excited.*) Aha—it's been discovered! Discovered . . .
(*Mavrusha's wailing can be heard.*) My God . . . we're
lost . . . (*Ducks behind the screen.*)

SCENE 7

*Varravin, followed by a crowd of clerks, Mavrusha among
them.*

MAVRUSHA (*yelling and weeping*): This way, gentlemen . . .
this way . . . oh . . . ah . . . oh . . .
VARRAVIN (*stopping at the threshold*): Phew, damn it, what
a smell!
CLERKS (*coming in, their noses covered, and starting to remove their rubbers*): Phew, phew—it's unbearable.
CHIBISOV: It's impossible to stay here even a minute!
MAVRUSHA (*yelling*): This way please, gentlemen, this way,
Sirs . . . oh . . .
VARRAVIN: Why is there such a penetrating odor here?
MAVRUSHA (*as before*): My dear Sirs . . . why shouldn't there
be . . . a smell . . . he died poor, ohhhh . . . I'm the
one who paid for the coffin, ohhhh, and there's nothing
left for the funeral, ohhhh. That's why he's lying there,
the poor soul, and smelling! Ohhhh . . .
VARRAVIN: Is there really nothing at all left to pay for his
funeral with?
MAVRUSHA (*as before*): Nothing, my dear, nothing at all.
Pretty soon the police will be here. They'll take everything they find; they'll grab his papers—and what kind
of papers—he himself used to always keep a-l-l of them
hidden away . . . ohhhh . . .
VARRAVIN (*eagerly*): He left papers behind, you say?

MAVRUSHA: That he did, Sir, yes.

VARRAVIN: Show them to me.

MAVRUSHA: Show them to you? Now, you mean? He has to be buried first, Sir; he smells so badly, it's just awful like this.

VARRAVIN (*aside*): He does have to be buried . . . My most confidential papers disappeared—that is, they were stolen, and stolen by whom?! . . . By *him*!! . . . And then suddenly he dies! Isn't there some kind of a trick here too?! . . . Nothing to be done, though—he has to be buried and then the papers found. Those papers absolutely have to be found, at any cost! . . . (*Turns to the clerks.*) Gentlemen, what must we do? You see, it's almost scandalous. There's nothing to bury him with, and if they find out about it in the city they'll say, He died of starvation; his comrades abandoned him; his superiors didn't look after him. That's no good at all; even public opinion will not take our side.

CLERKS: Yes, yes, it won't take our side.

VARRAVIN: Then here's what, gentlemen. Let's do the Christian thing; let's help a comrade, shall we? Even our superiors will look kindly upon us for that. Nowadays everything communal is fashionable, and from a philosophical standpoint, what is a community if not a pooling of resources?

CHIBISOV: Yes, gentlemen, His Excellency is right—even the magazines show it: community is pooling, and pooling is community.

CLERKS: Yes indeed, that's so.

CHIBISOV (*exaltedly*): Pooling! Community! Brotherhood!! (*Makes his way to the door and looks for his rubbers.*)

IBISOV (*affecting the same tone*): Yes, yes! . . . The Lord loves the gracious giver. (*Points to heaven with a finger, then makes his way to the door, also in search of his rubbers.*)

3RD CLERK: Splendid! . . . Splendid and warm! . . . From the common heart! (*The same movements as Chibisov and Ibisov.*)

4TH CLERK: Many a little makes a mickle. (*The same movements—a general flight.*)

VARRAVIN (*barring the door and holding the clerks back*):

Gentlemen, what are you doing?! Wait a while. You shouldn't do that! No, you shouldn't do that. (*Grasps Chibisov and Ibisov by the arms and leads them, along with the other clerks, toward the proscenium.*) Gentlemen, listen to me—we're one family after all, aren't we? (*Shakes them by the arms.*) Aren't we one family?

CHIBISOV and IBISOV (*jumping from pain*): Yes! Yes! We're one family.

VARRAVIN: Our younger brother is in need. (*Shakes them by the arms.*) Are we not warm people?

CHIBISOV and IBISOV (*jumping and twisting from pain*): Yes, yes—damn it—we're warm people.

VARRAVIN: Right you are!! We respond sincerely, with open hearts!!

CHIBISOV and IBISOV (*tearing free of him*): Yes indeed, sincerely, with open hearts! (*All start running out.*)

VARRAVIN (*catching them*): No, no—I'm telling you again, not like that. (*Aside.*) What vipers, they just won't give in! (*Aloud.*) If you please, gentlemen, we'll arrange it like this. (*Gathers the clerks around him.*) Are you ready now to perform a good deed?

CLERKS: Ready, ready.

VARRAVIN: Then for a good deed you'll willingly take money from another won't you, that is from another's pocket?

CLERKS: From another's pocket? Willingly, very willingly.

VARRAVIN (*tenderly*): In that case each of you take another ever so lightly by the collar. That's the way, good. (*Divides them into pairs.*)

OMEGA (*running up*): Your Excellency! There's nobody to take me by the collar?

VARRAVIN: Then you take yourself.

OMEGA (*bowing*): Yes, Sir. (*Withdraws and takes himself by the collar.*)

VARRAVIN (*reviewing the clerks*): Splendid, gentlemen, splendid! (*Tenderly.*) Now each of you take the other's billfold. (*Noise and scrambling; the clerks extract the billfolds from each others' pockets.*)

VARRAVIN (*feasting his eyes on the scene*): Lovely! Like brothers! There's true community! Now, count out three rubles apiece, but no more than three rubles! No more, mind!

CLERKS (*shouting*): Gentlemen, three each . . . But no more, no more! (*They count out the money. Varravin accepts it and advances to the proscenium.*)

VARRAVIN (*to the audience*): What warmth, what fervor! . . . They even have to be restrained . . . (*Moved.*) Such offerings as these move me deeply. (*To the clerks.*) Now, gentlemen, return the billfolds. That's the way. I thank you. Permit me to extend you my sincere, heartfelt thanks. You have done a fine deed—a good deed. Your younger brother is dying in want—and you at once . . . I thank you! I am moved—I am weeping—you weep, too! (*All weep.*) Embrace one another. (*They embrace each other.*)

OMEGA (*running up to Varravin*): Your Excellency, I have nobody to embrace.

VARRAVIN (*wiping a tear*): Embrace her. (*Points to Mavrusha. Omega embraces her.*)

MAVRUSHA: What are you doing, you sinner, you shameless person, you . . . What are you up to?! Get away . . .

VARRAVIN (*to Mavrusha*): Come over here, you poor woman! Are you an orphan?

MAVRUSHA (*wailing*): Yes, Sir, Excellency, an orphan! A pooooor orphan!

VARRAVIN: You remained alone? (*Puts the money in a billfold.*)

MAVRUSHA: Alone, Sir, alone, all alone. (*Sticks out a hand.*)

VARRAVIN (*putting the billfold in a pocket*): You should know, my dear, that there are good people (*points to heaven*) and heaven! (*To the clerks with feeling.*) Let's be off now, gentlemen! We have to bury Tarelkin!!

CLERKS (*approaching Mavrusha in high spirits and thumping her on the shoulder*): Yes, there are good people and heaven! (*They go out.*)

SCENE 8

Mavrusha remains motionless; Tarelkin dashes out from behind the screen.

TARELKIN (*throwing himself at Mavrusha and embracing her*): Yes, Mavrushenka, there are good people and heaven!!

MAVRUSHA (*breaking free of him*): The lot of you can go to hell! What did I get out of this little game of yours?

TARELKIN (*joyously*): Splendid, Mavrushenka, splendid; just splendid. Hooray!! . . . Like a mountain lifted from my shoulders! I'll never forget what you did for me.

MAVRUSHA: Never? You'll deceive me!

TARELKIN: Deceive you? I should say I won't. (*Walks around the room, thinking.*) Varravin'll finish it all off fast and arrange the funeral in the twinkling of an eye. Then he'll go tearing after the papers, and you lead him on . . . Don't give in quickly—but afterward hand him what he wants . . . Devil with him . . . the papers aren't worth a damn. I appropriated the really good ones. After you give him the papers, swear by everything that's holy that there weren't any other papers besides the ones you gave him. Tell him you know it for certain. Clear?

MAVRUSHA: I understand.

TARELKIN: Now on your way—and don't forget to spread more fish around. (*Mavrusha goes out.*)

SCENE 9

TARELKIN (*alone*): How should I plan my next steps? Which direction should I follow? What place should I warm next? Should I bide my time for a long time, and afterward, how can I just suddenly reappear? How should I go about screwing money out of Varravin? (*Gaily.*) In what sums, big or small? Eh? I think maybe small at first, but later on—I'll keep shaking him till he's dizzy—ha, ha, ha! (*Walks about. Noise. Leaps behind the screen.*)

SCENE 10

Varravin comes in. Tarelkin behind the screen.

VARRAVIN (*meditating*): Died! He must have died, beyond any doubt, because he's become so putrid! . . . There's no news that could have brought me such pleasure, I should say such delight . . .

TARELKIN (*behind the screen, aside*): You said it.

VARRAVIN: It's as though a whole mountain of filth, slops, and every kind of carrion tumbled from my shoulders.

TARELKIN (*aside*): Merci!

VARRAVIN: It's as though after long years of a wearying thirst I suddenly drew into myself limpid spring water—and became refreshed. The laziest and most restless creature that ever was crawled back into its hole.

TARELKIN (*aside*): Enough, don't you think?

VARRAVIN: The most loathsome toad returned to its burrow; the most venomous and dangerous snake lived out its life cycle and in a place ordained by fate rolled over and died! . . . Died! . . . The rottenest soul departed the foulest body. How could he not stink? In my opinion, he doesn't stink enough; the smell ought to be greater.

TARELKIN (*aside*): Thank you; that I didn't expect! Are those his parting words?! Hold on! —I'll have my own to say.

VARRAVIN: Everything's ready now—everything's ordered—everything's arranged: driver, roads, grave . . . I had them dig out a hole six feet deep—where he's going, that robber (*makes a gesture*) —and that'll be that!!

TARELKIN: And that'll be that? Really? We'll see. (*Improvizes.*)

> General Varravin, Sir,
> Said his parting words to me;
> But, alas, he never guessed
> What the outcome here would be.

VARRAVIN (*shouting*): Hey, you, where are you? —Are you there? —You, woman!

SCENE 11

Varravin; Mavrusha comes in. Tarelkin behind the screen.

VARRAVIN: Come here, you stupid wench.

MAVRUSHA (*approaching*): Yes, Sir.

VARRAVIN: Do you know who I am?

MAVRUSHA: No, I don't, Sir.

VARRAVIN: I'm a general.

MAVRUSHA: Yes, Sir, Your Lordship.

VARRAVIN: Do you know what a general is?

MAVRUSHA: No, I don't, Sir, Your Lordship.

VARRAVIN: General means that I can take you and have you ground to dust.

MAVRUSHA (*falling on her knees*): Have mercy, Sir, Your Grace.

VARRAVIN: Show me at once where his papers are.

MAVRUSHA: Spare me, Your Grace—I'll show you everything you want—everything. (*They go out.*)

SCENE 12

TARELKIN (*emerging from behind the screen*): Go look; go look for nothing—for the exercise—ha, ha, ha! (*Paces the room, rubbing his hands together.*) I have my treasure right here with me! (*Thumps himself on the chest.*) Inseparably, unquestionably, imperishably. (*Goes up to the door. Silence. Listens attentively.*) Aha . . . they're coming. (*Goes behind the screen.*)

SCENE 13

Varravin and Mavrusha come in.

VARRAVIN: No—there's nothing! . . . Incomprehensible. When I know, know for sure, that it was he—beyond a doubt—who stole those papers of mine! . . . Why once he even hinted at the likelihood of it in a kind of strange and impudent way. That stuff, he said, would be good for heating my future apartment. Oh! He was the kind of swindler it wouldn't be enough just to tear to pieces live.

SCENE 14

Rasplyuev comes in rapidly, followed by Shatala and Kachala, who stop at the door.

RASPLYUEV: I have the honor to present myself to Your Excellency for orders.

VARRAVIN: Who are you?

RASPLYUEV: Police Inspector Ivan Rasplyuev.

VARRAVIN: Why didn't you take measures to preserve the property of the deceased?

RASPLYUEV: All measures were taken.

VARRAVIN: Which ones?

RASPLYUEV: A guard was stationed outside; four officers. I myself was here, completely zealous in the fulfillment of my duty . . . Nothing has been lost—there is no cause for you to be upset.

VARRAVIN: Remember—the responsibility is yours.

RASPLYUEV: The sternest measures were taken! Judge for yourself—over there (*points to the door*) one officer merely stretched a hand toward the deceased's belongings, and I grabbed hold of it so he's still walking around even now with it in a sling. Please have a look for yourself. (*Points to the door.*)

VARRAVIN: Yet the maid here complains that the property was plundered. The deceased's papers were lost, she says.

RASPLYUEV: She's lying—permit me to interrogate her.

VARRAVIN: Interrogate.

RASPLYUEV (*to Mavrusha*): What papers were lost? —What property was plundered? Speak!

MAVRUSHA: Papers, Sir, papers; just like what Their Lordships are writing—the same sort. (*Varravin withdraws to a side, reflecting.*)

RASPLYUEV: Come here! (*Conducts Mavrusha to the opposite side of the stage and holds a fist up under her nose.*) How many teeth have you got left, tell me how many, you old hag—I'll settle everything.

MAVRUSHA (*loudly*): I don't know, Sir, I don't know. I just happened to say that—I didn't see anyone and I didn't hear anything.

RASPLYUEV (*to Varravin*): You see, Your Excellency. She says she saw nothing and heard nothing. Now you know the kind of people you're dealing with here. They'll lie through their teeth, but if you slap them down from the start you'll hear the different tune they'll be singing.

VARRAVIN (*thinking*): Curious . . . Well, carry out your orders. Remove the body—but as fast as you can; there's no point to keeping it here any length of time.

RASPLYUEV: We'll remove it at once, Your Excellency. (*To*

his police officers.) Hey, fellows, drag him out! (*Shatala and Kachala leave quickly, followed by Rasplyuev.*)

SCENE 15

Varravin; then Tarelkin.

VARRAVIN (*pensively*): Now where could those papers of mine have gone to? I'm losing my wits. I anticipate everything; I suspect everything. There's one thing I am afraid of: he took them and dispatched them in an insurance letter to my superior . . . Hm . . .

TARELKIN (*emerges from behind the screen and speaks in a voice different from his own*): Lamenting, Your Excellency? Have you lost a servant and now realize your loss?

VARRAVIN: Lamenting, yes; I've lost a comrade, a colleague. Did you happen to know him?

TARELKIN: I did, as a neighbor. Are you looking for something?

VARRAVIN: Yes. Some official little trifles.

TARELKIN: Certainly. Everything has its purpose in life. Well, have you found what you're looking for?

VARRAVIN: No, I'm afraid I haven't.

TARELKIN: That is regrettable. It happens, though. Seems that one thing's near and yet far, while another thing's far and yet near. (*Thumps himself on the chest. Aside.*) Well, crocodile? Every dog has his day.

VARRAVIN: What were you saying?

TARELKIN: I was saying, Your Excellency, that oftentimes we can't have what we see, while sometimes we have what we can't see. (*Noise. Shatala and Kachala appear carrying a coffin in the rear of the stage.*) Ah, there they go dragging him out. Your Excellency, please permit an old acquaintance to say a final word in parting.

VARRAVIN: By all means.

TARELKIN (*solemnly*): Organs of civil order—halt. (*The officers come to a halt.*) My dear Sirs, Your Excellency! Alas, Tarelkin is no longer! The silent abyss of the grave has opened before us its black mouth and Tarelkin has vanished into it! . . . He has spent himself and vanished into thin air—he is no more. And what lies before us? —An empty grave and only . . . A great puzzle, an incomprehensible occurrence. I now address my words to you, the cleverest of this world. Tell us, you discoverers of invisible worlds and calculators of innumerable stars, tell us—where is Tarelkin? Hm . . . (*Raises a finger.*) Come now!

Yes, esteemed visitors, we mourn the passing of Tarelkin! . . . Gone is the zealous doer, gone the commander of the advance regiment. Tarelkin was always and everywhere at the fore. No sooner would the sound of change taking place reach his ears or the roar of the attainment of perfection, then he would at once appear shouting, Forward!! . . . When a standard was borne, Tarelkin marched ahead of the standard; when progress was proclaimed, there he was—in advance of progress—so that Tarelkin was in the fore and progress brought up the rear! —When the emancipation of women came, Tarelkin shed tears over the fact that he was not a woman so that he could remove his crinoline before the public and show it . . . how one ought to emancipate one's self. When the existence of humaneness was announced, Tarelkin at once became so permeated with it he stopped eating chickens, as his weaker and, so to say, younger brothers, and turned instead to turkeys and geese, as the stronger. Tarelkin is no longer, and the warmer are needy in their ardor; those in the forefront have been left without their front, and those in the back have gotten the rear! Tarelkin is no longer, and the earth has begun to grow cold, progress has become sunk in thought, humaneness has been widowed . . .

But how, you ask, was he rewarded by his fellowmen for such a passion for action? . . . I shall tell you the answer—no, not the answer: Irony is before you! A simple coffin, a carter, a dray hearse and a cheap grave . . . However, take a look—beside this wretched coffin stands a dignitary (*points to Varravin*) —the lord and master of this world, girdled with power. What does his presence here reveal to us? Was he led here and placed beside this coffin in our midst by hypocrisy or by shrewdness, or by some self-seeking goal? Oh, no! By his very presence he pays respect to poverty in the ranks, to destitution in decorations, to a servant in uniform—a servant who will carry even into the grave with him the most treasured personal belongings of His Excellency . . .

VARRAVIN (*starting*): What do you mean?!

TARELKIN (*continuing*): Tears . . . (*To Varravin.*) I am speaking about your tears, Your Excellency. (*Varravin makes an affirmative gesture and slowly leaves.*) Thus let us show our esteem for this simple but distinguished coffin by our warm tears and let us say: Peace be unto your ashes, honest toiler in the bitter field of civil activity. (*Bows and withdraws in the direction of the proscenium.*)

RASPLYUEV (*to the police officers*): Carry him out. (*They carry away the coffin. The clerks follow them.*)

SCENE 16

Rasplyuev and Tarelkin.

RASPLYUEV (*donning a cocked hat*): Precisely. Your observation, my dear Sir, was quite correct—the soul is immortal.

TARELKIN (*taking him by the hands; in high spirits*): True, isn't it? Immortal, that means that mortals do not die.

RASPLYUEV: Yes indeed! —They do not die!! (*Muses.*) But how do you mean, "do not die"?

TARELKIN (*firmly*): They live . . . But, you know, over there (*pointing*) —far away!!

RASPLYUEV: Yes—far away!! Yes indeed. Tell me, what rank did he hold?

TARELKIN: Oh, a high one. Collegiate councillor. You know, he handled all the cases in Varravin's office.

RASPLYUEV: You don't say! Then why was he buried in such poverty, if I may say so . . . Why there wasn't even . . . anything to eat. That's something our religion usually prescribes, after all.

TARELKIN: Well, what can you do. He was virtuous, simple.

RASPLYUEV (*enthusiastically*): Yes! I understand . . . You know, I'll tell you something—virtue isn't rewarded in this world of ours.

TARELKIN: How right you are! It certainly isn't rewarded!
Who is there who'd reward it? People? Have you seen
them?

RASPLYUEV: I've seen them.

TARELKIN: What kind of a heart do they have, did you see
that too?

RASPLYUEV: I saw. A wolf's!

TARELKIN: Exactly—a wolf's! (*Takes Rasplyuev by the hand.*)
You've suffered then, have you?

RASPLYUEV (*winking at the audience*): So-so. —And you?

TARELKIN: Worse than a dog!

RASPLYUEV: You don't mean it. Why in the civil service, I
thought . . . that . . . doesn't happen—especially when
you've already got a title.

TARELKIN: On the contrary—that's when it's all the more
painful.

RASPLYUEV (*astonished*): All the more painful??! But just
among yourselves, never in public, huh?

TARELKIN: Of course, it stands to reason: only God and I
know!

RASPLYUEV (*chuckling*): Ha, ha! —Tell me, would you:
Who? How? Under what circumstances? It interests me.

TARELKIN: Why now? I imagine that after the funeral you
wouldn't refuse a little bite, would you?

RASPLYUEV: To tell the truth, I wouldn't mind it at all. This
work of ours is really a dog's—no sooner do you drag
a corpse away when you're sitting down to a good healthy
snack and a nice chat with an intelligent person.

TARELKIN: Then would it be convenient for you to come over
to my place for a bite after the ceremony?

RASPLYUEV: What ceremony? Cart him off in a wagon and
toss him into a hole. My men look after that end of
things, my dear Sir. I just have to drop by there a while
to take care of a yardkeeper, then I'll come over to you.

SCENE 17

TARELKIN (*alone*): Foresight—I thank you! How nice and
easy everything went. One thing now: prudence. —Away
from here! Tomorrow I'll give up the apartment and be
on my way! To the woods! To Moscow! —I'll hide out

there till the smoke blows over and everything quiets down again . . . I'll get packed immediately! (*Takes a suitcase.*) Immediately! Immediately!

CURTAIN

ACT TWO

(*The same room. Trunks and suitcases—everything packed. A buffet is set up in the middle of the room.*)

SCENE 1

TARELKIN (*alone; seated in a chair*): Yes indeed, only now do I understand happiness, feel it with my heart, sniff it with my nose. Here it is . . . (*Looks all around himself.*) Quiet, peace . . . independence!! There's happiness for you! . . . No boss over me, no creditors—not even friends to deprive me of a minute's rest. A fine thing I pulled off! With one stroke I shook off my old sins, all my chains crumbled to dust, all my debts have been paid off, and nature itself by the very act of my death signed: Paid in Full! In the meantime, right here, next to me, on my very heart—reserve capital! (*Takes out some papers.*) Personal papers of Varravin written in his own hand . . . A noose in which his damned head is sitting. A year or so, maybe two and everything'll quiet down, and then I'll produce them all right, produce them just for spite, damn it! It simply won't even enter his mind that I'm alive. Ha, ha, ha!!

SCENE 2

Rasplyuev comes in while Tarelkin is laying the table.

TARELKIN: Welcome.

RASPLYUEV: Thank you kindly.

TARELKIN: May I ask what delayed you?

RASPLYUEV: Couldn't help it. Had to poke around the cemetery. General Varravin himself accompanied us. (*Puts his sword and cocked hat in a corner.*)

TARELKIN (*pointing to the buffet*): Wouldn't you care to have something?

RASPLYUEV (*rubs his hands together and goes over to the table*): Don't mind if I do.

TARELKIN (*puts out wine and vodka*): As God has provided.

RASPLYUEV (*looking over the buffet with obvious pleasure*): He hasn't provided badly at all. (*Takes bread and some herring. Sighs.*) Ah me—human weaknesses. (*Wolfs down everything, then helps himself to wine.*)

TARELKIN: Wouldn't you like a little cheese with it?

RASPLYUEV (*coming over to the cheese*): Cheese? Why, of course. (*Takes some bread, breaks off a piece of cheese, wolfs them down and then empties a bottle.*)

TARELKIN (*aside*): What kind of a yap has he got?

RASPLYUEV (*chewing*): Exactly . . . you were quite right recently when you mentioned that the soul is immortal.

TARELKIN (*examining the empty bottle in the light*): Immortal, Sir . . . immortal . . .

RASPLYUEV (*helping himself to more cheese*): And you know —that it can't eat or drink. (*Chews.*)

TARELKIN (*gathering up all the empty dishes*): Yes, not at all.

RASPLYUEV (*chewing*): And if the soul asked for a little something to eat, there'd be nothing for it . . . nothing doing.

TARELKIN: Right, nothing doing. (*Wants to pour a liquor glass for Rasplyuev.*)

RASPLYUEV (*holding out a tumbler instead*): No, put it in this one. (*Drinks.*) Hey there, soul-my-girl, lift your feet!

TARELKIN (*bringing him more bread*): What a yap! A bottom-

less pit, that's what! Where on earth does he put it all?
(*Rasplyuev downs a chunk of bread.*) More yet! What
if he bursts? (*Aloud.*) Tell me, how do you feel?

RASPLYUEV: Well, I'll tell you—I still don't feel anything.

TARELKIN: Really?

RASPLYUEV: That's the kind of nature I've got: an organ!
(*Fills a tumbler of vodka.*)

TARELKIN: That's vodka.

RASPLYUEV: Vodka—yes, vodka. (*Drinks.*) It's all the same
to me, my friend. (*Tarelkin looks at the floor.*) You
looking for something?

TARELKIN: Just looking—maybe your bottom's bulging.
Doesn't it pass right through you?

RASPLYUEV (*sitting up in his chair*): No, Sir! I'm pretty
strong—it doesn't pass right through. Did you hear,
Paganini had a good instrument?

TARELKIN: I heard.

RASPLYUEV: Well, I've got a better one.

TARELKIN: I believe it.

RASPLYUEV: I'll tell you a story about this instrument of mine,
my good man. Once I come into this here tavern. I ask
for a roll and tea. Then my instrument starts up and
plays. What songs! Asking for work, it was. Nothing to
be done. Give me a portion of ham, I says, a little
caviar, I says, plenty of vodka, I says. Let's have a little
snack, I think to myself. Ate everything, I did, but just
imagine, my dear Sir, the instrument refuses to work!

TARELKIN: Tsk, tsk . . .

RASPLYUEV: All right, I think to myself. So I pull off another
hunk of bread, ask for some cheese, down some Sherry.
But you know—I feel like eating even more. Pfaugh, I
says, what is this: some kind of a trick you're pulling?
Let's have some pancakes, says I! Down went a dozen
of them. A second batch was despatched in pursuit—
this just got the teeth excited—and a third! No matter
what, though—the instrument still kept quiet!!

TARELKIN: Extraordinary!

RASPLYUEV: The situation, I see, is not good—all my abysses,
like they say, gaped open. Then, Sir, I ordered to be
served in our own style, in the Russian style: a loaf of
black bread, three herrings—each one solid like a log,
and a pitcher of *kvas*. Then I crossed myself—that's the

way I felt—and I dug into the eating. Well, it's as though I got stuck. This is a fire I've got here that can't be put out (*smacks himself on the belly*) and a worm that can't get enough to feed on.

SCENE 3

The same. Lyudmila Spiridonovna comes in.

LYUDMILA: Tell me, Sirs —Does Sila Silich Kopylov live here?

RASPLYUEV (*eating*): Here, dearie, here.

TARELKIN: What do you want, lady?

LYUDMILA: Well, where can I find him, huh?

TARELKIN: Why here he is—me.

LYUDMILA: But they told me you died.

TARELKIN: No, they're just playing stupid jokes, that's all, jokes.

LYUDMILA: Aha! Well then, I'm very glad. Where else could I lay my head. Come now, don't you remember your Lyudmilushka?

TARELKIN: What Lyudmilushka?

LYUDMILA: Lyudmila Spiridonovna—you tempter, you! (*Rasplyuev and Tarelkin laugh.*)

TARELKIN (*showing off and attempting to recall*): Amalia . . . or Rosalia . . . there was a certain Kapalia, I remember . . . But Lyudmila, no—I don't recollect any Lyudmila. Are you from the ballet, or from school?

LYUDMILA: From the laundry trade!

TARELKIN (*suspiciously*): From the laundry trade?!! I don't know anyone from any laundry trade.

LYUDMILA: Doesn't your heart tell you anything?

TARELKIN: I'm afraid not; it doesn't tell me a thing.

LYUDMILA: Here she is before you now.

TARELKIN: Really? Well now! This is some kind of a monster! No, devil with you—I don't understand such a woman.

LYUDMILA: You don't? Oh my! Don't you want to see the children?

TARELKIN: What children? What are you up to? I never had any children.

LYUDMILA (*to Rasplyuev*): Now you see how they are, Sir. First they give you children, then afterward they don't want to know you. (*Opens the door.*) Hey, children, come in here! (*Two small children come running in.*)

TARELKIN: What's going on here? —My God!

LYUDMILA: Well, children, here's your daddy . . . Handsome, isn't he, huh? Be kind to him, however he is. (*The children throw themselves on Tarelkin. He recoils from them.*)

TARELKIN: Away, away, you little devils, away I say!!! (*In despair.*) What, my whole life?! With a laundress?!! Never.

LYUDMILA (*falling on his chest and caressing him*): Enough now, Silich, enough. Let's make peace—it's not the first time we've quarreled, after all. Oh! Silich! Silich! Come now! You've gotten older . . . Yes, yes, you did get older. Why a person wouldn't recognize you. You're all pale, like a bare knee. It's really true, with the water here in Petersburg (*making a gesture with her hand*) how can you put on weight or get filled up enough? You know, Silich, the moment I saw you I felt two changes in me— one on account of my flaming passion, the other on account of your cruel coldness to me. (*Caresses him.*) Silich, dear.

TARELKIN: Get away from me, vile woman—away! I don't know you—away! And take those brats with you—or else I'll throw them out the window.

LYUDMILA (*to Rasplyuev*): Did you hear what he said, Sir? You're a witness! That's how he drives away his off-spring. I beg you, Sir, tame him, the animal that he is.

RASPLYUEV: Go to the police. You can file a complaint there to the sergeant on duty.

LYUDMILA: Yes, I'll go to them. Goodbye, Sir. (*Takes the children.*) I'll file it right away, I will . . . (*Goes out.*)

SCENE 4

Rasplyuev, Tarelkin, Varravin in disguise wearing a threadbare military great-coat, a wig, a bushy moustache, green spectacles. He speaks in a clipped military style, walks with a limp and supports himself with a crutch. A crowd of creditors. Noise and loud voices can be heard, followed by a knocking at the door.

TARELKIN: Who is it? Who's out there? (*The creditors come in noisily, Varravin after them.*) What do you want?

1ST CREDITOR: Please tell us, where is Kandid Tarelkin?

2ND CREDITOR: Where is collegiate councillor Tarelkin?

VARRAVIN (*changing his voice*): Where is that swindler Tarelkin? (*Bangs his crutch.*)

TARELKIN (*aside*): Ahhhh . . . My creditors. What ugly mugs . . . (*Aloud.*) Tarelkin? He died, gentlemen, he died.

1ST CREDITOR: Oh, that crook—he did it on purpose.

2ND CREDITOR: I don't agree, I demand him.

VARRAVIN: He cut his throat. With a dagger yet, no ordinary knife.

3RD CREDITOR (*in a whining voice*): There you have it! I ask you now, where are our laws? Why that's robbery!!

4TH CREDITOR (*his whole body trembling*): That's . . . dis . . . hon . . . est!!!

1ST CREDITOR (*shouting*): I tell you, I'll find him at the very bottom of hell if I have to!

2ND CREDITOR (*shouting*): What kind of nonsense are you talking? What hell?

1ST CREDITOR: Nevertheless, I can look for my property wherever I want.

2ND CREDITOR: Go look then; I spit on your property.

1ST CREDITOR: And I likewise on yours. (*Spits and rubs his leg.*) See!

1ST and 2ND CREDITORS (*getting excited, and together*): How dare you! At whom? I . . . I! . . .

VARRAVIN (*separating them*): Stop it, gentlemen, enough. You're not here for that. Let's have his personal effects! (*Bangs with his crutch.*)

CREDITORS (*shouting*): There you are! Let's have his personal effects?!

TARELKIN (*plugging his ears*): The police took every last thing there was.

1ST CREDITOR: Then his belongings are lost too? That—that's a catastrophe!!

3RD CREDITOR (*addressing the audience*): Well, I'm asking you, where are our laws?

4TH CREDITOR (*as before*): That's . . . dis . . . honest!!

2ND CREDITOR: Well then, let's go to the police—the police are our only salvation.

ALL THE CREDITORS (*shouting*): To the police! To the police!
TARELKIN (*accompanying them*): To the police! To the
police!
RASPLYUEV (*gets up from behind the table and moves downstage*): That's right, to the police! Our only salvation
is the police.
4TH CREDITOR (*lagging behind somewhat*): That's . . .
dis . . . hon . . . est!!! (*Turns quickly on his heels
and goes out. Tarelkin shows the creditors out, then
closes the door behind them.*)

SCENE 5

Rasplyuev and Tarelkin.

RASPLYUEV: Well, well. This Tarelkin had himself a fling—
hell with him . . . Some sight it'll be when these creditors start scrapping down at the police station. —My
God! I can just imagine the way it'll be: the crowd
of them, and some miserable stuff left behind not worth
a damn. They'll grab hold of some piece or other and
pull it this way and that (*makes a gesture*) . . . But
this Tarelkin, it seems, was a clever rascal. You know,
he knew how to live, and he knew when it was time to
give up the ghost . . . Where'd he be now, you think?
—He wouldn't have escaped the hell fires! They'd have
driven him out of the service—they'd have stripped him
bare—and he'd've sat it out a long time in prison. But
what about him now? Thank God—he's lying with his
belly up, paws all nicely folded over. Everything's nice
and peaceful—everyone's satisfied . . . Why even His
Excellency, General Varravin, visited his grave. There's
respect for you—a big shot like that and all of a sudden
he's condescended to accompany your mortal body to
the grave. And what's the body? —Manure, gizzards—
that's all. In property he's interested; right from the
funeral with me to the police station. Turned everything
inside out.
TARELKIN: Why, was he looking for something?
RASPLYUEV: No, nothing like that. I just suppose it was
reminiscing, that's all. Big shots are like that sometimes.

TARELKIN (*ironically*): Why, of course, he's very tender-hearted.

RASPLYUEV: I suppose so.

SCENE 6

Rasplyuev, Tarelkin, Varravin.

VARRAVIN (*comes in disguised; aside*): There's nothing there; the papers must be here then! (*Looks the room over.*) Undoubtedly must be here.

RASPLYUEV: What can I do for you, Sir?

VARRAVIN: Tell me—Tarelkin really died, did he?

TARELKIN (*throwing his arms up*): He died.

VARRAVIN: Died? Died? But tell me, how?

TARELKIN: By the law of nature and the will of the gods.

VARRAVIN (*shaking his head*): Tsk, tsk, tsk, tsk!

TARELKIN (*sizing him up*): You doubtless knew the deceased —God rest his soul.

VARRAVIN: Of course I knew him. He was a swine.

RASPLYUEV: But did you know him really very well?

VARRAVIN: Of course I did; we were friends.

TARELKIN (*surprised; aside*): Friends?! What kind of a bird is this? Never saw the likes of him before. (*Tarelkin and Varravin eye each other closely. Tarelkin, aside.*) What kind of a rascal is he?

VARRAVIN (*aside*): What a conniver's mug.

TARELKIN (*to Varravin*): Nevertheless, my dear Sir, I should point out that one shouldn't talk like that about the dead.

VARRAVIN: Then how else do you suggest that I call a pig?

TARELKIN: What do you mean?

VARRAVIN: Just this: let's say you've got somewhere—in a pigsty or cellar—a pig, and this pig, neither big nor well fed—but just a pig—should die. You wouldn't say then that a human being passed away in your cellar.

RASPLYUEV (*roaring with laughter*): That's a good one.

VARRAVIN: So you can imagine, my dear Sir, that this good-for-nothing Tarelkin . . .

TARELKIN: No, not at all, if you please.

VARRAVIN: Wha-a-at? If you please what? I've been humiliated, humiliated to the very most intimate depths of my

soul, and you don't allow me to relieve myself even
somewhat! . . . May I ask after this, who do you think
you are—well?

TARELKIN: Who am I? (*Points to Rasplyuev.*) Here's the
person you should ask— (*Rasplyuev makes an affirmative
gesture.*) And who may I ask are you?

VARRAVIN: I'm a creditor of the deceased.

TARELKIN: He never had such a creditor!

VARRAVIN: How dare you, Sir? —I—I'm a captain—Captain
Polutatarinov I am—you see? (*Points to his lame leg.*)
A Caucasian hero—I captured Shamil the Avar.

TARELKIN (*growing excited*): But I still say . . .

RASPLYUEV: Shhhh—gentlemen! No noise . . . (*To Varravin.*)
Please continue.

VARRAVIN: So you can imagine, my good man, this scoundrel,
doubtless already sensing that he was soon to die, borrowed from his friends money, goods—whatever he could
—and even from me wheedled out, in a treacherous way,
a watch, a splendid one—believe me, a "Brigette."

TARELKIN (*aside*): The rascal is lying about me as though I
were dead.

VARRAVIN: He took this watch from me and says: I'm on my
way to the theater, my dear; I've got a chain, but no
watch to go with it. Lend me yours like a good fellow.
So I did—out of friendship—believe me, just out of
friendship.

TARELKIN (*aside, clenching his fists*): I'm infuriated! To
know that he's telling lies and not be able to say: You're
lying! . . . (*Ironically.*) Well, so you lent it to him then?

VARRAVIN: Yes, I lent it to him. And do you know what that
rascal and son of rascals did? He took my watch, died,
and left me now like a fish out of water! That is why
I am one of his creditors for the amount of two hundred
rubles in silver. —But now, where is the watch? (*Looks
the room over.*) It's not down at the police station;
therefore, it must be here, it must be. And now please
let me ransack all these nooks and crannies. Maybe just
out of nastiness he shoved it into some little crevice.
Or maybe the crook left it in among books, papers, or
documents. Everything's possible! (*Walks about the
room scrutinizing everything.*) Everything's possible!!!

RASPLYUEV: Indeed! That's my rule, too—believe everything,

because everything's possible! (*Points to the door.*)
There's still some junk left—why don't you have a look?

VARRAVIN: Please place all of it under strictest sequestration.

RASPLYUEV: But that's useless now.

VARRAVIN: Why?

RASPLYUEV: Because there still wouldn't be a cent to pay off
the debts.

VARRAVIN (*angrily*): So! I'm really not surprised! Believe
me—what a scoundrel he was by nature or birth! Believe
me, his only aim was to take and afterward, naturally,
not to return, sensing that he was going to die. Great
God! If he fell into my clutches now, I'd make mince-
meat out of the bastard . . .

TARELKIN (*indignantly*): I beg your pardon!

VARRAVIN (*to Rasplyuev*): Believe me, noble Sir, that because
of such circumstances that mug of his was spat upon
more than once.

TARELKIN (*losing his patience*): This is unbearable.

VARRAVIN: He bore it.

TARELKIN: I must say that you're offending my moral sense.

VARRAVIN: Wha-a-at? Your moral sense? What sort of a drink
is that? —What kind of berries is it made out of? What
is it, some kind of delicacy? —Moral sense. —Why that
scoundrel offended all the senses.

TARELKIN: And may I inquire specifically what senses the
deceased offended?

VARRAVIN: All, I tell you, all! The sense of sight, because his
face was repulsive. The sense of hearing, because his
voice was jarring, like a cheap balalaika. The sense of
touch, because his skin, down to his very fingertips, was
covered with a clammy and malignant sweat! The sense
of smell, because he stunk of rotten meat.

TARELKIN: You're lying, Sir, he never did.

VARRAVIN: He stunk, my good man, stunk.

TARELKIN (*running to a side*): What kind of a devil is this?
Where did he appear from?

VARRAVIN (*to Rasplyuev*): So you see, noble Sir, all the senses!
All. And this bandit with his insinuating manner, with
his strength . . .

RASPLYUEV (*interrupting him*): Wait a moment!! This is a
case of the cleverest sort! These traits you pointed out

with such clarity just happen to exactly fit none other than Sila Kopylov.

VARRAVIN: How's that? My dear fellow, what are you saying?

TARELKIN: Exactly fit me? . . . How dare you? On what grounds? —By what right?

RASPLYUEV (*importantly*): Hold on there a moment. Don't start haranguing me—save your voice!

VARRAVIN: Come, come now! Wait, my dear fellow—we'll look into the matter. But I have the presentiment that I'll find my papers, that is to say my watch, here. I'm positive I will.

RASPLYUEV (*placing his arms akimbo and facing Tarelkin*): First of all—the face. (*To Varravin.*) Well? —In my opinion, you could say that the face is disagreeable.

VARRAVIN: Hm! —The face? Say it's a yap, it's a mug—but a *face*? No. Don't call it a face—you get me upset!

RASPLYUEV (*the same pose*): Almost, almost.

TARELKIN: There are many unattractive exteriors. That's no proof.

VARRAVIN: And the voice—you hear the voice?

RASPLYUEV: A cheap balalaika—yes! You're right!!

VARRAVIN: Yes—quite right!

RASPLYUEV (*the same pose*): The way you described him—just like a painting by Raphael.

VARRAVIN (*shaking Rasplyuev's hand*): Thank you.

TARELKIN (*trying to speak in a low voice*): Wait a moment, gentlemen, if you please—you're being much too rash.

VARRAVIN (*taking him by the hand*): Hands sweaty and clammy.

RASPLYUEV (*animatedly*): And the smell? (*Both approach Tarelkin and sniff him.*)

VARRAVIN and RASPLYUEV: What does he smell of?

RASPLYUEV: Something sweet almost.

VARRAVIN: Yes. But that's close, after all.

RASPLYUEV: Very close signs. A clever set of circumstances.

TARELKIN (*passionately*): Nevertheless, my dear Sir, wouldn't you care to take into consideration more fundamental traits? (*To Varravin.*) What can you prove by sniffing the air? (*To Rasplyuev.*) The late Tarelkin had beautiful hair and marvelous teeth; but I—as you see—have no hair (*indicates a completely bald head*) and no teeth (*opens his mouth*) ah . . . ah . . . ah . . . ah . . .

RASPLYUEV: Yes, that's so—quite so! . . . That's the boy, Sila Silich, you win! (*To Varravin.*) Well, Sir? Nothing left but to go home, I guess.

VARRAVIN: No, I shall go further and say, give him hair and teeth . . . and then . . .

RASPLYUEV: Oh, now . . . Captain—I was just running away with myself. No, no—it's quite out of the question! . . . The hair and teeth appear in the passport, and you can't get around them, brother, no matter how you try. As Antiokh Elpidiforych says: hair and teeth even the tsar can't give; nature, he says, gives them . . . Yes . . .

TARELKIN (*taking him by the hands*): Nicely spoken! (*They exchange bows and shake hands.*) I'll put it even stronger: God gives them!

RASPLYUEV (*with a swagger*): Ho, ho, ho (*raises a finger*) —climbing high!

VARRAVIN (*somewhat put down*): What? Perhaps, perhaps. However, while we're here we'll just have a look (*searches*) . . . Maybe Almighty God will help us somehow . . . let's see now . . . (*Opens a chest of drawers.*)

TARELKIN (*running up*): How dare you go burrowing about here, Sir?

VARRAVIN: Hello! What's this? (*Extracts a toupee and false teeth from the chest of drawers.*) Well?

RASPLYUEV (*looking in astonishment*): A toupee and teeth!

TARELKIN (*rushing at Varravin*): How can you . . .

VARRAVIN (*avoiding him*): But these aren't ones that appear in the passport. —Ha, ha, ha . . .

RASPLYUEV: Ha, ha, ha . . . Tricky business . . . What do we do?

VARRAVIN: What do you think? —Take and try the things on him.

RASPLYUEV: A most clever approach—agreed!

VARRAVIN (*to Tarelkin*): My dear fellow, would you please. (*Draws up a chair.*)

TARELKIN: What sort of nonsense is this—what stupid jokes —I don't want . . .

RASPLYUEV: We'll give you a hand. (*Takes Tarelkin and forcibly seats him in the chair.*) That's the way now! (*To Varravin, keeping Tarelkin in the chair.*) A towel, please.

VARRAVIN: Here you are, Sir. (*Hands him a towel.*)

RASPLYUEV (*tying Tarelkin's hands behind the chair*): We'll give you a hand all right.

TARELKIN: Oh, oh, oh, easier!

VARRAVIN (*putting the toupee on Tarelkin's head and straightening it out*): Now how do we go about sticking the teeth in his mouth?

RASPLYUEV: Nothing to it. You open his mouth with a stick —you saw yourself, he won't bite.

VARRAVIN (*performing the operation*): Quite right, Sir, he won't bite.

RASPLYUEV: But when the teeth are in, watch out—then he'll be able to bite. (*Tarelkin utters some unintelligible sounds when Varravin slips the teeth into his mouth.*)

VARRAVIN (*drawing back and examining Tarelkin*): My God! —What's this?! I don't believe my eyes!

RASPLYUEV: What is it, what is it?

VARRAVIN: It's Tarelkin!!

RASPLYUEV (*fear in his voice*): Really? —How could it be Tarelkin? Did you really know him well?

VARRAVIN: Like the palm of my own hand.

RASPLYUEV: My God! Wait! Don't you know that Tarelkin died, died beyond any doubt and was buried by me? General Varravin himself attended the ceremony. There can't be any doubt.

VARRAVIN: It is him! I'm telling you—it's him!

TARELKIN: Now this has gone far enough, gentlemen. Please —untie my hands—I ask you. —So what of it? —Just a coincidence—an accidental similarity, nothing else.

RASPLYUEV: Yes, yes—of course, just an accidental similarity.

VARRAVIN: Nevertheless, I advise you not to release this suspect and to take him under arrest.

TARELKIN (*attempting to free his hands*): How can you? Just try it—you'll see how far you get.

VARRAVIN (*to Rasplyuev*): You've done very well. I myself, you know, used to be in the service. It so happened that nobody could get past me, no matter how he tried. That's why I can say, hand on heart, (*puts his hand on his heart*) that there wasn't the rascal that could slip past me. (*To Rasplyuev.*) Ask him for his identity card.

RASPLYUEV: Let's have your card.

TARELKIN: Do me the favor—it's over there on the table.
VARRAVIN (*handing over the card to Rasplyuev*): Here it is—
have a look. (*Rasplyuev reads it.*)

SCENE 7

The same and Kachala with a package in his hand.

KACHALA (*handing Rasplyuev the package*): A paper, Sir,
from the department.
RASPLYUEV (*to Kachala*): Wait. (*To Varravin.*) Yes, it's so.
(*Shows him.*) Retired Aulic Councillor Sila Kopylov.
Yes . . . it's true, all right! . . . (*Taking the package
from Kachala.*) Let me have that paper. (*Breaks open
the seal and reads.*) What's this? Huh?! I don't under-
stand! (*Reads.*) I just don't understand. (*Reads.*) Draw
up a description of the personal effects of the suddenly
deceased resident of the third district Aulic Councillor
Sila . . . Sila . . . Kop . . . Kop . . . Ko-py-lov!! (*Looks
at everyone.*) Well? . . . Huh? . . . Well?!
KACHALA: But he died, Sir.
RASPLYUEV (*shouting*): What's this then? What?
KACHALA (*shouting*): He died in Schlüsselburg. As he lived,
so he died.
RASPLYUEV: But there he is, sitting in the chair over there!!!
KACHALA: It's not for me to know, Sir.
VARRAVIN (*banging himself on the forehead, aside*): Ohhhh
—the scoundrel—it's him!!!— (*To Rasplyuev.*) Be
careful! . . . It's . . . it's terrible!!!
RASPLYUEV (*pressing close to Varravin*): What's going on?
Eh? . . . I don't understand a thing. (*Tarelkin strains
in the chair in an effort to free himself. Rasplyuev shoves
Kachala onto him.*) Hold him, hold him, the devil!
(*Kachala leans against Tarelkin. Rasplyuev returns to
the papers. Varravin also reads.*) There's no doubt about
it. Kopylov died. Died of apoplexy! Died in the village
of Razgildyaevka, underwent an autopsy and was then
buried!! (*Bangs the paper.*)
VARRAVIN: Terrible!
RASPLYUEV: The same thing all over again. Tarelkin died!
Died—and was buried by me, (*thumps himself on the*

chest) by me!!! Now who the devil is the one in the chair?!!

VARRAVIN: Wait! I know who he is! It's . . . it's the greatest danger to the living.

RASPLYUEV (*taking fright*): What did you say?

KACHALA (*also growing scared*): The Lord be with us!

VARRAVIN: Listen to me, but take heart. (*Rasplyuev straightens up.*) Do you know what a lycanthrope is?

RASPLYUEV: No.

VARRAVIN: A werewolf?

RASPLYUEV: No.

VARRAVIN: A vampire?

RASPLYUEV: No.

VARRAVIN: A bloodsucker?

RASPLYUEV: No! No! No! —But I see—it's terrible!!

VARRAVIN (*pointing to Tarelkin*): You see—in the first place, he's already dead.

RASPLYUEV (*obviously confused*): I understand.

VARRAVIN: Sealed in a coffin and interred in the ground.

RASPLYUEV: I understand.

VARRAVIN: But, naturally, he wants to live.

RASPLYUEV: Naturally.

VARRAVIN: And what does he do? He abandons his dwelling-place—the grave—down there, and goes walking about.

RASPLYUEV (*trembling*): Brrrr . . .

VARRAVIN: But he's unable to sustain himself on grain or anything solid, because he'd have to be able to digest it—and what kind of digestion does he have, the devil? That's why he lives on warm . . . human . . . blood— it's ready food.

RASPLYUEV (*grasping himself by the head*): Oh my God! It's . . . it's hell itself . . . (*Approaches the proscenium.*) Would you believe, there's a chill running up and down my spine and I feel my blood running cold.

VARRAVIN (*quietly coming up to Tarelkin at the same time*): Now, snake, you're in my hands!

TARELKIN (*in dread*): Varravin!!

VARRAVIN (*hissing*): Meeee!! (*With the same motion takes a chair and places it in front of Rasplyuev.*) Now sit down. (*Rasplyuev seats himself.*) He has, you see, a snout.

RASPLYUEV: Ugh!!!

VARRAVIN: A snout as sharp as the sting of a scorpion and as hard as a diamond.

RASPLYUEV: Ugh! Brrrr . . .

VARRAVIN: He watches you for some time, then chooses a spot on your head (*picks out a certain place on Rasplyuev's head*) and strikes like this with his snout (*strikes Rasplyuev on the head with his crutch*). Right away this knocks you unconscious. You understand? —Unconscious. (*Rasplyuev is dumbstruck and can hardly speak; he makes a sign that he understands.*) After that, he begins to suck out . . . suck out . . . suck out your blood . . . (*Tarelkin makes another desperate attempt to break loose.*)

RASPLYUEV: Oh-oh! Hold him!

KACHALA (*drawing closer to Rasplyuev*): Ugh!

VARRAVIN (*rushing to Tarelkin and tightening his hands. Softly*): Give me back my papers, thief!

TARELKIN: I won't give them back!!

VARRAVIN (*tightening his hands more*): Watch out! (*Takes his hat and cane and raises his hands up; aloud.*) O righteous God! Spare my life!

RASPLYUEV (*seizing him*): Stop! Stop! I won't let you go.

VARRAVIN (*pointing to Tarelkin*): Keep him here, but be on your guard—he's a rare bird—there's been nothing like him since the creation of the world! . . . What an honor, an honor for the police—an honor for you!

RASPLYUEV: Don't leave us!

VARRAVIN (*leaving*): You'll get a medal for this, you most certainly'll get a medal!!!

RASPLYUEV (*grasping Varravin*): No, no—I won't let you go!!

VARRAVIN (*trying to break loose*): You have no right!

RASPLYUEV (*holding onto him*): In the name . . . in the name of the police, I order you . . . Kachala! Shatala! —Come here! Tie up this animal here for me—tie him up!! I'll give him the first interrogation right here and now in your presence. (*Kachala and Shatala throw a noose around Tarelkin.*) Twist it around him! Harder! (*They follow Rasplyuev's orders.*) Twist him some more —go on, it'll be my responsibility! More!

TARELKIN: Oh, oh—criminals—what are you doing?

RASPLYUEV: Aha! He's found his tongue again! Talk, anathema—who are you?

TARELKIN (*aside*): I'm lost . . . (*Lowers his head.*)

RASPLYUEV: Come on now, talk.

TARELKIN: What can I say? I already told you—I'm Kopylov.

RASPLYUEV: You lie, you hellish soul! Kopylov died. Here are the papers: he died, his guts were removed, and he was buried! (*To Kachala.*) Twist the rope tighter!

TARELKIN: Oh, oh, oh . . . Oh, all right, I am Tarelkin—oh, Tarelkin!

RASPLYUEV (*firmly*): You lie: Tarelkin's dead. General Varravin himself'll testify to that. Why are you trying to pull the wool over our eyes, anathema? (*To Kachala.*) Twist!

TARELKIN (*shouting*): Ow, good Lord, ow . . . I . . . I . . . I'm both of them.

VARRAVIN (*to Rasplyuev*): And both of them are dead.

RASPLYUEV (*seizing himself by the head*): It's terrible, terrible! (*Jumps up suddenly.*) Chains and handcuffs!! There's a crime been committed here! . . . No, on the contrary—there are two crimes been committed here!

VARRAVIN (*correcting him*): No, three crimes! (*Raises his hat high.*) To the head officials! . . . At once!

RASPLYUEV (*also waving his hat*): Yes!! To the head officials!! (*Takes Varravin by the arm and the two of them dash out waving their hats. Kachala and Shatala follow them, dragging Tarelkin still bound to the chair.*)

CURTAIN

(*Change of scene. Police Station. A hall; desks. An entrance door directly in front of the audience. To the right, a door leading to a dark corridor. To the left, a door opening into an office.*)

SCENE 8

Okh is sitting at a desk, a small decanter of vodka in front of him; Rasplyuev.

RASPLYUEV (*running in*): Where is the Inspector? Where?

OKH: I'm here.

RASPLYUEV: I . . . I have the honor to report . . .

OKH: Well?

RASPLYUEV: I'm beside myself.

OKH: What?

RASPLYUEV: I'm burning up.

OKH: Speak, what is it?

RASPLYUEV: Two people lived in our apartment.

OKH: So?

RASPLYUEV: Just like everyone, they lived, died, and were buried.

OKH: Well, so be it!

RASPLYUEV: But the two of them are one! And this one's alive!

OKH (*spitting*): Always telling stories like he was knocked silly.

RASPLYUEV: I swear it.

OKH: Maybe you're lying because you're hungry. Here, have a little vodka. (*Pours out some vodka for him.*)

RASPLYUEV (*passionately*): What do I need vodka for? — There's something that got me higher than vodka.

OKH (*drinking*): Higher than vodka?! —Unheard of!! (*Rises.*)

RASPLYUEV (*with mounting passion*): There's been nothing like this since the creation of the world!

OKH: Tell me all about it.

RASPLYUEV: Just imagine: a fugitive from the other world—! a revenant, a werewolf, a vampire, a bloodsucker—captured! Captured by me! I'm burning up from excitement!

OKH: Where was he captured?

RASPLYUEV: In the apartment of the late Tarelkin and the late Kopylov.

OKH: Where did this revenant appear from?

RASPLYUEV: He came up right out of the ground—he fell down from heaven; from two dead ones one living one was hatched. I'm getting dizzy . . . everything's growing dark . . . I'm in a daze.

OKH: Where is he now? Under arrest?

RASPLYUEV: He's here—tied up with a rope and captured! Over there (*points*) —sitting in the private office! . . . You can imagine the honor—the honor for me—the honor for the police—the rewards—the medals . . .

OKH: I'm afraid you've lost your mind.

RASPLYUEV: I captured him—I! In the face of the strongest resistance (*slaps himself on the chest*) and at the risk of my own life!

OKH: Sit down.

RASPLYUEV (*advancing downstage*): I captured Shamil!!!

OKH (*shoving him into the chair*): Sit down, I say, you're out of your mind!

RASPLYUEV (*jumping up*): I'll get a me-dal—a me-dal—the Order of St. George . . .

OKH (*interrupting him*): Oh, you damned chatterbox! Go to hell! (*Opens the door and thrusts him out.*)

RASPLYUEV (*in the doorway*): It's my conviction! (*Okh slams the door shut.*)

SCENE 9

Okh alone.

OKH (*musing*): Something extraordinary really must have happened! . . . Two people lived (*thinks*) —both of them died—perhaps killed? One of them has reappeared —and he's alive—damn! Even my head's cracking! — Hm! What a nuisance . . . you just can't get any sense out of him . . . (*Muses.*) How can I bring him back to his senses? Ah . . . wait a moment! (*Removes the handle from a broom.*) This way'll be all right . . . (*Opens the door.*)

SCENE 10

Okh and Rasplyuev.

RASPLYUEV (*breaking in*): It's . . . it's my conviction, (*strikes himself on the chest*) a me-dal . . .

OKH (*threatening him with the broomstick*): You see this? —If I let you have it right between your shoulders, your conviction (*points to the ceiling*) will go flying right in that direction.

RASPLYUEV (*composing himself*): Well, that's another matter . . . (*Casts a sidelong glance at the broomstick.*) Another matter entirely . . .

OKH (*sternly*): Make an official report, damn it! You know!

—Attention! (*Rasplyuev snaps to attention.*) Report to your superiors. (*Stands leaning on the broomstick; strikes a pose.*)

RASPLYUEV (*standing at attention*): Today I arrested a vaga-bond, a passportless vampire, in the face of the strongest resistance . . . (*becoming excited again*) at the risk of my own life . . . (*Strikes himself on the chest.*)

OKH (*raising the broomstick*): And this?

RASPLYUEV: What's the matter? —A person can be offended . . . (*Again reports officially.*) Having made my arrest, I have the honor to present him to you.

OKH: Does he have an identity card?

RASPLYUEV (*handing over papers*): As you see—the identity card of the deceased.

OKH (*examining the papers*): Yes, so it is! —See to it that he doesn't sneak away.

RASPLYUEV: All precautions have been taken. First of all, I cleverly seized his hands and bound them with a towel; then I roped him and twisted him 'round so that he really began howling—just like a wild animal.

OKH (*swinging the broomstick*): Fine! That's the way!

RASPLYUEV (*ducking the broomstick*): Your Excellency—put her down.

OKH: Her? Whom?

RASPLYUEV: The young lady you've got there.

OKH (*giving him the broomstick*): You're already acquainted with her, are you?

RASPLYUEV (*putting the stick in a corner*): Well, it's not that I'm acquainted with her, but I've seen her around, and if I've seen her from the distance from time to time, believe me—for a sensitive person, that's sufficient.

OKH: So it was his belongings General Varravin inspected?

RASPLYUEV: His—and not his. That's because this vampire split into two halves. One is Tarelkin, and the other Kopylov.

OKH: Whaaat? Where'd you get all this nonsense?

RASPLYUEV: From official investigation. I have the testimony of witnesses that these clerks did not die. They never died, but were sucked to death in the cruelest way you could ever imagine!!

OKH (*with amazement*): Sucked to death?!! —How could that be?!

RASPLYUEV: Just what I said. As regards that, I collected the fullest information.

OKH: Talk.

RASPLYUEV (*offering him a chair*): Please sit down; I'll explain everything in detail. (*Seats Okh and remains standing in front of him.*) You see, in the first place, he has a snout —a snout of unusual length. At the end of the snout there's a nipple—a nipple like the sting of a scorpion and hard as a diamond. As soon as he catches sight of a victim he lets the snout out with the greatest ferocity— through a sleeve or hidden in a handkerchief—it's all the same—and slowly, slowly picks out a spot in your head (*looks for something*) . . . I need something hard. (*Looks around.*)

OKH: There's the broomstick over there.

RASPLYUEV: Exactly, Your Honor, a stick! (*Takes the broomstick. Aside.*) You just wait, you old devil, I'll give it to you right on that baldspot of yours . . . (*Aloud.*) And he picks out the weakest spot on your head, and suddenly bangs it like this. (*Wallops him on the head.*)

OKH: Ouch!

RASPLYUEV: And then he begins sucking with extraordinary cruelty! . . . Sucking your blood until you're dead as can be!!

OKH (*rubbing his head*): Well, that's clear enough.

RASPLYUEV: Certainly. Captain Polutatarinov explained it to me twice like that and promised to appear at the inquiry. I'll testify the same, he says, at the inquiry. Evidently a very obliging person. He even escorted me here, to the police station itself with the prisoner. Watch out for him, he says, he's a rare specimen; since the beginning of the world the police never laid their hands on a werewolf like this.

OKH: Hm! Yes—two deaths, both sudden; an unknown person—whether he's a werewolf or a vampire or something of the sort, but in any case, there'll have to be an inquiry. Looks like there's nothing to be gotten from it except personal belongings.

RASPLYUEV: This captain says that we should expect big rewards. So please be so kind as to report to the chiefs as quickly as possible. He's the most evil of criminals and I don't want to be responsible for anything.

OKH: Of course, report to the chiefs; without them we won't get very far!

RASPLYUEV: Now please explain to them like this: One of my subordinates, Your Excellency, holding the position of inspector, by the name of Rasplyuev, singlehandedly captured and brought to the police station—in the face of the strongest resistance and at the risk of his own life—a most wicked criminal—a real offspring of hell.

OKH: Well, I can also report so it comes out that everything depends on one's care in choosing subordinates who, in such cases, can do nothing but execute their duties.

RASPLYUEV: As you wish.

OKH: Of course, my dear, as I wish. Give me my hat and my sword. I'll ride over to the chiefs right away.

KACHALA (*coming in*): Your Honor, Actual Councillor of State Varravin.

SCENE 11

The same and Varravin.

VARRAVIN: What's this I hear, something unusual going on here?

OKH: Quite so, Your Excellency.

VARRAVIN: Some kind of mysterious person is supposed to have been arrested with a great furor.

OKH (*hesitatingly*): We are ourselves perplexed.

VARRAVIN: Why, what is it? . . . Something supernatural?

OKH: It must be supernatural, Your Excellency. Such things do happen, don't they?

VARRAVIN (*affirmatively*): And I'll tell you, they happen often. Take the case of werewolves and vampires, for example; here there can't be any doubt. There's just one problem with them—getting hold of them and capturing them.

RASPLYUEV (*clapping his hands*): There you are! —Your Excellency! —Benefactor! Sir! I captured one, I swear it, I captured one, in the face of the strongest resistance and at the risk of my own life.

VARRAVIN: Is that so?! . . . That's astonishing; tell me about it.

RASPLYUEV: Your Excellency knows that the clerk Tarelkin

who worked under you passed away and was buried in a completely legal manner. You were there at the funeral yourself, weren't you?

VARRAVIN: Why, of course, it took place in my presence, before my very eyes!

RASPLYUEV: Another government clerk named Sila Kopylov, who lived in the same apartment, also died suddenly, and exactly at the same time!! (*Raises a finger.*)

VARRAVIN: Tsk . . . died too, did he?! Are you sure he really died?

RASPLYUEV: My heavens—not only did he die, but they opened him up on top of that, took out his guts, sewed him up again, and left such a mess behind in his belly he won't be able to straighten it all out until the Second Coming. That's no longer death, but the absolute end!

VARRAVIN: Yes, you're right, the absolute end.

OKH: And you see, Your Excellency, in the apartment of these two deceased clerks the police, in the course of their work, made the discovery . . .

RASPLYUEV (*interrupting Okh*): No, it was I, Your Excellency, I who made the discovery.

OKH (*to Rasplyuev, sternly*): The police—I'm telling you!

RASPLYUEV (*plaintively*): It was I, for God's sake, I! Your Excellency—they'd take the last piece of bread right out of a poor man's mouth.

VARRAVIN: Let him say what he has to.

RASPLYUEV: I made the discovery of a third person there—nobody knows who he is or where he's from. I investigated and it turns out that he's the cruelest villain, a vampire, who sucked the life blood out of the two clerks for his own subsistence!! What am I supposed to do in a case like this?

VARRAVIN: You arrested him, didn't you?

RASPLYUEV: Your Excellency—I captured him the way Suvorov took Warsaw in 1794! The resistance was the most ferocious, but it was my good fortune that Captain Polutatarinov happened along at just that time. He's a hero from the Caucasus, you know; captured Shamil the Avar singlehanded; a fearless fellow. He gave me help. He's unusually experienced and resourceful, you know, while I'm just a simple person—and apt to get excited and lose my head. I'm bursting, almost out of control, but he holds me back and says, Remember just one thing: you'll have a place in history; they'll award you a medal. He knows everything—such a learned man.

VARRAVIN: Ahhhh—so he's learned, you say?

RASPLYUEV: You can even see it in his eyes. They're small and green and they burn just like lamps. You can see at once —he's a professor.

VARRAVIN: Well done, Rasplyuev, my boy! This is a rare occasion. Imagine—he captured someone and didn't let him go.

RASPLYUEV: Your Excellency, I held onto him with my teeth even. My God! —I thought, I'd give up everything I had just so's the chiefs are satisfied!

VARRAVIN: Truly a heroic deed.

RASPLYUEV: You be the judge! Here's my head—here are my shoulders.

VARRAVIN: What do you intend doing now?

OKH: I'm riding over to the head office.

VARRAVIN: Hm.

OKH: I'll report the entire matter in detail.

VARRAVIN: Hm.

OKH: Let the chiefs themselves handle it the way they want.

VARRAVIN: Hm . . . You mean to say you want to deprive yourself of such a rarity and hand over your good fortune to someone else?

RASPLYUEV (*interrupting him*): For God's sake, what are you doing?

OKH: No, I'm not going to change my mind.

VARRAVIN: What? Then I don't understand you at all. There'll be an investigation, you know—that's inevitable.

OKH: Exactly.

VARRAVIN: Well, you know how the chiefs will handle it, don't you? They'll drape some fancy-cuffed violet-smelling dandy with a cherubic face around your neck, with special instructions—right?

OKH (*sighing*): Right, Your Excellency.

VARRAVIN: You know, you'll just be sitting around the anteroom to his office. You were the ones who did the capturing, but he'll be the one who'll do the grabbing. What do you think?

OKH (*sighing*): Things like that have happened, Your Excellency.

VARRAVIN: And will happen for fools! . . . My God, man, people wait ages for just such opportunities. That'd be a dainty morsel for anyone. Think of the rewards, the medals, the honors.

RASPLYUEV: Exactly! Word for word what Captain Polutatarinov was saying.

VARRAVIN: Any person in his right mind would say the same thing.

RASPLYUEV (*clasping his hands together in supplication*): Oh, Father, Father, teach us, what must we do?

VARRAVIN (*assuming a preceptorial air*): Now the first thing you must do is refrain from making so much noise. Then the matter must be kept in strictest secrecy—understand?

OKH: I understand.

RASPLYUEV: Ahhhh!

VARRAVIN: Make your report gently: such and such a person turned up, of suspicious appearance, origin unknown, and with a false passport. They'll order you to make an investigation—you do as they say. Begin with the little things and the details—take it slow and easy. Then, gradually, develop it; raise it higher and wider, wider and higher, and when it gets all tangled up and confused— that's the time to pull your catch in! —Just make sure to grab it and hang on to it! The choice is yours then: fame or fortune.

RASPLYUEV (*in ecstasy*): Ohhhh . . . what words! Golden words!

OKH (*similarly enraptured*): Indeed they are.

VARRAVIN: But remember: in the beginning don't sell yourself; on no terms! The main thing, do what I tell you. (*Lowers his voice and leading them to one side.*) Avoid water!

OKH: Water? What do you mean—avoid water?

VARRAVIN: Just that! Water acts like an electric charge on criminals of this sort. Give them some and the locks and chains haven't been made yet that can hold them. A calamity might result . . . he could escape!

RASPLYUEV: I'd sooner drop dead first!

VARRAVIN: That's why I'm telling you not to give the prisoner even a single drop of water.

RASPLYUEV: As you order. Not even the tiniest morsel will get into that mouth of his, Excellency!

VARRAVIN: Exactly. Then when he can't die in a way natural
to him, he'll slowly languish to death.

RASPLYUEV: I'll keep him all the time weak, all right!

OKH: Should he really be kept in a weakened state for a long
time, Your Excellency?

VARRAVIN: You'll see later.

RASPLYUEV: What are you getting yourself upset about,
Antiokh Elpidiforovich? You want to dandle the criminal, go ahead—but just say the word and I'll starve him
to death.

VARRAVIN: That's the spirit, well said!

RASPLYUEV (*shouting*): We'll do our best, Your Excellency!

VARRAVIN (*slapping him on the shoulder*): That's the good
fellow! And for my part I promise to take a hand in
the matter and to arrange things so that just the two of
you will conduct the investigation and nobody else.
You understand? . . . Goodbye now! (*Okh and Rasplyuev bow low.*) Remember: you have to begin small
and end big! (*Goes out. Okh and Rasplyuev accompany
him to the door with marked servility.*)

SCENE 12

Okh and Rasplyuev.

OKH (*in high spirits*): Well, Rasplyuev, well done! You really
pulled off something unusual.

RASPLYUEV (*ecstatically*): Oh, my friends! My friends! I
can't stand it any longer! Everything inside me's turning
upside down. My heart stops, then starts up again . . .
What did he say? What did the general say? . . . I don't
believe my ears! . . . What if they really do give me a
medal?!!

OKH: Do you happen to know what other power an investigator has?

RASPLYUEV (*somewhat crestfallen*): No, I don't know what
other power an investigator has!

OKH (*striving to make an impression; deliberate in tone*): An
investigator can take any person, no matter who, and
put him in solitary confinement!

RASPLYUEV (*breaking out in song and beginning a rhythmic

movement of his shoulders): Hel-lo, my darling, hel-lo my beauty . . . hel-lo my dark-eyed one . . . (*Poorly executes a lively dance, at the end of which he shouts.*) Hooray!! Everything's ours! . . . Now I can take and stick anyone I want in solitary . . . I understand . . . I understand! What a going-over I'd give them, Antiokh Elpidiforych.

OKH: We'll give it to them all right . . .

RASPLYUEV: To start off with, I'd grab the merchant Popugaychikov by the scruff of his neck and drag him off there! . . . For some time now I've been just itching to lay my hands on that Popugaychikov. That's because the good-for-nothing's lost all sense of responsibility and doesn't give a damn about it. You order him to do something and he just laughs. None of your tricks, he says; your time's passed already. How has our time passed already, Antiokh Elpidiforych?

OKH (*whipping out his sword*): You're mistaken, you are, merchant Popugaychikov—our time hasn't passed yet! (*Rasplyuev hands him his cocked hat. Both leave in unusually high spirits.*)

CURTAIN

ACT THREE

(*The same room in the police station.*)

SCENE 1

Rasplyuev alone.

RASPLYUEV (*putting a paper on the table*): A great day! (*Bangs the paper with a fist.*) Here's the warrant! . . . *I'm* the one who's going to be carrying out the strictest investigation! . . . *I'll* make the most detailed search.

Every single rat hole, every nook and cranny will be
turned inside out—on my orders! Hm . . . it wasn't so
long ago I was the one who was running from one hole
to another . . . I remember how I used to tremble at
the sight of these little loops here (*indicates the little
loops on his uniform*) —but now they'll all be trembling
at the sight of *me!* . . . They'll all be cringing!

SCENE 2

Rasplyuev; Okh comes in.

OKH: Well, what are you up to?

RASPLYUEV: Antiokh Elpidiforych, since I've been bestowed
honor, rank—I think . . .

OKH: So you think, do you? Look here now . . . just don't
forget your place! (*Makes a threatening gesture at him
with a finger.*) Understand?!

RASPLYUEV: My heavens! —Never.

OKH: I tell you—only two things matter with me: work and
obedience, obedience and work. Just remember that.

RASPLYUEV: As you say, Antiokh Elpidiforovich.

OKH: Others, you know, demand subservience besides. But
I don't have to have subservience. Because if I drive
you out of the government service and starve you to
death—then you'll be subservient to me.

RASPLYUEV: That's so, that's quite so. I always say a stick's
good—and how—but hunger, in my opinion, is still
better. With hunger, you can do everything; with hunger
you can even move a heart.

OKH: I'll move it, all right.

RASPLYUEV: I'll tell you about myself. Why did I become a
person? Because I discovered what hunger was. You
know—my stomach is of a special construction. It's not
so much that it's a wolf, but three wolves together. It
asks for a full portion of porridge, and they serve it a
thimble. And so I began feeling pangs of hunger, and
what pangs of hunger! I was almost driven mad because
of them. I walked the streets with my teeth chattering
. . . Holy Fathers, I swore, I'll be diligent, I'll be zealous,

even; only save my soul from this hell I'm in . . . So
they brought me to you and fixed me up.

OKH: Well, there you are.

RASPLYUEV: You see how I sacrifice myself, the kind of struggle I had to go through to get the vampire.

OKH: Well, did you interrogate him?

RASPLYUEV: I exercised him some.

OKH: And?

RASPLYUEV: At first he hemmed and hawed, but later on he
confessed. I died, he says, but now I'm alive again.
Afterward he says, I'd be glad to die, but I can't.

OKH: You think he was really telling the truth?

RASPLYUEV: Of course he was—why shouldn't he have been?
It's the second day already, after all, we haven't given
him anything to drink, so all the truth'd crawl to the
surface. He finally admitted that there's a whole gang
of them.

OKH: Evidently a conspiracy of some sort.

RASPLYUEV: I told you before and I'm telling you now: The
sternest measures are necessary if we're going to catch
them.

OKH: You'll be on your way soon.

RASPLYUEV: You know, the prisoner swears even that there's
a whole party made up of them—and he even intimated
that General Varravin himself is also one of them.

OKH: You don't mean it!

RASPLYUEV: He swears it's true. He says he—that is the general—was a snake and that he has fangs and the deadliest
poison. You examine him, he says—the general, mind
you!

OKH: So now what?

RASPLYUEV: So we examine him—ha, ha, ha! (*Both burst out
laughing.*) Everything belongs to us now! We'll demand
all of Russia!

OKH (*laughing gaily and waving his arms about*): Oh, you,
you!

RASPLYUEV: I am now of the opinion that our country is a
great pack of wolves, snakes and hares which suddenly
turned into people, and I suspect each and every person
of being such a changeling. That's why we have to es-
tablish a rule of subjecting everyone to arrest!

OKH: I should say!

RASPLYUEV: Indeed. We ought to suggest to the government that all the people in our country be checked. Who are they? Where did they come from? Did they transform themselves and take on other shapes? Do they have stingers and poison? Are there any who are alive but have really died, or any who died but in the meantime live, in opposition to the law?

OKH: I can imagine what would turn up.

RASPLYUEV: The hunting we'd have! . . . What we'd catch just from among the merchants!

OKH: It'd be no worse than a cholera epidemic.

RASPLYUEV: What do you mean, cholera epidemic? What are you saying? Cholera—cholera's a disease; the last time it hit here it reaped such a harvest, people are talking about it even to this day. But we're dealing with changelings, bloodsuckers, vampires, in other words: crime—and all they deserve is Siberia and chains.

OKH: Did you ask for the landowner Chvankin, on account of his correspondence with the prisoner?

RASPLYUEV: Certainly.

OKH: Good. And the merchant Popugaychikov?

RASPLYUEV: Likewise. —He'll appear.

OKH: All the witnesses here?

RASPLYUEV: Some of them have turned up.

OKH: Well, begin then! But don't forget our rule not to believe anything during interrogations.

RASPLYUEV: I'm weak on that point, though; I believe everything.

OKH: Don't, I'm telling you. I'm like this: let's say you come to me and tell me that Shatala, let's say, arrived, so what do I do? I don't believe what you say, but go and have a look for myself.

RASPLYUEV: But I'm not like that. If you should tell me for example that His Excellency the Commissioner of Police is out begging alms on the sidewalk, I'd believe you. Get him, I'd say! And I'd drag him in right by the collar!

OKH (*throwing up his hands*): The Commissioner?! Have you gone mad? What's the matter with you?

RASPLYUEV: I can't help it. That's my nature.

OKH: Then control yourself.

Scene 3

*The same. Doctor Krestyan Krestyanovich Unmoeglichkeit
comes in; speaks in a heavy German accent.*

DOCTOR: Ach so . . . You have a sick prisoner, Antiokh Elpidiforych? Suffering he is, no?

OKH: Yes, he's having some trouble with his stomach; certain
—pangs . . .

DOCTOR: Those are sufferings of the spinal cord.

OKH (*ironically*): Yes, that's it!! (*Aside.*) Wide of the mark.

DOCTOR: *Verstehen Sie*, spinal cord is near stomach. If spinal
cord is inflamed, stomach is inflamed, *auch*. Like fire—
here a fire, there a fire. He must have the water treatment.

OKH and RASPLYUEV (*both waving their hands*): What are you
saying, Krestyan Krestyanovich? You've gone completely
mad! We'd lose our heads.

DOCTOR: My head is never lost.

OKH: Of course not; not at all!

DOCTOR: I tell you—water help him.

OKH: I forbid it.

DOCTOR: You have no right. I'm doctor.

OKH: And I'm an examining magistrate—besides which I
happen to have the most confidential reasons.

DOCTOR: Well, this case maybe different. Maybe he is a
very important criminal.

OKH: And how!

DOCTOR: Political.

OKH: Worse.

DOCTOR: *Was ist das?* Worse than political criminal?

OKH: A changeling.

DOCTOR (*shuddering*): *Teufel!* —What do you mean, Antiokh
Elpidiforych? I never know of such a thing.

OKH: And God grant you never do.

DOCTOR: Is it—is it a Freemason?

OKH: Worse still; but most important, more harmful.

DOCTOR: *Mein Gott!* Well, I make out some prescription for
him.

OKH: That's completely out of the question.

DOCTOR: Well, a pill then.

OKH: A pill is possible.

DOCTOR: What should I prescribe . . . (*Thinks.*) Salis maybe
. . . Salis . . . no, no . . . (*Thinks.*) Extractum maybe
. . . Extractum . . . no, no—well, asafetida. That's it!
Wunderbar! I give him some *Teufelsdreck*—that's . . .
manure! Yes, that's it—devil's manure!

OKH: Marvelous! If it's from the devil then it'll be just right
for his guts. Now, Krestyan Krestyanovich, you have to
make out your prescription in such a way that it should
appear in any case that medical science has given its
help.

DOCTOR: *Ach so—gut, gut.*

OKH: And if anything should happen, well, medical science
isn't responsible for it.

DOCTOR (*with particular conviction*): Oh no! . . . Medicine
is never responsible . . . never! Never. (*Goes out.*)

OKH (*to Rasplyuev*): Now you can begin, Ivan Antonovich.

RASPLYUEV (*shouting in the direction of the main office*):
Hey there, Vanechka, come over here!

SCENE 4

*The same. Vanechka comes in with papers and takes a seat
at a separate desk.*

RASPLYUEV: Now listen, you son of a bitch, pay attention
here! You don't say a word, understand? And no trying
to collect any money—or I'll give it to you, hear?! . . .
Hey, Kachala! Did anyone come yet?

KACHALA: The woman Brandakhlystova, Your Honor.

RASPLYUEV: Well, show this Brandakhlystova in.

SCENE 5

The same. Lyudmila Spiridonovna Brandakhlystova comes in.

RASPLYUEV (*to Lyudmila*): Your name, please?

LYUDMILA (*timidly*): What?

RASPLYUEV (*shouting*): Your name, please?

LYUDMILA: Lyudmila, Sirs, Lyudmila Spiridonovna Branda-khlystova.

RASPLYUEV: Well now, Lyudmila Spiridonovna, did you know Sila Kopylov?

LYUDMILA: I did.

RASPLYUEV: And did you know Kandid Tarelkin?

LYUDMILA: No, I didn't.

RASPLYUEV: Well, they just showed you Sila Kopylov, didn't they? —Did you take a good look at him?

LYUDMILA: I did.

RASPLYUEV: Did you recognize him?

LYUDMILA: I did.

RASPLYUEV: Well then, is it he?

LYUDMILA: It is, Sirs, and it isn't.

RASPLYUEV (to Okh, meaningfully): There you are! (To Vanechka.) Take it all down.

LYUDMILA (continuing): What's his name, you say?

RASPLYUEV: Sila Silich Kopylov.

LYUDMILA: Then it's him.

RASPLYUEV: And from his appearance?

LYUDMILA: From his appearance it isn't him.

RASPLYUEV (to Okh): There you are . . . Have him take it all down.

OKH: Of course. (To Vanechka.) Write.

RASPLYUEV: That's good, dear. Now this is the situation: We suspect Sila Kopylov of being a vampire, a changeling.

LYUDMILA: That could be, Sirs; anything is possible with him. A little while ago he didn't even acknowledge his own children. He's a scoundrel—anything is possible with him.

RASPLYUEV: You lived with him, didn't you?

LYUDMILA: I lived with him.

RASPLYUEV: Well, did he change over, you know, turn about when you were with him?

LYUDMILA: All the time.

RASPLYUEV: What did he use to turn about to?

LYUDMILA: To a wall.

RASPLYUEV: A wall? What are you talking about?

LYUDMILA: Why, as soon as I'd crawl into bed, right away the rascal he'd turn that face of his to the wall. That's how I suffered with him eleven years. I cried my eyes out over him, the robber. All the time—I cried and cried, and couldn't even get any sleep at night because of it, while he'd just doze. The more I cried the more he'd doze, like you make a fire and then fan it. And now, the big horse, he's renounced me and he's renounced the children; he doesn't want to take care of them any more. Those aren't my children, he says. Whose children are they, I say, if they're not yours? Tell me, whose? But he doesn't have anything to say about it.

RASPLYUEV: But when you saw that he kept on turning over to a wall, weren't you afraid to go on sleeping with him?

LYUDMILA: I was afraid, Sirs, but what could I do? I had my duties as a wife.

RASPLYUEV (*to Okh*): She contradicted herself in her testimony, she cohabited with a criminal—shouldn't you order her taken into custody?

OKH: I suppose so—she'll be taken in.

LYUDMILA: Oh, Sirs, my benefactors, for God's sake, how can you arrest me? I have children; they have to be taken care of.

OKH: A neighbor can look out for them, my good woman.

LYUDMILA: A neighbor? I've got a vulture for a neighbor; she'd let them starve just out of spite.

OKH: No she won't; but if she does, she'll have to answer for it. We won't let anyone get away with a thing.

LYUDMILA: Well, as long as you say she'll have to answer for it . . . (*They show her out.*)

Scene 6

The same and the landowner Chvankin.

CHVANKIN (*comes in with a great swagger*): What's going on here, eh? Well? Tell me, who's in charge here?

RASPLYUEV: Police officer Okh.

CHVANKIN (*pacing the room*): Ah! Police officer—police officer—and how dare he, this police officer, trouble me? Well? How dare he?

RASPLYUEV: Would you please straighten it out with him. (*Points to Okh.*)

CHVANKIN (*vehemently*): Oh, no; I'm just asking: How dare he? Doesn't he know who I am? Well? I . . . I have

some authority myself! I am the landowner Chvankin!!
I have two hundred souls in the Saratov district! And
another two hundred in the Simbirsk! The devil knows
where the devil I have how many others! Why I . . . He
. . . (*Paces the room and pounds on the desks.*)

RASPLYUEV (*to Okh*): What are your orders? —You won't
get anything out of him here.

OKH (*winking at Rasplyuev*): Invite him into the secret
chamber.

RASPLYUEV: Can I?

OKH: You can. (*To Vanechka.*) Write a declaration, you
know—according to the form: incoherent speech . . .
something oppressing the soul and so forth.

CHVANKIN (*wheeling about suddenly to face Rasplyuev*):
What soul? Tell me, whose? Mine? You know that I
have three hundred souls in the Saratov district, and in
the Simbirsk dis . . .

RASPLYUEV (*to Kachala and Shatala*): Off with him to the
secret chamber! (*The officers seize Chvankin under the
arms.*)

CHVANKIN (*shouting*): What do you mean, secret chamber?!
Wait! You! —Hey! Wait! What for? . . . I protest;
(*dangling his legs in the air*) I'll appeal!! Right to the
throne, you hear—I'll go right to the throne! (*His voice
fades away in the corridor.*)

SCENE 7

The same. The merchant Popugaychikov comes in, bowing.

RASPLYUEV: Your given name and patronymic?

POPUGAYCHIKOV: Flegont Egorych, Sir.

RASPLYUEV: Family name?

POPUGAYCHIKOV: Popugaychikov, Sir.

RASPLYUEV: Occupation?

POPUGAYCHIKOV: I'm in business, Sir.

RASPLYUEV: What business?

POPUGAYCHIKOV: Spirits, Sir.

RASPLYUEV: You knew the accused, did you?

POPUGAYCHIKOV: Begging your pardon, Sir, why should I
know?

RASPLYUEV: Why shouldn't you?

POPUGAYCHIKOV: How should I know?

RASPLYUEV: You must know.

POPUGAYCHIKOV: For the life of me, I didn't know.

RASPLYUEV (*after a brief silence*): We won't let you go, my dear.

POPUGAYCHIKOV: As you like.

RASPLYUEV (*to Okh*): Should I continue?

OKH: Continue.

RASPLYUEV (*pounding on the desk with his fist*): You know what kind of a case we're investigating, huh? A changeling, a werewolf, a vampire, a bloodsucker!! —Captured! —Sitting in chains—and giving testimony!! (*Pounds on the desk again.*) Now what do you say . . . (*After looking askance at Rasplyuev, Popugaychikov takes out a banknote and hands it to Okh.*)

OKH (*continuing to read some papers he has in his hand and not looking at Popugaychikov*): What's that?

POPUGAYCHIKOV: Gratitude, Sir.

OKH: What sort?

POPUGAYCHIKOV: The twenty-five-ruble sort.

OKH: I can't.

POPUGAYCHIKOV: Please.

OKH: I can't.

POPUGAYCHIKOV: Don't insult me, Your Honor.

OKH: I can't, I tell you. I'd be glad to, but I can't.

POPUGAYCHIKOV (*sighing*): Please. (*Proffers another banknote.*)

OKH: Listen, Flegont Egorych, do you know me?

POPUGAYCHIKOV: Why certainly!

OKH: Well then, my friend, you realize I'm a man who doesn't go in for any tricks, no beating about the bush—not a kopeck less than a hundred rubles.

POPUGAYCHIKOV: You insult me, Antiokh Elpidiforych.

OKH: Where's the insult?

POPUGAYCHIKOV: You insult me.

OKH: Don't you believe in God? . . . Well?

POPUGAYCHIKOV: I do.

OKH: Well, I can't accept your offer.

POPUGAYCHIKOV: Why are you insulting me this way?

OKH: How am I insulting you? There's no insult. The insult's

when something's willful, but where's the damned will-
fulness here when I need . . . No, I just can't.

POPUGAYCHIKOV (*sighing*): Have it your way then. (*Hands
him a hundred-ruble note and approaches the other desk.
To Vanechka.*) Well, nit, where do I sign?

VANECHKA (*handing him a pen*): Here you are, Flegont
Egorych, Sir —Here's a pen. Everything'll be just fine,
Sir! Be so kind . . . Flegont Egorych . . .

POPUGAYCHIKOV: There, you pack of shysters! (*Gives him
some money and leaves.*)

RASPLYUEV (*to Kachala*): Who else is there?

KACHALA: The yardkeeper Pakhomov.

RASPLYUEV: Let's have Pakhomov then. (*Okh goes out.*)

SCENE 8

*Rasplyuev and Pakhomov, who is brought in forcibly by a
police officer.*

RASPLYUEV (*to Pakhomov*): Come here. (*Pakhomov remains
standing at the door.*) Come here, I say. (*The police
officer gives him a shove.*) Come here to the desk,
damn it! —Or you'll be given nothing to eat later.
(*Pakhomov moves.*) Well, you're a witness?

PAKHOMOV: Who, me?

RASPLYUEV (*mimicking him*): Yes, you.

PAKHOMOV: A what, Sir?

RASPLYUEV: That you . . . (*Reprimandingly.*) You're a witness, aren't you?

PAKHOMOV (*hesitatingly*): A what, Sir?

RASPLYUEV (*poking him in the mouth with a fist*): You're
a witness, aren't you?

PAKHOMOV (*trying to bolster his spirits*): A witness, Sir, a
witness.

RASPLYUEV (*approaching the proscenium*): Just now I'm beginning to really feel my strength. (*To Pakhomov.*) Did
you know your tenant, Aulic Councillor Sila Kopylov?

PAKHOMOV: What, Sir?

RASPLYUEV (*making a threatening gesture at him*): Now . . .

PAKHOMOV: I knew him, Sir, I knew him.

RASPLYUEV: Fine! Now—tell me, did you ever notice—didn't he used to turn himself into something?

PAKHOMOV: Eh?

RASPLYUEV (*standing directly in front of him, his hands on his hips*): You good-for-nothing bastard!! What am I supposed to do, wait around for you all day long? I've got another twenty-five more of your rotten kind to question yet. You think you're going to hold me up? I should say you're not!!

PAKHOMOV (*timidly*): As you like, Sir.

RASPLYUEV: That so? —As I like. —Fine. Here's what I like. Hey, Shatala! (*Shatala comes over.*) You stand right here! (*Positions Shatala behind Pakhomov.*) Now, when I ask him a question, you whack him, but whack him so that his answer will come flying out like a bullet . . . Understand?

SHATALA: What's there not to understand, Your Honor? (*Prepares to strike Pakhomov.*)

RASPLYUEV (*staying his arm*): Idiot! Wait! —Not now, but when I put a question to him.

SHATALA: Right, Your Honor.

RASPLYUEV (*standing in front of Pakhomov*): Now, my dear, you tell me what you noticed peculiar about your tenant, Sila Kopylov.

PAKHOMOV (*glancing behind himself*): What . . . I . . . noticed about Kop . . . (*receives a blow in the back of the head*) ouch . . . owwww . . . Jesus . . .

RASPLYUEV (*to Shatala, obviously annoyed*): Ass! Why did you have to interrupt him just when he started to talk? Well? I gave you an order . . . (*Approaches him with clenched fists.*) You don't listen to what I tell you, it seems, huh? (*Shatala looks at him wide-eyed.*) Wait, you stupid ox—I'll show you a thing or two . . . Hey Kachala—come here! (*Kachala approaches.*)

KACHALA: What is it, Your Honor?

RASPLYUEV: Stand over here behind this ox. (*Stations him behind Shatala.*) That's the way, (*raises one of his hands*) like this! When I give the signal, push him in the back of the head . . . (*To Shatala.*) Now you'll learn, you horse's ass, when you're supposed to strike a witness. (*Withdraws to a side and looks everything over.*)

Well, friends, quite a setup I've arranged here, eh? . . .
Quite a setup . . . (*Shatala and Kachala maintain their
pose; Rasplyuev delights in the sight of them.*) Now I
can relax. (*Sits down in a chair.*) The machinery will
operate by itself. (*In high spirits, stretches out in the
chair and rocks to and fro.*) Now, friend—tell me what
you noticed peculiar about your tenant, Sila Kopylov.
(*Gives a signal. Kachala wallops Shatala, Shatala Pakhomov, Pakhomov leaps into the air and lands on Rasplyuev. They fall on top of one another and roll across
the floor. Noise and confusion.*)

PAKHOMOV: Ow, ow, ow . . . God Almighty . . . they . . .
mur . . . dered . . . mur . . . dered . . . me . . .

RASPLYUEV (*panting for breath and getting up with difficulty*): Ow . . . wait . . . Oh—I broke my back . . .
owwww . . . damn it!! Executioners! (*Straightens himself out.*) Damn idiots, dunces . . . Had to shove their
fat faces in . . .

OKH (*coming in*): What's this? What's been going on here?

RASPLYUEV: I've been interrogating the yardkeeper here,
Antiokh Elpidiforych, but I just can't get anywhere with
him.

PAKHOMOV: Oh-h-h-h . . . they mur . . . dered . . . mur . . .
dered . . . me . . .

OKH (*to Shatala, after casting a glance at Pakhomov*): What
are you brawling about, blockhead?

SHATALA: His Honor said strike—so I struck.

OKH: But you could kill a man that way.

SHATALA: Not at all, Your Honor; I know just how to do it.
I hit him only on the back of the neck. His honor gave
me a strict warning: If you kill anyone on me, he says,
I'll beat you to within an inch of your life. I keep that
in mind.

PAKHOMOV (*throwing himself on his knees*): Oh, Sir, Your
Excellency, have mercy on me; I'll tell you whatever you
want to know. They won't even let me turn my neck
around. I'll tell you whatever you'd like. (*Wipes away
his tears with a hand.*)

OKH: Certainly you will—and you, idiots, you can all go
straight to hell. (*Chases out Kachala and Shatala. To
Pakhomov.*) Well, talk now; but I'm telling you, I want

everything in detail; no beating around the bush. Did you ever see Kopylov turn himself into an animal or beast of some kind?

PAKHOMOV: No, Your Honor, cross my heart, he never did; he never turned himself into any animal.

RASPLYUEV: You're lying.

PAKHOMOV (_trying to convince_): I swear it, he never did. Do what you want, he never did. To a wall, yes—the only turning he ever did was to a wall.

RASPLYUEV (_excitedly_): Aha! . . . That's it!

OKH (_to Pakhomov_): In what way?

PAKHOMOV: Coming down a straicase—well, that's another matter—it'll happen—he'll turn around to a wall.

RASPLYUEV: To a wall? . . . And you saw it?

PAKHOMOV: Of course I saw it, Your Honor.

RASPLYUEV: What did you see?

PAKHOMOV: That I couldn't see his face.

RASPLYUEV: So you saw that you couldn't see his face?

PAKHOMOV: Yes, Sir.

RASPLYUEV: And where was his face?

PAKHOMOV: In the wall.

RASPLYUEV (_excitedly_): Oh, oh! And was the wall big?

PAKHOMOV: The way our wall is.

RASPLYUEV: You . . . God Almighty! What's the length?

PAKHOMOV: A hundred and seventy-three feet.

RASPLYUEV: And the height?

PAKHOMOV: Thirty-four and a half feet.

RASPLYUEV (_to Vanechka_): Write it down!! (_To the audience._) That's how the cold penetrates everything. (_To Okh._) Extraordinary, Your Honor, isn't it? (_Okh makes an affirmative gesture._) And what he says agrees with the testimony of the Brandakhlystova woman! . . . The testimony of two witnesses—that's all the proof we need!!

OKH: Right! (_To Vanechka._) Draw up an indictment, and order the yardkeeper taken into custody.

PAKHOMOV (_on his knees_): Your Honor—don't destroy me!

OKH: Come now, my good man, don't act like that; you can't do that.

PAKHOMOV: But, Sir, for God's sake, who'll sweep the street?

OKH: Do you have a wife?

PAKHOMOV: How could it be otherwise; of course I have a wife.

OKH: Well then, your wife'll do the sweeping.

PAKHOMOV: My wife do the sweeping? No, she won't.

OKH: In that case, a police officer will come, take a stick to her, and she'll do the sweeping all right.

PAKHOMOV: She won't do it even then. (*They lead him away.*)

OKH (*to Kachala*): Well, show that landowner in now . . . (*Kachala cautiously opens the door leading to the dark corridor; Rasplyuev jumps behind Okh.*)

SCENE 9

The same. Chvankin slowly comes in from the dark corridor.

CHVANKIN (*looking around*): Gentlemen . . . my respects. (*Exchanges bows with Okh.*) If you wish to question me, I am quite willing. (*Bows.*)

OKH: Would you please . . .

CHVANKIN: With pleasure; even with great pleasure. If you had come right out and said so from the beginning, I would have been at once glad to . . . (*To Vanechka.*) A pen, please, my dear—I'll have to write a few little answers . . .

RASPLYUEV: Well then—did you know Tarelkin?

CHVANKIN (*with obvious willingness*): Tarelkin? —No, I didn't know him.

RASPLYUEV: And Kopylov?

CHVANKIN: Kopylov I knew.

RASPLYUEV: Our investigation revealed that you and the accused have been conducting a strange and secret correspondence.

CHVANKIN: Nothing secret about it—we were corresponding about wenches.

RASPLYUEV: About what?

CHVANKIN: I bought three wenches from him.

RASPLYUEV: Three? Three wenches? You bought them. (*To Okh.*) The law forbids it . . .

OKH: Strictly . . . Continue.

RASPLYUEV: When, and to what purpose, did you permit yourself to purchase wenches, and especially in such a quantity?

CHVANKIN: Well, you see—to tell the truth, I myself was puzzled.

RASPLYUEV: That's no excuse—we can't accept that.

OKH (*to Rasplyuev*): Keep quiet. (*To Chvankin.*) Ignorance of the law, Sir, is never an excuse. Please tell us the story.

CHVANKIN: I was living in Moscow at the time. One day some peasants from my estate in Simbirsk came to see me. Master, they said, buy some wenches for us. —Now where am I supposed to buy wenches for you, you old bunch of bastards? —We've already reached a bargain. —You have, have you? —We have, they say. —For how much? —For twenty-five rubles. —For a hundred? —Heavens no, they say, per piece. —Good ones? —First-class, they say . . . —Cheap enough, I think to myself! . . . What do you say to that, a whole first-class wench, you know like what . . . for twenty-five rubles!

RASPLYUEV (*enthusiastically*): Cheap! . . . A whole first-class wench . . . like this (*makes a gesture*) I'd pay the twenty-five myself!

CHVANKIN: So I ask them, Where do they sell wenches like that?

RASPLYUEV: Yes, that's interesting; where do they sell them?

CHVANKIN: The peasants tell me you can buy them nearby on the princess's estate, from the manager Sila Silich Kopylov. So I addressed a letter to Kopylov, he answered it—and that's how our correspondence started.

OKH: Correspondence—no correspondence, but the matter's serious; trading in wenches, Sir, is not allowed.

CHVANKIN: You don't understand—it was to reduce taxes; the peasant families would sell their daughters to cut down the amount of tax they had to pay according to the size of the family.

OKH: Oh, we'll see for whose benefit it was done. Under the circumstances it'll be absolutely necessary to undertake a local inquiry, so would you be so kind, first of all, to countersign your testimony. (*Chvankin takes a seat and puts his signature on each page of his testimony.*)

RASPLYUEV (*lost in musing*): My God!! (*Slaps the back of his head.*) Cheap!!

OKH (*to Rasplyuev*): Wake up—lazybones. (*To Chvankin.*) And in the second place, Sir, please sign a statement that you will not leave the city under any circumstances.

CHVANKIN (*continuing to sign sheets of paper*): What do you
    need a statement for? What kind of a statement? I'm
    not planning to leave the city anyway, statement or no
    statement.

OKH: It's a matter of form.

CHVANKIN (*more firmly*): I'm telling you I won't leave, so
    you can believe me. (*Gets up.*) It seems to me that
    among honorable people a word of honor should be
    sufficient. (*Takes his hat and starts to leave.*)

OKH: You can't, Sir.

CHVANKIN: Damn it, when I tell you I won't, it ought to be
    enough! (*Goes quickly to the door.*)

OKH (*giving a signal to Kachala and Shatala*): Hey, Kachala!
    . . . (*Kachala and Shatala grasp Chvankin under the
    arms.*)

CHVANKIN: What are you doing? . . . Hold on! . . . Are you
    taking me again to the secret chamber?!

OKH: Yes, Sir; we're inviting you there again. (*To Kachala
    and Shatala.*) Carry him away. (*They carry Chvankin in
    the direction of the corridor.*)

CHVANKIN (*swinging his legs in the air*): All right, I'll give
    you the statement; I prefer it better . . . Wait! . . .
    Damn you!! (*They carry Chvankin into the corridor.*)
    I'll give you the statement, I said!! Two statements!!

OKH (*to Kachala and Shatala*): All right, men! Bring him
    back!

CHVANKIN (*tearing loose from their hands*): I'll give you the
    statement . . . even three statements . . . with pleasure,
    with great pleasure, damn it.

VANECHKA (*handing him a pen*): Please sign. (*Chvankin
    signs.*)

OKH (*sighing*): It's only a matter of form, Sir, only a matter
    of form. (*Chvankin bows and then leaves.*)

SCENE 10

Okh, Rasplyuev; then Varravin.

VARRAVIN: Well, gentlemen, how are things going with you?

OKH: We're conducting the investigation, Your Excellency.

We've already gotten two testimonies. The witnesses
prove it!

VARRAVIN: Prove what?

OKH: That he used to change over!

VARRAVIN: Good. (*To Rasplyuev.*) How is he, by the way?

RASPLYUEV: Suffering greatly.

VARRAVIN: You didn't give him any water, did you?

RASPLYUEV: Not a drop.

VARRAVIN: So as a result he's very exhausted and without any
strength at all, right?

RASPLYUEV: How could he have any strength—he's prac-
tically dead.

VARRAVIN (*rubbing his hands together*): Good.

RASPLYUEV: For some time he was as ferocious as ever, but
then he got weak. He made a confession—tried to say
that he worked under you in the same department, but
he's confused and just lying. It'd be a mistake to look
for any real sincerity in him.

VARRAVIN: You wait, my friend, we'll get it yet. (*To Okh.*)
Bear in mind that as a witness I'm able to give you
some very important testimony regarding Tarelkin. While
he was still alive he told me once as his superior—quite
unexpectedly—that sometimes he becomes a rabbit!

OKH: The law says that a personal declaration is the best
testimony of all.

VARRAVIN: Exactly! —And he went on to tell me that when
he was in that state, that is, when he was a rabbit, his
creditors chased after him through all the streets, and
that, as he told me himself, he suffered untold hard-
ships . . .

RASPLYUEV: Extraordinary, Your Excellency. Well, we already
have the testimonies of two witnesses that the prisoner
used to change over, and besides that, now his personal
confession to you . . .

OKH: According to the law, that's complete proof!

VARRAVIN: Well then, the case is shaping up splendidly! . . .
Right now there's just one matter I have to query him
about. (*To Okh.*) Have him brought in here.

OKH: At once, Excellency. Hey, Kachala! Bring the prisoner in.

Scene 11

The same; Tarelkin is brought in, still tied to the chair by a rope.

TARELKIN (*in a weak voice*): Water . . . oh, water . . .

VARRAVIN (*withdrawing to a side, to Rasplyuev*): Begin your interrogation.

RASPLYUEV (*solemnly*): Tell the truth now, who are you really?

TARELKIN: Oh . . . I'm Kopylov.

RASPLYUEV: Nonsense.

TARELKIN: All right, I confess then, I'm Tarelkin . . . only let me have some water . . . oh . . . I'm so thirsty . . .

RASPLYUEV: We don't believe that either. We don't believe anything you say.

TARELKIN: Just let me have some water—I'll tell you whatever you want, just some water . . .

RASPLYUEV: Talk—are you an evil spirit?

TARELKIN: All right, an evil spirit.

RASPLYUEV: Are you a werewolf, a vampire?

TARELKIN: Yes, yes . . . oh . . .

RASPLYUEV: Who are your accomplices?

TARELKIN: All Petersburg and all Moscow.

RASPLYUEV (*to Okh*): There you are! . . . (*Aloud.*) Be specific; give us their names!

TARELKIN: There are too many of them!

RASPLYUEV: Give us them, I'm telling you! . . . At least tell us who the chief instigators are!

TARELKIN: Maksim Varravin, sergeant-at-arms Zhivets, police officer Okh, and district inspector Rasplyuev.

RASPLYUEV (*confused*): Well, did you ever . . . (*To Okh.*) What should be done now?

VARRAVIN (*to Rasplyuev*): Go on!

RASPLYUEV (*to Tarelkin*): Talk, what did you do?

TARELKIN: Oh . . . we killed people . . . Just like you're killing me now . . . oh . . .

RASPLYUEV (*sternly*): Don't you beat around the bush with me . . . Who did you kill?

TARELKIN: We killed Muromsky.

RASPLYUEV: What did you do, suck his blood out?

TARELKIN: Yes, we sucked all his blood out . . . Can't you give me some water, you pack of snakes you . . . What's happening to me? . . . I feel so hot all over . . . Like the sun was baking me . . . I'm going to Algeria . . . to Timbuktu . . . what a desert; there aren't any people here—just monsters . . .

VARRAVIN (*quietly, to Okh and Rasplyuev*): You can leave now—I'll interrogate him myself. (*Okh and Rasplyuev leave for the main office.*)

SCENE 12

Varravin and Tarelkin.

VARRAVIN (*approaching Tarelkin*): I'm here, you fool!! You're in my hands now. Everything's out in the open—I know everything—you're lost!!

TARELKIN (*plaintively*): Oh . . . oh . . . doesn't make any difference to me any more . . .

VARRAVIN: Confess, you stole certain papers . . . (*Silence.*) Give them back—or you'll find yourself in Siberia . . .

TARELKIN (*raising his eyes to Varravin*): It's by not giving them back that I won't go to Siberia!!

VARRAVIN: You'll die.

TARELKIN: So I'll die—but I still won't give them back!

VARRAVIN: You'll die a slow, painful death. I'll kill you by thirst . . . Hey, Kachala! (*Kachala comes in.*) Bring me a glass of water like a good fellow.

TARELKIN: Oh, what torture . . . what's the matter with me . . . I'm so hot . . . (*Kachala hands Varravin the glass of water.*)

VARRAVIN (*drinking*): Good water. What is it, tap or spring water?

KACHALA: Spring water, Excellency, right from the river.

VARRAVIN: All right, thank you, you go now.

TARELKIN (*exerting himself*): Ow . . . o-o-o . . . my God . . . what torture . . . (*To Varravin.*) Here you are! . . . Take them! . . . (*Removes the papers from under his jacket.*) Here they are . . . your papers . . . just give me some

water . . . (*Stretches out his hand.*) Give me some
. . . give me . . .

VARRAVIN (*taking the papers*): Wait a moment . . . maybe
you're trying to trick me . . . (*Examines the papers.*)
Yes, yes—these are the ones! (*Gives Tarelkin the water.*)
Oh, you traitor . . . you thief, you. (*Tarelkin drinks.*)
Oh, you snake, you miserable little snake!

TARELKIN (*whining*): What can I do with myself now, Maksim Kuzmich? (*Straightens himself out.*) It'd be best
for me to go away somewhere . . .

VARRAVIN (*untying the rope around Tarelkin*): Go to the
devil, go to hell—only get out of my sight.

TARELKIN (*getting up and straightening himself out*): Please,
Your Excellency, Maksim Kuzmich . . . please don't be
angry at me—treat me like a son. (*Bows.*) Forgive me!
—What's to be done; I lost—you won . . . (*Laughs.*)
Only for God's sake help me now—let me have back
those papers of Kopylov; where can I go without them?
Give me his identification papers and service record—
and I'll crawl off at once to Moscow. (*The two of them
go over to the desk and search among the papers.*)

VARRAVIN: Here are the identification papers and service
record—take them! (*Gives him the documents.*)

TARELKIN: And his references, his references!

VARRAVIN: Here are the references (*gives them to him*)
—now get the hell out of here.

TARELKIN: I'm going, I'm going, God knows I'm going . . .
only, Maksim Kuzmich . . . (*assumes a supplicatory
pose*) a little something for the road . . . you know . . .
you could manage . . .

VARRAVIN (*despairingly shoving his hand in a pocket*): Here,
go on take it . . . you devil, you goddamn bloodsucker!
(*Gives him money.*) You sucked out my blood!! (*Pushes
Tarelkin toward the door.*)

TARELKIN: (*Standing at the rear of the stage, he takes off his
toupee, removes his false teeth, stoops, and again assumes the appearance of Kopylov. Then he turns around
and approaches the proscenium, slowly scrutinizing the
audience.*) Gentlemen, perhaps you need someone to
manage your estates? I have references here (*shows the
references*). As to my experience, there's nothing to be

said: I've been through fire and water! And as for my
honesty—you've seen yourselves how I suffered for
truth! . . . I can present a certificate from any Society
of Rural Idle Talk . . . but I feel a particular inclination
toward the distillery business. This is just my nature
speaking . . . I'll set up for you a system of crop ro-
tation with any kind of fertilization you like: composts,
or if you prefer, bone, or liquid, or perhaps you think
something harder'd be better—whatever you like, I can
do everything! Or if you want Libich Powder, why I
can make it with my own two hands. To make a long
story short, I'll bring you progress: rational economy
based on hired labor . . . I'll arrange everything in such
a way that you'll just gasp in amazement . . . Really
now, do think it over . . . A fi-i-i-ne opportunity! (*Short
pause.*) Well? No! . . . You're not interested? (*Turns
to one of the audience.*) Would you be so kind, my
dear Sir, to please take down my address, in case you
should happen to change your mind: His Honor, Aulic
Councillor Sila Silich Kopylov—care of His Excellency
Maksim Kuzmich here (*points to Varravin*); he'll see
that it's delivered. (*Bows and runs offstage.*)

VARRAVIN (*shouting after him*): I'm telling you, go straight
to hell. There they won't turn you away—they'll welcome you!

CURTAIN

In case *The Death of Tarelkin* should be staged, the author finds it necessary to make the following observations.

Because of its humorous character the play should be performed in a lively, gay, loud manner—*avec entrain*. The dialogue, in particular, should be mastered thoroughly and spoken distinctly and boldly. Otherwise, in view of the rather complex movement of the characters on the stage, *words*, that is, the very essence of the matter, may be missed by the audience with the result that instead of real life all they will see before them is a familiar sort of *bustle*.

The choice of costume is broad and arbitrary. Some roles can be slightly overacted in the style of caricature. For example: Brandakhlystova, Chvankin, Kachala and Shatala and the entire group of creditors, whose costumes may be of any description and—as happens with moneylenders—depend on the apparel they take in pawn. The role of Brandakhlystova (if necessary) can be played by a man.

The author begs whomever will play the role of Tarelkin-Kopylov to pay attention to the *twofold* transformation of Tarelkin into Kopylov *onstage*, that is, *in full view of the audience*. This transformation should be executed quickly, suddenly, and accompanied by a change of the expression of the face and its features. This is a matter of mimicry and a task for an artist. Here one could point, for example, to the French comic Levassor, who developed this into a high art and acquired a very great reputation because of it. He carried the play of his facial muscles to such a degree of mobility that he could even change the shape of his nose at will and with the aid of a toupee, beard and moustache almost instantaneously assume the external appearances of the most varied types.

In conclusion, the author considers that he has the right to protest as energetically as possible against those actors who appear before audiences without mastering their roles, and therefore permit themselves to change the text in the most outrageous manner. To the author who conscientiously labored

long and hard over his work such liberties are utterly exasper-
ating. The public should stop the actor who strays from the
text. On all the stages of the civilized world such negligence
is prosecuted by the theater-going public *unmercifully*. And
rightly so.

Afterword

If, after all this, the question should be put to me: Where
have I seen such *Pictures?*—then I would have to answer,
placing my hand on my heart:

Nowhere!!! — and — everywhere!
*Wer die Natur mit Vernunft ansieht, den sieht sie auch
vernünftig an.*
As ye sow, so shall ye reap!